*Ex umbris et imaginibus
in veritatem.*

*From the shadows and images
into the truth.*

(John Henry Newman)

Contents

Abbreviations

The standardized abbreviations for certain works cited in this essay are:

Insight
: *Insight: A Study of Human Understanding, Collected Works of Bernard Lonergan,* Vol. 3, eds. Frederick E. Crowe and Robert M. Doran (Toronto: University of Toronto Press, 1992). Earlier edition of 1958 cited in parentheses.

Verbum
: *Verbum: Word and Idea in Aquinas,* ed. David B. Burrell (Notre Dame: University of Notre Dame Press, 1967).

Collection
: *Collection: Collected Works of Bernard Lonergan,* Vol. 4, eds. Frederick E. Crowe and Robert M. Doran (Toronto: University of Toronto Press, 1988).

Grace and Freedom
: *Grace and Freedom: Operative Grace in the Thought of St. Thomas Aquinas,* ed. J. P. Burns (London: Darton, Longman & Todd; New York: Herder and Herder, 1971).

Method in Theology
: *Method in Theology* (London: Darton, Longman & Todd; New York: Herder and Herder, 1972. Second edition Herder and Herder, 1973. Reprinted by University of Toronto Press, 1990).

Second Collection
: *A Second Collection: Papers by Bernard J. F. Lonergan, S.J.,* eds. W.F.J. Ryan and B. J. Tyrrell (London: Darton, Longman and Todd; Philadelphia: Westminster, 1974).

Caring About Meaning
: *Caring About Meaning: Patterns in the Life of Bernard Lonergan,* eds. Pierrot Lambert, Charlotte Tansey, Cathleen Going (Montreal: Thomas More Institute, 1982).

Preface

In many of his later writings Bernard Lonergan spoke of what he called the "startling" event of intellectual conversion. Virtually all of Lonergan's writings point toward this foundational event. Lonergan indicated that he himself experienced an intellectual conversion while studying in Rome in the mid-1930s.

What is intellectual conversion? This book will try to answer this question by focussing on this event in Lonergan's early life. It traces the early influences on his work and the stages of his developing thought up to 1935–1936. It highlights what we know of this major event in his thinking at that time. In addition, it sets out the developing expression of his intellectual conversion in his writings during the late 1930s and the 1940s. It brings Lonergan's early story up to the clearest expression of the meaning of intellectual conversion in his major work, *Insight: An Essay on Human Understanding*, written between 1949 and 1953.

Grateful acknowledgement is made to the following who have allowed me to reprint selected passages from Bernard Lonergan's writings:

> The trustees of the Lonergan Research Institute, Toronto, Canada, for permission to quote from Lonergan's unpublished writings and from *A Second Collection*.

> The University of Toronto Press for permission to quote from *The Collected Works of Bernard Lonergan: Insight* (Volume 3); *Collection* (Volume 4); and *Understanding and Being* (Volume 5); and also *Method in Theology*.

> The Thomas More Institute, Montreal, Canada, for permission to quote from *Caring About Meaning*.

I would also like to express my gratitude to the many benefactors who have helped me and encouraged me in this work. In the first place, I want to thank all my friends and family who have trusted that in some way these several years of study and research in a seemingly esoteric project were worthwhile. I would like to thank the recent Archbishops of Newark who have allowed me to continue my own studies in and around other pastoral assignments: the Archbishop Emeritus,

Peter L. Gerety and my present Archbishop, Theodore E. McCarrick. Also, I wish to thank Thomas Peterson, O.P., and Seton Hall University for allowing me a sabbatical year during which much of the writing of this work took place. A special word of thanks to Joseph Flanagan, S.J., and his colleagues at Boston College for the postdoctoral fellowship in Lonergan Studies during the year 1990–1991. I also thank Richard Conway and Paul Holmes for their invaluable computer expertise; and George Lawless, O.S.A., for his insights into St. Augustine. I am grateful as well to Afra Maffey and my local "Lonergan Group" for convincing me of the "existential" importance of Lonergan's work. I certainly want to thank my sister, Therese Liddy, Anthony Ruggiero, and other friends, who have proofread and commented on various sections of the manuscript. Finally, I thank Frederick Crowe, S.J., whose personal interest in this project and gentlemanly example has exemplified for me "what it's all about."

Most of all, I am grateful to the mysterious ways of the Lord for allowing my path as a student in Rome to cross that of Bernard Lonergan's and, through him, for allowing me to meet so many other pilgrim thinkers in our common journey to the Eternal City.

Introduction

I met Bernard Lonergan for the first time in the fall of 1960 soon after I arrived in Rome to study for the priesthood. At that time Lonergan was fifty-six years old, a Jesuit professor of theology at the Gregorian University. The first time I caught a glimpse of him was in one of the Roman restaurants, *Il Buco,* where some of the older American students had invited him for a meal. He seemed to enjoy it, but he also seemed to be a quiet retiring man. But my major exposure to him came in the classroom. There I listened for two years as Lonergan, with an English-Canadian twang combined with classical Latin, sought to bring some light to the Christian mysteries of the Trinity and the Incarnation. To this day some graduates of the North American College in Rome bring howls of laughter to their confreres by imitating Lonergan's sing-song Latin cadences.

There were about six hundred of us from all over the world in the great aula of the Gregorian, and so—by tradition and necessity—the only pedagogical method was the lecture. Years later Lonergan referred to those teaching conditions as "impossible": so many people from many different countries listening to a professor lecturing in Latin about the mystery of the Trinity![1] And it was obvious that Lonergan was definitely over the heads of most of us. Only the bravest students— and there were a few—approached the brilliant professor outside the classroom to quiz him on his exact meaning. Those who did so, and followed out his thought, seemed to be "caught" by something. But the rest of us were not sure what that "something" was. The name of his 785-page philosophical work, *Insight: A Study of Human Understanding,* was on our horizon and many of us at least owned our own copy. But in the midst of the many classroom and seminary demands, few of us had broached it. I remember at one point getting lost in the introduction!

It was the early 1960s and Rome was an exciting place. Many Catholic theologians were making the headlines in the world's newspapers

---

[1]Lonergan felt the challenge. Years later he would say: "They were about six hundred and fifty strong and between them, not individually but distributively, they seemed to read everything. It was quite a challenge." *Second Collection,* 276.

and new subjects and topics were in vogue. Historical studies, especially Scripture and patristics, liturgical studies, various types of psychology, were all becoming the focus of interest. And of course, it was the time for "involvement," the American Peace Corps, and (welcome relief!) pastoral work outside of the seminary. "The Church in the world," with a concern for issues of social justice, was just beginning to emerge into our consciousness.

During the summer of 1964, after my ordination in Rome and my return to the United States, I was asked by my bishop to return to Rome in the fall to study philosophy in preparation for teaching in the local seminary. At the time I wondered whether I might not be compromising my "activist" principles in agreeing to this use of my time. And indeed, I wondered whether there was anything to philosophy at all. The neo-scholastic philosophy that we had been taught in our early seminary days seemed quite discredited and its vocabulary not just significantly absent from the documents of Vatican II, but rapidly disappearing from the horizon of most Catholics. In its place, personalist categories had entered into our vocabulary. The documents of Vatican II were purposely couched in the non-scholastic and interpersonal language of the Bible.[2]

Nevertheless, in spite of misgivings, I agreed to study philosophy. As a graduate student, I had much more time to follow out my own interests, and the encouragement of the people I trusted pointed me in the direction of Lonergan. One was a classmate from seminary days, David Tracy, now a well known teacher and writer at the University of Chicago. But there were others as well, intently studying Lonergan's thought.

I spent a good part of one whole year working through *Insight*. In a little room at the back of the library of the Casa Santa Maria, the graduate house of the American College, I spent day after day poring over that book. I often remember studying as the lights dimmed in the early evening when Rome's electric power was especially taxed— a fitting symbol, I thought, of the search for enlightenment. I was reminded of the pain and effort in reading *Insight* when I read the story George Huntston Williams recounts of the young seminarian, Karol Wojtyla, as he worked nights in the Solvay Iron Works during the Nazi occupation of Poland. He too struggled with one book, a philosophical work influenced by the school of Louvain.

[2]The most graphic example of this transition took place in the context of the Council's debate over the document on divine revelation. A highly scholastic schema prepared by a preparatory commission was scrapped entirely to make way for a text that the Council fathers felt was more biblical, more personal, more pastoral.

Wojtyla . . . remembers that the most difficult book for the future Pope, and perhaps the one that started him out on a career in philosophy, was one given him to study by Father Klosaka. It was entitled *Ontology or Metaphysics* and was written by Rev. Prof. Kazimierz Wais (1865–1934) of Lwow. . . . Workers saw Wojtyla puzzling over it while he awaited the periodic purification of water used in the boiler room he tended in Solvay. Fellow seminarian Mieczyslaw Malinski remembers Wojtyla, in his blue-grey overalls and clogs without socks, carrying the book on his way to the Solvay chemical factory and responding to an enquiry about the *Metaphysics* of Wais thus: "Yes, it's hard going. I sit by the boiler and try to understand it—I feel it ought to be very important to me." That was in September 1942. . . . Years later, in his pontifical garb, he would say to his priestly friend of so many years something more: "For a long time I couldn't cope with the book and I actually wept over it. It was not until two months later, in December and January (1942–43), that I began to make something of it, but in the end it opened up a whole new world to me. It showed me a new approach to reality, and made me aware of questions I had only dimly perceived. . . .[3]

This was the way I felt about *Insight*. Though I do not remember crying over it, I have a vivid memory of struggling and paining over it. Pages would go by with hardly a glimmer of understanding. Then, slowly, connections began to be made. Flipping pages, I would compare later sections with earlier ones. I would spend hours going over just one short passage. I spent time consulting books on mathematics, physics, relativity theory, etc., to check out some of the scientific examples Lonergan was using. To the extent that I read and searched, I came to realize that he was penetrating into the fundamental questions of the sciences.

In fact, the very fact that I did not understand and was seeking to understand was the key to the whole thing. For Lonergan's main point was the centrality of the human act of understanding.

Thoroughly understand what it is to understand, and not only will you understand the broad lines of all there is to be understood but also you will possess a fixed base, an invariant pattern, opening upon all further developments of understanding.[4]

The promise was extraordinary, but the basic issue was eminently experiential and personal. Just prior to embarking on *Insight* I had been reading some works of contemporary psychology and I was intrigued by Carl Rogers' *On Becoming A Person*. I was especially impressed by

---

[3]George Huntston Williams, *The Mind of John Paul II* (New York: Seabury Press, 1981) 86–87.

[4]*Insight*, 22 (xxviii).

Rogers' insistence on being "experiential" in one's efforts at self-knowledge: letting one's words flow from one's feelings. Rogers aimed at refining the ability to identify levels of present feelings and at helping people to find the words that express those feelings. Rogers called appropriated truths "significant learnings."[5] There was a truth here I wanted to maintain and I remember saying to myself something like: "Lonergan can't contradict any of the truths *I know* or I'll know he's wrong. Anything he says will have to take into account and develop the truths I've already *experientially* appropriated or he won't be worth my while."

And I doubted he could do it. His work appeared so patently intellectual and all my leanings—and the leanings of the culture around me—were "experiential." By that term I understood chiefly the in's and out's of human feelings. Lonergan's work seemed too "cold," too intellectual to acknowledge all those levels of feelings. And besides, anything that seemed "scholastic" had, for the most part, been omitted by the Council then taking place in Rome.

But strangely, there was an experiential aspect to *Insight*. In fact, it began to appear that the whole aim of the work was the appropriation of human experience: not just the experience of one's feelings, but also the experience of the subtle acts of understanding.

> The crucial issue is an experimental issue, and the experiment will be performed not publicly but privately. It will consist in one's own rational self-consciousness clearly and distinctly taking possession of itself as rational self-consciousness. Up to that decisive achievement, all leads. From it, all follows. No one else, no matter what his knowledge or his eloquence, no matter what his logical rigor or his persuasiveness, can do it for you.[6]

Fortunately, at the time there were others in Rome who were wrestling with the same book. This community acted as a check on the adequacy and accuracy of my own understanding. And indeed, that community continues, as there is a Lonergan journal, newsletter, workshops, Lonergan Centers in numerous countries, etc. Gradually, I moved from an adversarial relationship to the conviction that there was indeed "something there." What was, and is there, is the subject of this book.

In 1965 I began work on a doctoral dissertation on an American philosopher of art, Susanne K. Langer. Lonergan had highly praised

---

[5]Lonergan later adverted to the parallel between Rogers' appropriation of feelings and his own appropriation of understanding. Cf. *Second Collection,* 269.

[6]*Insight,* 13 (xviii–xix).

Langer's early work on aesthetic and artistic consciousness, but her later work, especially her *Mind: An Essay on Human Feeling,* consisted in the reduction of all "higher" human activities to feelings and feelings to electro-chemical events.[7] Langer represented the whole empiricist tradition in philosophy. As I studied her work, I gradually discovered that there was an unbridgeable gulf separating what Langer was saying about science and human consciousness and what Lonergan was saying. As Lonergan once wrote of the various major schools of philosophy: "Empiricism, idealism, and realism name three totally different horizons with no common identical objects. An idealist never means what an empiricist means, and a realist never means what either of them means."[8]

Of course, the issue between these basic schools of philosophy had real implications. On a strictly logical level, the empiricist horizon has no room either for the existence of God or for an immortal dimension of the human person. As Langer once wrote, spelling out the implications of her view of the human mind and spirit:

> That man is an animal I certainly believe; and also that he has no supernatural essence, "soul" or "mind-stuff," enclosed in his skin. He is an organism, his substance is chemical, and what he does, suffers, or knows, is just what this sort of chemical structure may do, suffer, or know. When the structure goes to pieces, it never does, suffers, or knows anything again.[9]

This conflict in underlying philosophies became a conflict in myself. I remember one evening in particular. I was studying in my room in Rome in the mid-1960s as twilight spread over the city. I remember saying to myself quite clearly: "Who's right here—Lonergan or the empiricists? Both can't be right—between them there's a basic conflict about the human person, the human mind, indeed about reality." I questioned my own motivation: "If you come down on Lonergan's side of this issue, is it because he's religious, a Jesuit priest and you yourself are a life-long Catholic and a priest as well?" I could admit all the underlying motivations that might incline me toward a more religiously amenable answer; but the question itself was not directly a religious one. In the first instance it was a question about the mean-

---

[7]Cf. Richard M. Liddy, *Art and Feeling: An Analysis and Critique of the Philosophy of Art of Susanne K. Langer* (Ann Arbor: University Microfilms, 1970). Also my review of Susanne K. Langer's *Mind: An Essay on Human Feeling* I, *International Philosophical Quarterly* 10 (1970) 481–84.

[8]*Method in Theology,* 239.

[9]Susanne K. Langer, *Philosophy in a New Key* (New York: New American Library, 1948) 44.

ing of the whole modern development of the natural sciences. But it was also a question about the meaning of human consciousness in general and the meaning of my own *self*. It was a question about what I was doing then and there. It was a question whose adequate answer I could find only within my own self. As Newman once wrote: "In these provinces of inquiry egotism is true modesty."[10]

Previously, in various philosophy courses, I had learned many things about what the great philosophers had said about the mind. But those facts had tended to pass through my own mind and on to test papers without connecting with my own basic self-knowledge. I could repeat from memory the various positions on knowledge and the various schools of philosophy. But my personal convictions were not clear. They were vulnerable to the many challenges coming from the contemporary sciences and philosophies. The challenge I faced at the moment was the challenge of modern empiricism that invoked science in its own defense.

In some ways the latter was easy to understand—or at least imagine. The empiricist emphasis on feeling, imagination and electro-chemical events was rather obvious. What was not so easy to understand was Lonergan's position. I sensed there really was something to his emphasis on the centrality of understanding—for how else explain all that transcends the merely biological: all of human culture and civilization? Still, Lonergan seemed to imply that there was a residual materialism, or "naive realism," even in someone like myself who had studied six years of Catholic philosophy and theology. Moreover, such naive realism could be found even in the scholastic philosophy I had been taught. It was that residual materialism that was at the basis of much conflict and division in the Church as well as in the world at large.[11]

---

[10]John Henry Newman, *A Grammar of Assent* (London: Longmans, Green, & Co., 1913) 384. In spite of oppositions and conflicts among people on matters philosophical, ethical, and religious, still a serious inquirer "'brings together his reasons and relies on them, because they are his own, and this is his primary evidence; and he has a second ground of evidence, in the testimony of those who agree with him. But his best evidence is the former, which is derived from his own thoughts; and it is that which the world has a right to demand of him; and therefore his true sobriety and modesty consists, not in claiming for his conclusions an acceptance or scientific approval which is not to be found anywhere, but in stating what are personally his grounds . . . .'"

[11]Lonergan often recommended E. I. Watkin's *The Catholic Centre* (New York: Sheed and Ward, 1939) for its analysis of the implicit materialism in much Church life and thought.

What *Insight* called for was a radical change of mind about mind itself. Later he would write of that radical change as an intellectual conversion:

> Intellectual conversion is a radical clarification and, consequently, the elimination of an exceedingly stubborn and misleading myth concerning reality, objectivity, and knowledge. The myth is that knowing is like looking, that objectivity is seeing what is there to be seen and not seeing what is not there, and that the real is out there now to be looked at.[12]

As I wrestled with Lonergan's writings, I found this myth in myself. The myth is rooted in the world of immediate experience, "the world of immediacy," and it confuses that immediate world with the far larger world, the world Lonergan calls "the world mediated by meaning." This latter world is the world we grow into as we grow up: it is the "real world" that is far larger world than the world of immediacy and it is brought to us through the language and memories of other people, the pages of literature, the labors of scholars and scientists, the reflections of saints, the meditations of philosophers. It is the world filled with meaning.

> This larger world, mediated through meaning, does not lie within anyone's immediate experience. It is not even the sum, the integral, of the totality of all worlds of immediate experience. For meaning is an act that does not merely repeat but goes beyond experiencing. What is meant is not only experienced but also somehow understood and, commonly, also affirmed. It is this addition of understanding and judgment that makes possible the larger world mediated by meaning, that gives it its structure and its unity, that arranges it in an orderly whole of almost endless differences; partly known and familiar, partly in a surrounding penumbra of things we know about but have never examined or explored, partly in an unmeasured region of what we do not know at all. It is this larger world mediated by meaning that we refer to when we speak of the real world, and in it we live out our lives. It is this larger world, mediated by meaning, that we know to be insecure, since besides truth there is error, besides fact there is fiction, besides honesty there is deceit, besides science there is myth.[13]

The myth of "naive realism" overlooks the fact that the real world is not known by childish procedures. Our human tendency is to think that we get at the real world just by "taking a good look." On the other hand, intellectual conversion takes place when we understand that reality is attained, not just by experiencing, but by the addition

[12]*Method in Theology*, 238.
[13]*Collection*, 233.

and development of the properly human activities of understanding, judging, and believing.[14]

The myth of knowing as looking is at the core of philosophical issues.[15] In *Insight* Lonergan speaks of the "startling strangeness" one experiences as one makes the breakthrough from the residual materialism of naive realism, to the "critical realism" of thinking about our minds on their own terms. It is a breakthrough to a whole new world. It is a discovery that one has not yet made "if one has no clear memory of its startling strangeness."[16] Compared to the rest of life this "startling" breakthrough is as distinctive an experience as the difference between winter twilight and the summer noonday sun.[17] One has not yet experienced it if one has not yet made the discovery

> that there are two quite different realisms, that there is an incoherent realism half animal and half human, that poses as a halfway house between materialism and idealism, and on the other hand that there is an intelligent and reasonable realism between which and materialism the half-way house is idealism.[18]

I never realized the autobiographical character of those words of Lonergan until I did this study. As a student in England in the late 1920s, Lonergan rejected a version of scholastic realism and, under the influence of English empirical thought, he identified himself as a "nominalist." Later, after reading Plato and Augustine, he came to a "theory of intellect as immanent act" and, as he later confessed, experienced the fear of becoming an idealist. Finally, under the influence of the Jesuit writers Joseph Maréchal and Bernard Leeming, he came to realize the meaning of the scholastic teaching on the "real distinction between essence and existence," and that was the key to what he later called his own intellectual conversion to a "critical realism."

At the conclusion of this work I will describe one very vivid moment in my own intellectual biography as I wrestled with Lonergan's work. Let me now just mention that in the 1960s, after reading through *Insight*, I went back and read Lonergan's previous major work on St. Thomas Aquinas, *Verbum: Word and Idea in Saint Thomas*. There I discovered that what Lonergan was calling for in *Insight* did not hang in mid-air. It came out of a dialogue with Aristotle and Thomas Aquinas. I have since discovered that Lonergan's roots in Aquinas' thought ex-

---

[14]*Method in Theology*, 238.
[15]Ibid., 238–39.
[16]*Insight*, 22 (xxviii).
[17]*Insight*, 13 (xix).
[18]Ibid., 22 (xxviii).

tended into his own early philosophical development: in his interest in modern logic and mathematics, in the writings of John Henry Newman, in the early dialogues of Plato and Augustine, in his own encounter with some Thomistic writers while studying in Rome. It was through his encounter with all these influences that he came to the major breakthrough of his own intellectual development and then invited others, in *Insight*, to share in that breakthrough.

And that is what this book I have written is about: Lonergan's early development leading to his own intellectual conversion in the mid-1930s and the expression of that conversion in his writings up to the completion of *Insight* in 1953. It is about his intellectual life during the twenty-eight years he mentions in the Preface to *Insight*. "Now I have to make a brief acknowledgement of my manifold indebtedness, and naturally I am led to think in the first place of the teachers and writers who have left their mark upon me in the course of the twenty-eight years that have elapsed since I was introduced to philosophy."[19] There he mentions his "more palpable benefactors," mostly brother Jesuits, who encouraged him in his work. Here I tell the story of his "less palpable benefactors," mostly the classic writers who influenced him on the way to his own intellectual conversion. My aim has *not* been to write a Lonergan biography. Others are working on and will work on that great project.[20] My aim has been to ask specifically about the sources of his great "change of mind" that took place during the mid-1930s, and to show how that conversion found expression in his writings up to the completion of *Insight*.

Lonergan was aware of the possibility of interpretative biographies that attribute mysterious and fictitious motivations to historical figures. And yet he left a record of his own early days: some early articles and letters as well as later testimonies to the teachers and writers who profoundly influenced his thought: his mathematics teacher at Heythrop, Joseph O'Hara, S.J.; H. W. B. Joseph's *Introduction to Logic*; John Henry Newman's *Grammar of Assent*; J. A. Stewart's *Plato's Doctrine of Ideas*; Augustine's early dialogues written at Cassiciacum in northern Italy; the Jesuit scholastic writers, Peter Hoenen, Joseph Maréchal and Bernard Leeming. All of these writers contributed to "the great change of mind" that was Lonergan's intellectual conversion during 1935–1936. All contributed pieces to the puzzle of human knowledge until the whole picture fell into "a unique explanatory perspective."[21]

[19]*Insight*, 9 (xv).
[20]Cf. the works of Crowe, Mathews, and Rice in our bibliography.
[21]*Insight*, 3 (ix). In many ways the present work is a commentary on Lonergan's article of 1971, "*Insight* Revisited," *Second Collection*, 263–78. There he outlines the intellectual

The first part of this book chronicles Lonergan's early intellectual journey. Regarding the writers who influenced him, I have concentrated on the sections of their writings that obviously became an integral part of Lonergan's own future thought. My question has been: "What did Lonergan understand in the works that made such a great impression on him—Newman's *Grammar of Assent*, Stewart's book on Plato, Augustine's Cassiciacum dialogues, etc.? What is the key to the influence each of these writings had on his thought?" It has often occurred to me that reading these works through the eyes of Lonergan's later writings is a liberal education in itself. For one can repeat all the words of the great thinkers—as so many "survey" courses in school do; but unless one *means* what those great writers meant, then "one will not be raising oneself up to their level but cutting them down to one's own size."[22]

The second part of the book chronicles the early expressions of Lonergan's intellectual conversion especially in his writings on Thomas Aquinas. There is no doubt that his years of study of Aquinas represented a tremendous deepening of his own personal intellectual conversion.

> After years reaching up to the mind of Aquinas, I came to a two-fold conclusion. On the one hand, that reaching had changed me profoundly. On the other hand, that change was the essential benefit.[23]

The third part of the book brings the story to 1953, the publication of *Insight*. No adequate account of what happened in Lonergan's own mind in the 1930s could omit this developing expression of the meaning of intellectual conversion. *Insight* is the fullest expression of that conversion. This period is marked by Lonergan's growing focus on the nature of scientific method. It is also marked by a growing concern to invite others to share in the same intellectual breakthrough he himself had experienced.

Since Lonergan's *Insight* can be quite daunting, I have thought that one way to introduce readers to some glimmer of its meaning is to point out the course of Lonergan's own development. At the same time it is important to remember a caution he himself gave when he summarized his view on human knowing in the beginning of *Method in The-*

---

influences that went into the writing of *Insight* and the new context that emerged in his writing of *Method in Theology*. The reader is advised to read "*Insight* Revisited" as a succinct statement of what is spelled out in detail in this book.

[22]"Method in Catholic Theology," *Method: Journal of Lonergan Studies* 10 (Spring 1992) 10–11.

[23]*Insight*, 769 (748).

ology. "Please observe that I am offering only a summary, that the summary can do no more than present a general idea, that the process of self-appropriation occurs only slowly, and usually, only through a struggle with some such book as *Insight.*"[24] The present writer has undertaken this work in the hope of setting out the historical context in which intellectual conversion took place in Lonergan's own life under the influence of some classic philosophical texts. It is, in this sense, a "Companion to *Insight.*"

I can think of no more profound benefit from "reaching up" to the mind of Bernard Lonergan than a change in the reader's understanding of his or her own mind. And I can think of no greater tribute to Bernard Lonergan than to say that he helped me to know myself. His influence upon me is comparable to the influence of Platonic thought on St. Augustine. As Peter Brown wrote,

> the Neo-Platonists provided [Augustine] with the one, essential tool for any serious autobiography: they had given him a theory of the dynamics of the soul that made sense of his experiences.[25]

Presently the University of Toronto is publishing the twenty-two volumes of *The Collected Works of Bernard Lonergan*. Hopefully that will address, to some degree, the relative neglect of Lonergan in the academic community. As Hugo Meynell wrote of him: "of all the contemporary philosophers of the very first rank, Bernard Lonergan has been up to now the most neglected."[26]

My own experience of the immense value of wrestling with Lonergan's work has been confirmed by the women and men from many countries and from many walks of life whose lives have been significantly enriched through the effort of appropriating his thought. My perception has been that this has opened them up to understanding the true meaning of their own lives. In their lives the philosophy of knowledge has come to have "existential" import.

[24]*Method in Theology,* 7.
[25]Peter Brown, *Augustine of Hippo* (Berkeley and Los Angeles: University of California Press, 1969) 168.
[26]Hugo Meynell, *An Introduction to the Philosophy of Bernard Lonergan,* 2nd ed. (Toronto: University of Toronto Press, 1991) 1.

BERNARD J. F. LONERGAN
(1940)

Part One

The Way to Intellectual Conversion

When I was a boy, I remember being surprised by a companion who assured me that air was real.

Astounded, I said, "No, it's just nothing."

He said, "There's something there all right. Shake your hand and you will feel it."

So I shook my hand, felt something, and concluded to my amazement that air was real.

Whether my conclusion was correct, we need not consider. The point is that all of us in childhood have to solve implicitly a whole series of questions in cognitional theory, epistemology, and metaphysics.

Bernard Lonergan
"The Natural Theology of *Insight*"

Chapter One

Beginnings

1. Canada

Bernard Joseph Francis Lonergan was born in the small town of Buckingham, Quebec, on December 17, 1904. His father, Gerald, was a third generation Irish-Canadian whose forebears settled among the English speaking residents of that largely French area of Canada. His mother, born Josephine Helen Wood, was descended from English colonists who in the late eighteenth century had chosen to move to Canada at the time of the American revolution. Both her grandfathers had become Catholics in adult life.[1]

Lonergan's father had graduated from McGill University where he studied engineering. Eventually he became a Dominion surveyor and, when Bernard was in elementary school, he was appointed Inspector of Surveys. Much of his working life was spent in leading surveying parties in the Western territories of Canada. Apparently he was often absent from the family as a result of long surveying expeditions, but young Bernard had a high regard for him. He once quoted someone's remark about his father: "The most honest man I ever met."[2]

His mother was a pious woman who saw to the education and religious development of her three sons: "She joined the Third Order of St. Dominic and said the beads three times a day for the rest of her life, as far as I know. The Scholastics teaching me at Loyola would come and visit me at the hospital, and they thought she was a very holy woman."[3] She enjoyed music and painting. In his later years, hearing some music, probably a variation of the Kreutzer Sonata, reminded Lonergan of sitting outside on the lawn as a child and listening as his mother played the sonata in the house.[4] He retained a life-long love of listening to Beethoven.

[1] Valentine Rice, "The Lonergans of Buckingham," *Compass* (Journal of the Upper Canada Province of the Society of Jesus, March 1985) 4–5.

[2] *Caring About Meaning,* 40.

[3] Ibid., 138.

[4] William Mathews, "Lonergan's Apprenticeship," *Lonergan Workshop 9,* ed. F. Lawrence (Boston College, 1993) 48.

3

Bernard Joseph Francis was the oldest of three boys. The second son, Gregory, later also became a Jesuit. The third son, Mark, became an engineer and raised a family in Montreal, a home Bernard enjoyed visiting in his later years. Bernard as a young boy must have been inquisitive, for he recounted this incident later in his life: "When I was a boy, I remember being surprised by a companion who assured me that air was real. Astounded, I said, 'No, it's just nothing.' He said, 'There's something there all right. Shake your hand and you will feel it.' So I shook my hand, felt something, and concluded to my amazement that air was real."[5] What was meant by "real," of course, and how we know the real, took him years to figure out.

It seems that Lonergan was a shy young man whose interests at an early age turned to books. He once spoke to me of being alone and bored one summer at his aunt's farm, and someone saying to him, "Well, what do you do when there's nothing to do? You read a book!" And so Bernard read his first book, Robert Louis Stevenson's *Treasure Island*.[6] It was the beginning of a life-long process of entering into the "real" world revealed by books:

> For words denote not only what is present but also what is absent, not only what is near but also what is far, not only the past but also the future, not only the factual but also the possible, the ideal, the ought-to-be for which we keep on striving though we never attain. So we come to live, not as the infant in a world of immediate experience, but in a far vaster world that is brought to us through the memories of other men, through the common sense of the community, through the pages of literature, through the labors of scholars, through the investigations of scientists, through the experience of saints, through the meditations of philosophers and theologians.[7]

Lonergan attended the ungraded elementary school in Buckingham, run by the Brothers of Christian Instruction: "There were three sets of three grades in the Brothers' school for the English in Buckingham; the French had a different grade for everybody. I've told you Gerald MacGuigan's reason why his brother Elliott is so superior? I had the advantage Elliott had, you see; in the ungraded school you kept working. If, like Gerald, you had one teacher talking all day long, you just wasted your time."[8] Lonergan once spoke of education as giving people

[5]Bernard Lonergan, "The Natural Theology of *Insight*" (an unpublished paper given at the University of Chicago Divinity School, March 1967) 3.
[6]*Caring About Meaning*, vii.
[7]*Collection*, 232–33.
[8]*Caring About Meaning*, 131–32.

the space and time and inspiration to have their own insights. Apparently that is what went on in the young Lonergan. He remembered being able to listen as a young boy to what was going on in the higher grades. As a result, by the time he got to those higher grades he knew all he was expected to know.

From his earliest years he found himself interested in mathematics: "In elementary school I liked math because you knew what you had to *do* and could get an answer. . . ."[9] I remember in algebra doing a problem and getting a minus answer. I was sure I was wrong and I asked, but was told, 'Oh no, that's right.' It was the revelation of negative numbers."[10] On the other hand, "English Composition was quite a problem for me. Only in my last year at elementary school was I able, confident enough, to write a good English composition. . . . I didn't know what to say!"[11]

From Buckingham Lonergan went on, at the age of thirteen, to board at the Jesuit high school and junior college of Loyola in Montreal. He stayed there from 1918 to 1922: "My father went to Ottawa University for college before going to McGill but by the time I was eligible, it was practically entirely French. Ottawa boys were going to Antigonish (my mother thought that was rather far away) and some Buckingham boys were at St. Alexander's College, run by the Holy Ghost Fathers, up at Gatineau. I liked Loyola much better, judging it by circulars they sent out. I was very impressed, in the *Loyola Review*, that the boys wrote poetry—wow! I had no hope of doing that myself, of course."[12] The program at Loyola was the typical classical Jesuit education of the time: "When I was sent to boarding school when I was a boy, there were no local high schools—that sort of thing didn't exist, you were sent out to a boarding school—the one I went to in Montreal, in 1918, was organized pretty much along the same lines as Jesuit schools had been since the beginning of the Renaissance, with a few slight modifications. So . . . I can speak of classical culture as something I was brought up in and gradually learned to move *out of*."[13] It was a literary education, emphasizing the Latin and Greek classics, while also including English and French literature, mathematics, history and, of course, religion. Lonergan was a good student who skipped some grades and was advanced into classes with older boys—something he did not find

[9]Ibid., 2.
[10]Ibid., 133.
[11]Ibid., 2–3.
[12]Ibid., 133–34.
[13]*Second Collection*, 209–10.

too much of a strain.[14] Going through Loyola, he said, "I acquired a great respect for intelligence."[15]

While at Loyola in early 1920, at the age of sixteen, Lonergan developed a serious illness after playing hockey in an outdoor rink: his ears froze, his jugular became blocked and he developed mastoiditis. He was hospitalized for about a month, during which time his mother stayed with him. At one point he received the sacrament of the sick. He missed the rest of the school year, but eventually he recovered and was allowed to return to Loyola in the fall. Around this time one of the priests at Loyola suggested to him the idea of a religious vocation. Lonergan dismissed the idea because he did not think his health was good enough: "Then he raised with me the question of vocation and I said, 'There won't be any question of that. I'm ill;' and he said, 'There's nothing organically wrong with you; you had some operations but you recovered.' So that raised the question again."[16]

Another possible road he could have taken at the time was a career in economics or finance. According to his brothers, from an early age he read the business pages of the newspapers, and of course, during several periods in his life he turned his attention to analyzing the nature of economic activity.[17] Finally, he made his vocational decision: "I went out to the Sault to make a retreat, an election, and I decided on the street-car on the way out. (It was a two-hour trip on the tram.)"[18]

It was a simple decision—uncomplicated. On July 29, 1922, he entered the novitiate of the Society of Jesus at Guelph in Ontario, where he remained for four years. There he engaged in the Jesuit regimen of prayer, asceticism, work, and study. It was a monastic-type environment, withdrawn from the world. Lonergan never spoke a great deal about the spiritual side of his vocation to the Jesuits. Perhaps a hint of his life can be given by his description years later of the experience of the hidden workings of the Lord in the life of a religious: "Without any experience of just how or why, one is in the state of grace or one

[14]*Caring About Meaning*, 143.

[15]Ibid., 142. At the same time, a letter of many years later contains some rather critical remarks about his early Jesuit education: "At Loyola my acquired habits did not survive my first year: by the mid-term exams I was in 3rd High; by the end of the year I was fully aware that the Jesuits did not know how to make one work, that working was unnecessary to pass exams, and that working was regarded by all my fellows as quite anti-social." Letter of May 5, 1946, to his provincial (John L. Swain); quoted in Frederick E. Crowe's *Lonergan* (Collegeville, Minn.: The Liturgical Press, 1992) 5.

[16]Ibid., 137.

[17]Mathews, "Lonergan's Apprenticeship." Mathews writes of the "ambiguities" of Lonergan's vocational decision.

[18]*Caring About Meaning*, 131.

recovers it, one leaves all things to follow Christ, one binds oneself by vows of poverty, chastity, and obedience, one gets through one's daily dose of prayer and longs for the priesthood and later lives by it. Quietly, imperceptibly, there goes forward the transformation operated by the *Kurios*, but the delicacy, the gentleness, the deftness, of his continual operation hides the operation from us."[19]

His was the typical Jesuit ascetical training of the day: "one's heavy dose of prayer." *The Spiritual Exercises of St. Ignatius* were given, but as he realized later, they were accompanied by a nineteenth-century interpretation that emphasized "examining one's motives" in the light of the three powers of the soul: memory, intellect, and will: "It was a rather big block in the spiritual life. It was the reduction of St. Ignatius to decadent conceptualist scholasticism. . . . That was the stone offered when I was asking for bread (not that I thought of it that way), and so was the other business: 'examine your motives.' When you learn about divine grace you stop worrying about your motives; somebody else is running the ship."[20]

Characteristic of his generation, Lonergan did not speak easily of his own spiritual life. Later on he noted that in his early training there was a great fear of illusion in the spiritual life and great hesitancy to speak of mystical experience. Years later he would frequently speak and write of the experience of "falling in love" and "being in love" with God: "It is as though the room were filled with music though one can have no sure knowledge of its source. There is in the world, as it were, a charged field of love and meaning; here and there it reaches a notable intensity; but it is ever unobtrusive, hidden, inviting each of us to join. And join we must if we are to perceive it, for our perceiving is through our own loving."[21] Still, this experience is mysterious. It need not be the focal point of attention. As Lonergan once remarked, "You can be a mystic and not know it."[22]

After the novitiate years in Guelph there were two years of the juniorate, 1924–1926, which consisted in languages and literary studies, mostly Greek and Latin, with some English and mathematics: "During the vacations we were allowed to read novels, to wit: Dickens, Thackery and Scott. I read Thackery and kept a list of all the words,

---

[19]*Collection*, 230–31.

[20]*Caring About Meaning*, 145.

[21]*Method in Theology*, 290. Crowe quotes a letter from Lonergan to Louis Roy, dated August 16, 1977: "After twenty-four years of aridity in the religious life, I moved into that happier state and have enjoyed it now for over thirty-one years" (Crowe, *Lonergan*) 7. That is, there was a breakthrough in Lonergan's prayer life sometime in 1946.

[22]*Caring About Meaning*, 27.

to know the meaning well enough to use them myself. I looked them up in the dictionary and wrote them down and went over these lists; if I still didn't know the meaning, I would look up the dictionary again. I improved my vocabulary tremendously. But I went to England for philosophy and all the lads there where talking that well!"[23]

2. England

Lonergan was, then, an ordinary young Canadian in the Society of Jesus. He enjoyed music and sports, mathematics and literature. He was a bright student who in 1926 was sent, along with two other Canadians, to study philosophy at Heythrop College in England, the Jesuit seminary north of London:

> My early education, up to about the age of 21 was in a classicist tradi-
> tion; everything always has been and ever will be substantially the same.
> There was no historical-mindedness involved in it. At that age I was
> shifted from Canada to England where even the Jesuits regarded the *Ratio
> Studiorum* as quite outdated and the shift started me on a process of think-
> ing for myself: moving away from the way I had picked up of thinking
> up till then, without being aware that I had a way of thinking.[24]

Lonergan joined a number of other young Jesuits already studying at Heythrop: "I studied philosophy at Heythrop from 1926 to 1929. At the same time I was to prepare for a degree as an external student at the University of London. Many of my fellow students had a similar lot, and classes on the Latin and Greek authors were regularly held by Fr. Harry Irwin and on mathematics by Fr. Charles O'Hara. Philosophy, accordingly, had no monopoly on our time or attention."[25]

The external degree at the University of London was a publicly recognized degree that would be very useful for future teaching: "I certainly didn't work hard at philosophy or theology when I was a student. In philosophy, anyone at Heythrop with any brains was getting a university degree; that was his main concern. If you were teaching in a school, there would be a government grant if you had a degree, and very modest help for the school if its teachers were without degrees."[26] The one course that caught Lonergan's eye in the London curriculum was a course in methodology: "I was very much attracted by one of the degrees in the London syllabus: Methodology. I felt there

---

[23]Ibid., 217.

[24]Unpublished transcript by Nicholas Graham of discussion, Lonergan Workshop, Boston College, June 21, 1979.

[25]*Second Collection*, 263.

[26]*Caring About Meaning*, 8.

was absolutely no method to the philosophy I had been taught; it wasn't going anywhere. I was interested in method and I wrote to Father Fillion: 'instead of classics, what about methodology?' He said, 'No, do classics.' It was just as well because my own method is much better than what I would have gotten in London.''[27] Later Lonergan would remark that he had the same experience studying theology in Rome: if the courses were to be anything more than a "heap," he would have to concentrate on methodology.[28]

In the meantime, he had his hands full at Heythrop. He had the external degree in London which included mostly classics but also some modern mathematics and logic. He was being tutored in classics and mathematics. In addition, there were the regular series of courses in philosophy. Of these courses Lonergan says: "The textbooks were German in origin and Suarezian in conviction. The professors were competent and extremely honest in their presentation of their wares."[29] "Suarezian in conviction"; that is, Lonergan's introduction to philosophy came through the scholastic thought of the Renaissance Jesuit, Francisco Suarez (1548–1617). It might be helpful to outline the background of this philosophy that Lonergan received at Heythrop.

In 1879 Pope Leo XIII had issued the encyclical *Aeterni Patris*, which proclaimed the Catholic Church's official option for the Aristotelian method of St. Thomas Aquinas in her philosophical and theological instruction. That had sparked a renewal in scholastic philosophy, the opening of centers focussed on the study of St. Thomas, and the beginnings of a great deal of historical study of Thomistic and scholastic thought. Leo XIII's aim, and the aim of the Jesuit scholastic philosophers who advised him, was to combat the relativist and idealist philosophies of the nineteenth century by a return to the realist philosophy of St. Thomas. Gerald McCool defines the underlying vision behind this decision virtually to canonize the thought and method of St. Thomas:

> St. Thomas' epistemology, they argued, was an Aristotelian realism hinged upon the abstraction of the concept from sense experience and its return to sensible reality through the judgment. The unity of sense and intellectual knowledge in Aristotle's judgment demanded the subsistent unity of soul and body in the man who made it. Aristotelian unity

---

[27]Ibid., 10. (Fr. Frederick Crowe informs me that the superior's name was spelled "Filion"). Cf. also Elaine Cahn and Cathleen Going, eds., *The Question as Commitment: A Symposium* (Montreal: Thomas More Institute Papers, 1979) 77:10.

[28]Unpublished transcript by Nicholas Graham of discussion, Lonergan Workshop, Boston College, June 19, 1979.

[29]*Second Collection*, 263.

in the knower demanded in turn the Aristotelian metaphysics of form, matter, substance and accident. The union and distinction of the various forms and powers of knowing could be achieved more coherently in the tradition of St. Thomas than in any of the Post-Cartesian traditions. And because of that the unity of man and his world could be given a more satisfactory explanation. This was no small advantage for Catholic theology, threatened as it was by the fideism, rationalism, and pantheism from which the more recent traditions could not protect it.[30]

A major concern was certitude. If there was nothing certain in natural knowledge, how be certain of the supernatural? Was there any alternative to a blind faith, a fideism? That position had been condemned in the First Vatican Council nine years before Leo's *Aeterni Patris*. The Council had also vindicated the possibility of a natural knowledge of God: "The same holy mother the Church teaches and holds that God, the beginning and end of all things, can certainly be known by the natural light of reason from the things that are created."[31] What was the foundation of this knowledge? Was there anything certain in natural knowledge? The scholastic philosophers felt that the scholastic account of knowledge vindicated the certainty of natural knowledge and thus prepared the way for the certitude of faith. As Lonergan described the early scholasticism he was taught: "Our philosophy started off with the rejection of universal skepticism; you had to be certain about something or you would be a universal skeptic. (What to be certain about was a further question you didn't go into.)"[32]

As Gerald McCool points out, the ultimate result of this renewed intellectual emphasis in the Church was the emergence of a de facto pluralism in scholastic thought and several interpretations of the thought of St. Thomas. The Franciscan religious order, in fact, tended to favor the scholastic philosophy of John Duns Scotus over that of Thomas. The Dominicans, fellow religious of Aquinas, interpreted his thought according to the great commentators, Thomas de Vio Cajetanus ("Cajetan" 1469–1534) and John of St. Thomas (1589–1644). The famous twentieth century convert and scholastic philosopher, Jacques Maritain, followed the latter in his interpretation of St. Thomas. On the other hand, the Jesuit order tended to interpret Aquinas according to the thought of the Spaniard, Francisco Suarez. Among the em-

---

[30]Gerald A. McCool, "Neo-Thomism and the Tradition of St. Thomas," *Thought* 62 (June 1987) 137. Cf. also McCool's *Catholic Theology in the Nineteenth Century* (New York: Seabury Press, 1977).

[31]Denziger & Schönmetzer, *Enchiridion symbolorum, definitionum et declarationum de rebus fidei et morum*, 3004.

[32]*Caring About Meaning*, 47.

phases of Suarez' thought was his denial of the "real distinction" between the essence of a thing and its existence, a thesis other Thomists tended to defend. According to Suarez, existence is nothing else but the actual essence itself, a "mode" of essential being. This issue became a central bone of contention among twentieth century Thomists and was in fact central to what Lonergan later called his own "intellectual conversion."[33]

Suarez' thought did not lack influence. Diverse Renaissance and Enlightenment thinkers had been influenced by him: Descartes, Leibniz, Spinoza, Wolff, Berkeley, Schopenhauer, Vico—among others. In fact, when many modern continental thinkers thought of scholastic thought, they were often thinking of Suarezian scholasticism. Perhaps because of this interpenetration by continental thought, German Jesuits had also been greatly influenced by Suarez. Among these were a number who were influential in Rome in the latter nineteenth century. Johannes Baptist Franzelin was a Suarezian Thomist who was the central theological influence on the decrees of Vatican I. A fellow Jesuit, Joseph Kleutgen, exercised the major influence on Leo's writing of *Aeterni Patris.*

A typical Suarezian textbook that Lonergan would have been exposed to at Heythrop was written in Latin by the Jesuit, J. Urraburu, a five-volume series first published in 1886. For Urraburu human knowing took place through a mental process of abstracting "species" or concepts from sensible objects and comparing these terms with each other to see whether or not they attained to the concrete existence of things. The predicate is not seen in the subject, but each is conceived separately and compared with each other to arrive at existence. Every judgment contains a perception of the identity or discrepancy among terms arrived at through a comparison of the terms.[34]

It was this brand of scholastic philosophy that Lonergan received at Heythrop. And it was this brand of scholasticism that he rejected.

[33]For an account of the twentieth-century scholastic controversy over the real distinction between essence and existence, cf. Helen James John, *The Thomist Spectrum* (New York: Fordham University Press, 1966).

[34]Cf. Urraburu, *Psychologiae, Pars Secunda,* vol. 5, 919: "Judicium affirmativum in nobis dicitur, et est compositio, negativum autem divisio . . . quod si rationem quaeras, cur nos judicare nequeamus nisi componendo vel dividendo terminos, ea repetenda est ex imperfectione intellectus nostri, qui, quoniam species, quibus utitur ad res cognoscendas, utpote abstractae a sensibus, imperfectae sunt, non potest per unam solam perfecte cognoscere res; hinc non vidit in subjecto predicatum, sed unumquodque seorsim concipere debet, et unum cum alio conferre, ad hoc ut esse vel non esse illud cognoscat, atque enuntiet." Further on he adds, " . . . judicium omne continere perceptionem identitatis vel discrepantiae terminorum, quae subaudit comparationem quandam inter se."

Speaking of Father Bolland, his professor of cosmology and natural theology, he said: "He read his Suarez very faithfully. (And on the feast of St. Thomas he would say the Mass of the ferial!) He taught cosmology and natural theology. You have to hold the formal objectivity of color otherwise you can't refute Kant: that was the thesis he was certain was right in cosmology. And the thesis he thought was right in natural theology was the *praedeterminatio physica* (it was wrong, you see). He knew that Vatican Council I had defined the possibility of proving the existence of God but didn't tell us which was the proof that held."[35] Speaking of his first year philosophy professors, Lonergan notes: "In my first year of philosophy in England two were outstanding: the professor of logic and epistemology whose efforts were devoted generously to making sure we didn't think that there were any pat answers; and the professor of metaphysics who had other and more important duties and gave us only three classes in the whole year. He relieved me of the labor of learning what I would have had to unlearn later on."[36] As is evident from these quotes, Lonergan was disillusioned with the scholastic philosophy he received during his training in England. He shared what he called "the common view" that held the philosophy manuals in little esteem.[37] He certainly did not work hard at philosophy at Heythrop and indeed said he had no interest in it.[38] Later it would be evident that his major disillusionment was with the Suarezian—and before him, Scotist—theory of knowledge. It just did not cohere with his own self-knowledge.

Nevertheless, there were several positive academic influences during Lonergan's time at Heythrop. And these cohered with his own native interests. Perhaps the major influence was Fr. Charles O'Hara,

[35]*Caring About Meaning,* 29. Lonergan continues: "At Heythrop I heard a story about all professors of cosmology in the Society being assembled in Rome to find out what on earth they were to do about cosmology. Bolland . . . got up at the meeting—he was a little fellow—and said that he always taught the theses in the book and never changed them. If he could demonstrate a thesis he gave one argument; if he couldn't demonstrate it, he would give about twelve probable arguments; and if he couldn't find even probable arguments, he would say: 'I base my argument on the authority of St. Thomas Aquinas.' The Spaniards and Germans were strongly anti-Thomist and they cheered to the rafters! The French and the Italians were strong Thomists and they didn't remember this story at all. In Spain it became a tradition."

[36]Unpublished transcript by Nicholas Graham of discussion, Lonergan Workshop, Boston College, June 21, 1979. Cf. *Caring About Meaning,* 43, where Lonergan speaks of being grateful to his metaphysics professor who gave only three classes all year, "so I never had to unlearn all that nonsense."

[37]*Second Collection,* 38. Also cf. Lonergan's "Questionnaire on Philosophy," *Method: Journal of Lonergan Studies* 2:2 (October 1984) 1–35, regarding his philosophical education.

[38]*Caring About Meaning,* 8, 47.

a tutor in mathematics for those who were preparing university degrees:

> O'Hara took me for special lessons in coordinate geometry, and there was also projective geometry to do. He was quite a pedagogue; he had methods. One of his methods was: flag the diagram. Draw a diagram; mark all the values you know on it. You should be able to see an equation or two equations—whatever you need—and get the solution. Don't learn the trigonometrical formula by heart; just flag the diagram and read off the formula[39] . . . . He also developed a whole technique of teaching math. He would write an elaborate equation on the blackboard and remark, "Now, if you have an X-ray mind" and we all wanted to have an X-ray mind "you will see that this is a quadratic." He could expatiate on the great discovery of zero—which made the decimal notation possible—the superiority of Leibniz's ds/dt over Newton's y with a dot over it, and other somewhat more recondite discoveries. He was strong on the history of mathematics. . . .[40]

It was to O'Hara that Lonergan attributed his dawning awareness of the scientific revolution. "He wasn't talking much about quantum mechanics but he certainly was talking about relativity and had read books on it."[41] Central also in this growing awareness of scientific method was Lonergan's detailed reading of H.W.B. Joseph's monumental *An Introduction to Logic*:

> I had done an intermediate exam at London (I had taken logic) and had studied H.W.B. Joseph's *Introduction to Logic*. Joseph was a witty fellow. He had Mill's method of difference illustrated by the example of a man who finds that his inability to sleep may be due to his run around the quad before going to bed, and his morning stiffness due to the coffee he takes. He gives up coffee and still has stiffness in the morning; he gives up running around the quad and finds the stiffness gone—so by the method of difference he solves his problem. Joseph's was a thorough book on logic, some six hundred and fifty pages long.[42]

---

[39]Ibid., 2. Lonergan also remarks on taking the wrong train on the way to his mathematics exam in London: "I got to the exam twenty minutes late, I read the paper, picked a question, had it out in three minutes and began to feel I was all right! It was a tricky question but I saw one of O'Hara's tricks to solve it, using the square root of minus one."

[40]Unpublished transcript by Nicholas Graham of discussion, Lonergan Workshop, Boston College, June 21, 1979.

[41]Ibid., 4.

[42]Ibid., 3. He also read the following scholastic authors on logic and quotes them in his student papers: P. Coffey, G. H. Joyce, and C. Frick.

The actual illustration in Joseph's text is somewhat different than Lonergan recalled.[43] But Joseph's point in this section is one that will be central in Lonergan's future thinking. According to Joseph, contrary to John Stuart Mill's radical empiricism, causal connections are not perceived; they are understood.

William Mathews has pointed out that many of the categories that were to find their way into Lonergan's *Insight* of 1957 had their origin in Joseph's book. Joseph's categories themselves were highly influenced by Mill, the most influential of English logicians of the nineteenth century. At the same time, Joseph's book is deeply rooted in Aristotelian logic and it continually asks how that logic is related to the concrete processes of the human mind.[44] Thus, in treating of scientific processes, Joseph seems to describe what Lonergan years later will call insight and explanatory understanding: "In demonstrative reasoning we have a real insight into the connexions of things. Where this is possible, though Aristotle thought that we used syllogism, yet, as we have seen, there is not really any subsumption. The conclusion need not be less general than the premisses; there need be no application of a rule invoked *ab extra*; the connexions may be traced in an individual subject, though between characters in it that are universal. . . ."[45]

Joseph employs a term that Lonergan will later use to characterize scientific insight, that is, the term "explanation":

> Thus repeated observations of ice floating on water, in various times and places, of various sizes and shapes, may lead me to conclude that ice is lighter than water; for as it floats irrespectively of size or shape, time or place, I can connect its floating with nothing but a less specific gravity. That it should be lighter, however, remains a brute fact, nowise appar-

[43]"A man may run for an hour round his garden on a frosty night, and when he wakes up next morning may notice that his legs are stiff, and the dahlias in his garden blackened. If he had really no other experience of such events than in this succession, he might equally well conclude that the frost had made him stiff and his running blackened the dahlias, as vice versa. But it is involved in the causal relation that if two things really are cause and effect, the one never exists without the other; and hence by comparison of that experience with others, he might conclude that running round the garden did not blacken dahlias, because at another time they had not gone black after he had been running round it; and that frosty nights did not make his legs stiff in the morning, because he had waked up after another frosty night without stiffness in them. So far he would have only disproved the connexions to which his mind had jumped. To prove that frost does blacken dahlias, and that it was the running that made his legs stiff, is a more difficult matter; for the mere fact that one has been followed by the other many times constitutes no proof." H.W.B. Joseph, *An Introduction to Logic* (Oxford: The Clarendon Press, 1916) 428–29.

[44]Ibid., 421 ff. where Joseph inveighs against Mill's empiricism.

[45]Ibid., 398.

ently necessary. But if I could show that water expands in becoming ice, then, though this indeed is still a brute fact, yet, granting this, I see that ice must float; so far, I have explanation, insight into the necessity of the connexion of facts, demonstrative thinking.[46]

The significance of Joseph's book, besides giving Lonergan the rudiments of Aristotelian logic, was that it helped him to ask the basic question in philosophy, "What on earth are they doing?" or, more accurately, "What on earth are *we* doing?"[47]

---

[46]Ibid., 399. Also cf. 382 ff. where Joseph invokes Aristotle's distinction between the *priora quoad se* and the *priora quoad nos;* that is, between things that are first in our knowledge and those that are first in themselves. Cf. also 411 where Joseph refers to Poincaré's statement that a physical law is a differential equation.

[47]Cf. *Caring About Meaning,* 10.

Chapter Two

John Henry Newman

My fundamental mentor and guide has been John Henry Newman's *Grammar of Assent*. I read that in my third year philosophy (at least the analytic parts) about five times and found solutions for my problems. I was not at all satisfied with the philosophy that was being taught and found Newman's presentation to be something that fitted in with the way I knew things. It was from that kernel that I went on to different authors.[1]

The major influence on Lonergan's thought during his early years was John Henry Newman, the nineteenth-century convert to Roman Catholicism and the author of a number of classic works. Lonergan had read some of Newman's writings in his earlier years, but while at Heythrop he picked up Newman's *Grammar of Assent*. It is this book that he mentioned on a number of occasions to have read five or six times. What was Lonergan looking for in Newman during this time when he was "beginning to think for himself"? Someone whose presentation "fitted in with the way I knew things." The ultimate touchstone was his own self-knowledge: "I was looking for someone who had some common sense, and knew what he was talking about. And what was Newman talking about? About judgment as assent; about real apprehension and notional apprehension, notional assent and real assent. He was answering the liberal view that all judgments are more or less probable but nothing is certain. And he could give examples."[2]

In order to understand Newman and his influence on Lonergan, one has to realize both Newman's profoundly religious spirit and his profoundly intellectual desire to dialogue with the philosophical cur-

[1]Bernard Lonergan, "Reality, Myth, Symbol," *Myth, Symbol, and Reality*, ed. Alan M. Olson (Notre Dame, Ind.: University of Notre Dame Press, 1980) 32–33. Lonergan had some previous familiarity with Newman: In Loyola he had read *The Present Position of Catholics* and in the juniorate *The Idea of a University*; cf. *Caring About Meaning*, 15. In his early paper, "True Judgment and Science," Lonergan refers to *The Arians of the Fourth Century* and *The University Sermons*.

[2]*Caring About Meaning*, 14; cf. also 46.

rents of his own age. As a young man Newman had read some of the anti-religious writers of the time, such as Thomas Paine, David Hume, and Voltaire.[3] Soon after, through the influence of a young English clergyman, Newman experienced a profound religious conversion, a conversion that had a strong intellectual component: "When I was fifteen, (in the autumn of 1816,) a great change of thought took place in me. I fell under the influence of a definite Creed, and received into my intellect impressions of dogma, which, through God's mercy, have never been effaced or obscured."[4] In many ways this "first conversion" could be said to be the fundamental conversion in Newman's life, for it was from this that all else followed: his commitment to a serious religious and moral life, his movement from evangelicalism to High Church Anglicanism, the Oxford movement, his conversion to Catholicism and finally, all his activities and writings as a Catholic.

It is significant that the work that had the greatest influence on Lonergan, the *Grammar of Assent*, was published in 1870, that is, toward the end of Newman's life. It was the only book he wrote that was not written under the pressure of an immediate public challenge. And yet it was the book in which he addressed the underlying philosophical issue of the nineteenth century—one might also say, of the twentieth century. That issue, which percolates beneath the surface of all of his writings, is the defense of Christianity precisely as *true* against the prevailing rationalistic and skeptical philosophies of the time. When Newman was named a Cardinal by Pope Leo XIII in 1879, he summarized the major thrust of his life's work as a resistance to "the spirit of liberalism in religion" which he defined as, "the doctrine that there is no positive truth in religion, but that one creed is as good as another, and this is the teaching which is gaining substance and force daily. It is inconsistent with any recognition of any religion as *true*. It teaches that all are to be tolerated, but all are matters of opinion."[5]

---

[3]"When I was fourteen, I read Paine's *Tracts against the Old Testament*, and found pleasure in thinking of the objections which were contained in them. Also, I read some of Hume's *Essays*; and perhaps that on *Miracles*. . . . Also, I recollect copying out some French verses, perhaps Voltaire's, in denial of the immortality of the soul, and saying to myself something like 'How dreadful, but how plausible!' " John Henry Newman, *Apologia pro vita sua* (London: Longmans, Green, & Co., 1913) 3.

[4]Ibid., 4.

[5]John Henry Newman, " 'Biglietto' Speech" (Rome: Libreria Spithöver, 1879) 6–7. Cf. Katherine Parisi, *Newman and Liberalism*, doctoral thesis defended at Drew University, May 29, 1992. Cf. Newman's earlier statement on rationalism: "Rationalism is a certain abuse of Reason; that is, a use of it for purposes for which it never was intended, and is unfitted. To rationalize in matters of Revelation is to make our reason the standard

But that defense of Christianity precisely as true involved Newman in the perennial issue of determining "What is truth?" As a young man Newman had, like Lonergan himself, devoted a great deal of time to the study of Aristotelian logic. He had come under the influence of Richard Whately, who involved him in the writing of his textbook *Elements of Logic*, which remained the standard text at Oxford until it was replaced by John Stuart Mill's text in the 1850s. Soon afterwards he began to read the Church Fathers and was deeply attracted to their Platonism.[6] At the same time, it was the need to speak to the underlying philosophy of his own age that led Newman throughout his busy years to read the writings of such men as John Locke and John Stuart Mill. Although he was in fundamental opposition to modern liberalism in religion, he was sympathetic with some of the major aims of modern thought and indeed, as a Catholic, he was considered among the most liberal of men.[7]

Indeed, in his writings Newman evidenced an uncanny ability to enter into the minds and views of his opponents. Before refuting liberal views he always insisted on presenting them with their full force. He had read Voltaire, Locke, Hume, and Gibbons as a teenager; he read John Stuart Mill when Mill's texts became standard reading at Oxford. Always, Newman framed his thoughts in a manner to be understood by the people of his time. As Lonergan articulated one of his major debts to Newman: "Newman's remark that ten thousand difficulties do not make a doubt has served me in good stead. It encouraged me

---

and measure of the doctrine revealed. . . . It is Rationalism to accept Revelation and then to explain it away; to speak of it as the Word of God, and to treat it as the word of man; to refuse to let it speak for itself. . . . The Rationalist makes himself his own center, not his Maker; he does not go to God, but implies that God must come to him. . . . Rationalism takes the words of Scripture as signs of Ideas; Faith of Things or Realities." *Essays Critical and Historical* (London: Longmans, Green, & Co., 1895) 1:31–35.

[6]Cf. Newman, *Apologia pro vita sua*, 26: "The broad philosophy of Clement and Origen carried me away; the philosophy, not the theological doctrine. . . . Some portions of their teaching, magnificent in themselves, came like music to my inward ear, as if in response to ideas, which, with little external to encourage them, I had cherished so long." Elsewhere in the *Apologia* Newman mentions his own early temperament as being attracted to the world of the unseen, leading him to "rest in the thought of two and two only absolute and luminously self-evident beings, myself and my Creator." Ibid., 4.

[7]Cf. Newman's " 'Biglietto' Speech," 9: " . . . It must be borne in mind, that there is much in the liberalistic theory which is good and true; for example, not to say more, the precepts of justice, truthfulness, sobriety, self-command, benevolence, which, as I have already noted are among its avowed principles and the natural laws of society. It is not till we find that this array of principles is intended to supersede, to block out religion, that we pronounce it to be evil."

to look difficulties squarely in the eye, while not letting them interfere with my vocation or my faith."[8]

For Newman the core issue in the *Grammar of Assent* was the nature of the human mind. What does it mean to know? How can a coherent theory of human knowing be framed in such a way as to cohere with the experiential emphases of Mill and Locke on the one hand, and with the experience of conscience and the assertion of Christian doctrine as true on the other? For Newman, in line with the general emphasis of English philosophy, the major focus was human experience, but it was a far richer notion of experience than that of the empiricist philosophers.

Certainly a major influence on Lonergan was Newman's very method. For Newman was not a scholastic. He was influenced by the Fathers of the Church and by modern English philosophy. Such philosophy was down-to-earth and practical; it focussed on sense experience and perception. If its empiricist tendencies were to be refuted and transcended, it would have to be accomplished by someone who carefully analyzed our human mental processes.

For Newman the ultimate court of appeal for the knowledge of human mentality would be the mind's own knowledge of itself. As he trenchantly expressed it, "in these provinces of inquiry egotism is true modesty."[9] This necessary egotism at the foundation of mental and philosophical science points to the inevitabilities that we necessarily employ in our human operations, whether or not we advert to what we are doing. The following words must have rung a bell for the young Lonergan who was beginning to "think for himself":

> I am what I am or I am nothing. I cannot think, reflect, or judge about my being, without starting from the very point which I aim at concluding. . . . I cannot avoid being sufficient for myself, for I cannot make myself anything else, and to change me is to destroy me. If I do not use myself I have no other self to use. . . . What I have to ascertain are the laws under which I live. My first elementary lesson of duty is that of resignation to the laws of nature, whatever they are; my first disobedience is to be impatient at what I am, and to indulge an ambitious aspiration after what I cannot be, to cherish a distrust of my powers, and to desire to change laws which are identical with myself.[10]

In spite of oppositions and conflicts among people on matters philosophical, ethical, and religious, still a serious inquirer, "brings

[8]*Second Collection*, 263.

[9]John Henry Newman, *A Grammar of Assent* (London: Longmans, Green, & Co., 1913) 384.

[10]Ibid., 347.

together his reasons and relies on them, because they are his own, and this is his primary evidence; and he has a second ground of evidence, in the testimony of those who agree with him. But his best evidence is the former, which is derived from his own thoughts; and it is that which the world has a right to demand of him; and therefore his true sobriety and modesty consists, not in claiming for his conclusions an acceptance or scientific approval which is not to be found anywhere, but in stating what are personally his grounds. . . ."[11]

From the point of view of Bernard Lonergan's life and work, it is interesting to note that one of the major break-throughs in Newman's own intellectual journey was the awareness of the distinction between various levels of human consciousness. Newman had been working on an analysis of mind for over thirty years. It was "like tunnelling through the Alps"—though fittingly enough, the "beginning of my success dates from 1866—when in Switzerland. . . ."[12] "At last, when I was up at Glion over the lake of Geneva, it struck me 'You are wrong in beginning with certitude—certitude is only a kind of assent—you should begin with contrasting assent and inference.' "[13]

This was the foundation for the *Grammar of Assent*. In this work Newman focusses on the unconditional character of the act of assent and distinguishes it from notional and real apprehension and formal and informal inference.[14] Newman analyzes these mental activities in the worlds of common sense and religion. In the following pages we will present some of Lonergan's own writings from his school days in England and relate them to what he learned from Newman.

1. "The Form of Mathematical Inference"

In recent years attention has begun to be focussed on some early papers Lonergan wrote as a student at Heythrop in the journal, *The Blandyke Papers*. " 'Publication' here means simply that the author, having had his article duly refereed, copied it by hand into a notebook which was left in the common room for perusal by the college 'public.' "[15] In the first of these papers, "The Form of Mathematical Infer-

---

[11]Ibid., 385–86.

[12]John Henry Newman, *Letters and Diaries: The Vatican Council*, vol. 25 (Oxford University Press) 35.

[13]Ibid., 29.

[14]For the unconditional character of the act of assent cf. *A Grammar of Assent*, 8, 13, 16, 35, 38, 75, 157, 172–74, 188–89, 259.

[15]Notes to "The Form of Inference" in *Collection*, 256. The name "Blandyke" comes from a village near Liège where the students had their weekly holiday in the years when English laws forced the Jesuit seminary across the English Channel. Cf. Frederick E. Crowe, *Lonergan* (Collegeville, Minn.: The Liturgical Press, 1992) 32.

ence," of January 1928, Lonergan's concern is the specific question of what in fact happens when we draw mathematical conclusions. It is obvious that, in spite of Newman's vindication of the whole human world of the "non-logical," Lonergan, like Newman, is very interested in determining what happens in the world of logical and mathematical thinking. In this article the young Lonergan finds the scholastics "not very enlightening" in their view that in mathematical thinking there is a conceptual inference in which the predicate is understood to be necessarily an attribute of the subject, *"exigitive de ratione subjecti."*[16] Such a conceptual approach is based on universal concepts such as "triangularity as such."

In opposition to such "conceptual thinking," Lonergan's own analysis is factual and empirical. He adverts to what he calls a "universalization" on the level of sense. He invokes Aquinas' *vis cogitativa* as the faculty of such concrete apprehension. Thus, the solution to a geometric and mathematical problem involves a "generic image," a "phantasm," a "visualization," a "kinetic image," that can be manipulated and "gyrated" so that one "sees" the solution to the problem. Both axioms and inferences are "intuited" in the concrete. One senses here the pedagogical influence of Father Charles O'Hara, his tutor in geometry.

In this article one of the common themes of Lonergan's later writings is sounded: the schematic image is more important for thought than is ordinarily believed. The truth of the particular is not a consequence of the truth of the general; rather, the general is grasped in the particular. Something similar can be found in Newman. In an unpublished philosophical fragment on "the faculty of abstraction" Newman wrote:

> Now, when we come to the subject of making abstractions or taking views or aspects itself which all men have to a certain point, and which in some men rises to genius, what account are we to give of it? Does it imply generalization or comparison? No, if we imply in these words the presence of a subject matter of "many" individuals: for did we see but one horse or dog, we could gain from it an idea of the sciences of physiology, anatomy, physical chemistry, etc., etc., in other words we could view it under the aspects of its life, organization, structure, vital action, etc., etc.[17]

[16]"The Form of Mathematical Inference," 129.

[17]Edward Sillem, ed., *Philosophical Notebook of John Henry Newman*, vol. 2 (Louvain: Nauwelaerts Pub. House, 1970) 13. To this quote Edward Sillem appends the editorial note: "The question is whether a universal is merely formed by induction from particulars. A Nominalist must reply in the affirmative. Newman replies in the negative. In principle a universal can be formed from one particular."

Elsewhere in his notes Newman says: "There is a universal which is not abstract, and an abstract which is not universal."[18]

2. "The Syllogism"

The second of the *Blandyke Papers* was read by Lonergan before the "Philosophy and Literature Society" at Heythrop on February 26, 1928: "At Heythrop there was the 'Phil and Lit Society' and in my second year I read a paper there on 'The Form of Inference.' (Later on it came out in *Thought* and in the first volume of *Collection*.) The hypothetical syllogism is the real thing; it relates propositions—wow! The place was crowded and no one understood what on earth I was talking about."[19] This second of his papers originally was entitled "The Syllogism."[20] In it Lonergan repeats some of the themes of the previous article: the emphasis on concreteness, the perceptual scheme, the visualization. He is opposed to any "mechanical" theory of syllogistic reasoning on the analogy of a slot machine: "put in a penny, pull the trigger, and the transition to box of matches is spontaneous, immediate and necessary."[21] On the contrary, reason acts "only because of a reason," and consequently the form of syllogistic reasoning can most easily be seen in the hypothetical syllogism of the form:

> If *A*, then *B*
> But *A*
> Therefore *B*.

In this simple form of syllogism, the middle term indicates both the *ratio ratiocinandi* and the *ratio essendi* of the attribute belonging to the subject. By this is meant that the reason for knowing something is rooted in the reason for a thing's own being: "The cause of the attribute belonging to the object in the real order, is the reason why the mind attributes the predicate to the subject in the act of inference."[22]

Lonergan's emphasis is very decidedly against the importance of universal concepts in the processes of thought. By "manhood" or "triangularity" one means, in all strictness, the more notable characteristics of a man or a triangle. No valid conclusions can mechanically be

[18]John Henry Newman, *The Theological Papers of John Henry Newman on Faith and Certainty*, eds. de Achaval and Holmes (Oxford: Clarendon Press, 1976) 57.

[19]*Caring About Meaning*, 13.

[20]Cf. the editorial notes to "The Form of Inference" in *Collection*, 256–58.

[21]"The Syllogism," 1.

[22]Ibid., 6. Cf. H.W.B.Joseph, *An Introduction to Logic*, 305: "We have already, in discussing the modality of judgements, met with this distinction between the reason for *a thing being* so and so, and the reason for *our knowing* it to be so—between *ratio essendi* and *ratio cognoscendi*." Cf. also ibid., 205–06.

inferred from such universal concepts. On the other hand, there is the central importance of proper images, the proper perceptual schemes, etc., in order to grasp meaningful relationships.[23]

In this article Lonergan adds a note on predication, which he distinguishes between phenomenal and noumenal: "Predication [phenomenal] consists in saying that a thing-in-itself distinguished and denoted by the presence of certain phenomena also presents some other phenomenon. For example, 'this flower is yellow': 'this flower' means 'a thing-in-itself' designated by means of the phenomena common to all flowers and by the gesture 'this'; 'is yellow' means that 'this flower,' the subject, has besides the phenomena indicated by its name, a further phenomenon indicated by the word 'yellow.' "[24] As far as noumenal predication, Lonergan concedes that phenomena cannot be conceived as independent of the thing-in-itself, but how it is "to be" the thing-in-itself "only God knows."

There is here a definite agnosticism with regard to "things in themselves," that, as J. M. Cameron has brought out, is found in Newman and is a definite strand in English empiricism, an empiricism first articulated by David Hume in the eighteenth century. According to this view—Cameron calls it the empiricist myth—the foundation upon which knowledge rests consists in impressions which rise from the senses and, as Hume states, "their ultimate cause is, in my opinion, perfectly inexplicable by human reason, and 'twill always be impos-

---

[23]It is interesting to note that Newman, contrary to Mill in his *System of Logic,* makes a clear distinction between imagination and conception. He reflects on Mill's reflections on the definition of a circle: " 'We cannot *conceive* a line without breadth; we can form no mental picture of such a line.' Does he not here confuse conception with imagination? We cannot imagine such a line—but there are many things which we conceive, or (whatever word we use) which we hold before our intellect, which we cannot imagine. Abstract words imply conceptions which are not still imaginations. What would he call the operation by which we hold in the mind the idea of whiteness? Why is not length without breadth as good an idea or conception as whiteness? It is an abstraction from facts⟨phenomena⟩. Take again the notion of *relation;* e.g., paternity or friendship. This something which *goes between* two objects. It cannot exist without those objects and without a process in fact—but we can conceive it in itself, etc.; it is like a line without breadth." "Papers of 1857 on Mill's Logic," *Philosophical Papers on Faith and Certainty,* 41. Elsewhere he notes: "Mill says, contrary to Whewell, that the ellipse is no *fact* in addition to the numerical *observations* in detail on which it is founded. But surely the *relations* of facts are facts; and therefore new facts above the facts. Hence . . . the ellipse which expresses the relation of the observations *to each other* is something new. . . . Question. What Whewell and Mill call 'conception' p. 304, is the object of it the same as 'formal cause'?" Ibid., 43. Readers of Lonergan's writings will see concerns similar to those of Newman in the latter part of the nineteenth century.

[24]"The Syllogism," 8.

sible to decide with certainty, whether they arise immediately from the object, or are produc'd by the creative power of the mind, or are deriv'd from the author of our being."[25]

Edward Sillem highlights this characteristic in Newman's thought: "At what period of his life he arrived at the doctrine which he held firmly in later life, namely, that the material world is a world of things or substances of which we can know nothing, because what we perceive of them are merely their sensible phenomena, it is difficult to say with any precision. One thing, however, is quite certain: he did not take his doctrine from Locke."[26]

How then did Lonergan deal with this issue? How had Newman dealt with it? It was at this point that the young Lonergan picked up off his shelf Newman's *Grammar of Assent*.

3. "True Judgment and Science"

Newman's early influence on Lonergan can be seen most clearly in the third of the *Blandyke Papers*, "True Judgment and Science," which he gave before the "Phil and Lit Society" on February 3, 1929: "The next year I spoke on Newman and there were about six people there! The first fellow who spoke (he went after ordination to South Africa on the missions and died there quite young) said, 'If it isn't a left-handed compliment, the talk was much better than I expected.' "[27] This paper contains the most ample references to Newman in all of Lonergan's extant writings. In it Lonergan vindicates Newman's contention that we can know with certainty more than we can formally or scientifically prove. In other words, science and logic are not the ordinary human criteria for truth: "If true judgment may be consciously true, then science ceases to be the one measure of certitude."[28]

In logic the only certain conclusions are deductions from self-evident propositions. On the other hand, scientific hypotheses may have any

[25]David Hume, *A Treatise of Human Nature* (Oxford: 1896) 84; quoted in James M. Cameron, *The Night Battle* (London: Catholic Book Club, 1962) 225–26.

[26]Sillem, *The Philosophical Notebook of John Henry Newman*, vol. 1, 187. The theme is sounded even in Newman's *Apologia* where he speaks of the doctrine of transubstantiation: "For myself, I cannot indeed prove it, I cannot tell *how* it is; but I say, 'Why should it not be? What's to hinder it? What do I know of substance or matter? just as much as the greatest philosophers, and that is nothing at all;'—so much is this the case, that there is a rising school of philosophy now, which considers phenomena to constitute the whole of our knowledge in physics." *Apologia pro vita sua*, 240.

[27]*Caring About Meaning*, 13. Two other shorter papers from 1929, largely logical in scope, were "Infinite Multitude" (February 1929) and a letter on "Creation from Eternity" (Easter 1929).

[28]"True Judgment and Science," 1.

degree of probability but cannot be certain, for absolute verification is logically impossible. Still, in many of the ordinary true judgments of life, absolute verification is possible. Here Lonergan refers to Newman's doctrine of "the illative sense":

> The illative sense is just such an absolute verification. The mind in a given case may be able to determine the limit of converging probabilities, and so disregard as nugatory the nebulous possibilities which prevent an inference from being logically valid. . . . In this action . . . the illative sense concludes a process which is too manifold in its data, too elusive in its procedure, too intimate in its discernment, for adequate analysis to be possible or for a criterion of the abstractly self-evident to be fair. Thus we know the truth and know we know it but prove it we cannot.[29]

Lonergan uses as his example his certainty that "there is a country called Tibet," just as Newman had used the example, "England is an island." Such ordinary judgments are rational, and can be certain, but they are not reducible to the rationality of deduction from self-evident principles.

Lonergan's adversaries in this article are not only the anti-religious rationalists who championed "science" as the one way to truth, but also the scholastics who championed a purely logical and conceptual approach to human understanding. Lonergan was familiar with the critical attacks on the *Grammar of Assent* on the part of scholastic philosophers. Thus, he had read the first major criticism by Fr. Thomas Harper in *The Month* of June 1870. Harper had attacked the very conception of informal inference: "Either my inference is formally valid or it is not. If it be formally valid, it is *ipso facto* moulded by logical law; if it is not, it is no inference at all."[30] On this view human reasoning could theoretically be reduced to a series of syllogisms which would have self-evident propositions for their ultimate premises. On the contrary, Lonergan quotes Newman:

> Our reasoning ordinarily presents itself to our mind as a single act not a process or series of acts. We apprehend the antecedent and then the consequent, without explicit recognition of the medium connecting the two, as if by a sort of direct association of the first thought with the second. We proceed by a sort of instinctive perception from premise to conclusion. . . . We perceive external objects and we remember past events without knowing how we do so, and in like manner we reason without

[29]Ibid.
[30]Thomas Harper, "Dr. Newman's Essay in the aid of a *Grammar of Assent*," *The Month* 12 (1870) 599–611, 677–92; 13 (1871) 31–58, 159–83.

effort and intention or any necessary consciousness of the path which the mind takes in passing from antecedent to conclusion.[31]

Newman's contention was that we should be satisfied with this account of judgment, because we cannot analyze all our grounds for making judgments. Such is the character of "the illative sense," which Newman called a solemn word for an ordinary thing.[32] Lonergan quotes approvingly the *Grammar's* assertion that the mind can know more than it can say in words: "Common sense, moral perception, genius, the great discoverers of principles do not reason. They have no arguments, no grounds, they see the truth but they do not know how they see it; it is as much a matter of *experiment* with them, as if they had to find a road to a distant mountain, which they see with the eye; and they get entangled, embarrassed, overthrown, in the *superfluous* endeavor."[33]

As opposed to the Cartesian principle of methodic doubt, of doubting everything that can be doubted, Lonergan states: "Instead of pronouncing all our assents as untrustworthy from a nervous fear of error, we take ourselves as we find ourselves, wrong perhaps in not a few opinions but for the most part right. By the digestion of these views and by the assimilation of new ones which come to us as the mind develops and experience increases, error is automatically purged away."[34] He quotes Newman in the application of this principle to the world of religion: "This is the secret of the influence by which the Church draws to herself converts from such various and conflicting religions . . . it is by the light of those particular truths, contained respectively in the various religions of men . . . that we pick our way slowly perhaps but surely into the religion which God has given; taking our certitudes with us not to lose but to keep them more securely and to understand and love their objects more perfectly."[35]

Later in his life Lonergan would formalize this procedure under the rubric of "dialectic": that is, develop positions that are true and reverse false positions by bringing out their contradictions to the invariant features of mind and reality. The whole process is basically positive: beginning from what we know and developing what we know in such

[31]*Grammar of Assent*, 259–60.

[32]Cf. C. Stephen Dessain, "Cardinal Newman on the Theory and Practice of Knowledge: The Purpose of the *Grammar of Assent*," *The Downside Review* (1957) 11.

[33]*Grammar of Assent*, 380. Newman concludes this quote with a line elsewhere quoted by Lonergan: "It is the second-rate men, though most useful in their place, who prove, reconcile, finish, and explain."

[34]"True Judgment and Science," 2.

[35]*Grammar of Assent*, 249.

a way as to dissolve the false beliefs we have picked up on the road of life. In this article Lonergan quotes from Newman for the first time what he will often refer to through the years in his analysis of belief:

> Of the two I would rather maintain that we ought to begin with believing everything that is offered to our acceptance, than that it is our duty to doubt everything. . . . We soon discover and discard what is contradictory to itself; and error having always some portion of truth in it, and the truth having a reality which error has not, we may expect that when there is an honest purpose and fair talents, we shall somehow make our way forward, the error falling off from the mind and truth developing and occupying it.[36]

Lonergan adds some notions on judgment:

> To lay it down that truth cannot be known unless directly or deductively self-evident seems mistaken, not only because the illative sense does posit truth without self-evidence, but also because such a canon is at odds both with our mental constitution—for mind judges rather than syllogises—and with the evidence at our disposal which is far too manifold for us *a priori* to limit ourselves to the self-evident and burk the remainder. Again it is fallacious to urge that assent must be proportioned to evidence, for evidence is the mark of truth not the measure of assent, and truth once known is to be assented to unconditionally.[37]

He also refers to Newman's assertion of the unconditional character of assent:

> If assent and inference are each of them the acceptance of a proposition, but the special characteristic of inference is that it is conditional, it is natural to suppose that assent is unconditional. Again, if assent is the acceptance of truth, and truth is the proper object of the intellect, and no one can hold conditionally what by the same act he holds to be true, here too is a reason for saying that assent is an adhesion without reserve or doubt to the proposition to which it is given.[38]

Charles Hefling has commented on Newman's doctrine on assent:

> There are any number of philosophers who either have failed to notice any distinction between meaning and truth, understanding and judgment, apprehension and assent; or else have denied that such a distinction exists. Newman, by contrast, would seem to be pushing, apparently on his own and perhaps without altogether knowing it, towards something he could not, in any case have learned from any modern thinker

[36]Ibid., 377.
[37]"True Judgment and Science," 3.
[38]*Grammar of Assent*, 172.

who preceded him: a significance, beyond the copulative, conveyed by *is*. Grant that *is* has such a further significance, correlative not with apprehension but with assent, and quite alot of the *Grammar* falls into place.[39]

But though assent is always unconditional, that is, it has the absolute character of truth, still it can differ according to the quality of the apprehension which precedes it. Accordingly, Lonergan goes on to present Newman's ideas on notional and real apprehension. He quotes Newman on the tendency of logicians to "starve" words of their life so that they become mere "notions": "Words, which denote things, have innumerable implications . . . but it is the very triumph of [the logician] . . . to have stripped them of all their connatural senses, to have drained them of that breadth and depth of associations which constitute their poetry, their rhetoric and their historical life, to have starved each term down till it has become the ghost of itself. . . ."[40]

He then presents his analysis of Newman's doctrine:

> The distinction of real and notional apprehension I take to be one of degrees not of kind. The real is not of reality as it is in itself—such is had only by God—while the notional is not unreal in the sense that it is not representative, but only less real. It is the apprehension of a few definite aspects of a thing which is apprehended in all its aspects in real apprehension. . . . Real apprehension may be described as impressional, that of one who enters onto the object by sympathy, intuition, unformulated interpretations, while notional apprehension stands over against the object, successively views its relations, analyses, formulates.[41]

Lonergan refers to Newman's assertion that in notional apprehension we regard things not as they are in themselves, but mainly as they stand in relation to each other.[42] On the other hand, real apprehension is concerned, not primarily with ideas, "the aspects of things," but with things themselves of which we have an "impressional" apprehension.

Lonergan then quotes Newman regarding the moral dimension of the search for truth:

> Shall we say that there is no such thing as truth and error, but that anything is true to a man which he troweth? and not rather as the solution

[39]Charles C. Hefling, "On Apprehension, Notional and Real" (paper presented at the Lonergan Workshop, Boston College, March 18–19, 1988) 7.
[40]*Grammar of Assent*, 267.
[41]"True Judgment and Science," 4.
[42]Cf. *Grammar of Assent*, 31.

of a great mystery that truth there is, and attainable it is, but that its rays stream in upon us through the medium of our moral as well as our intellectual being; and that in consequence that perception of its first principles which is natural to us is enfeebled, obstructed, perverted, by the allurements of sense and the supremacy of self, and, on the other hand, quickened by aspirations after the supernatural.[43]

The issue of truth, then, in the life of the individual is the issue of wisdom: "The evolution of thought in which truth gains the upper hand and error is purged away, is to be accompanied and supplemented by a growth in the moral character. Not science so much as wisdom is to be the individual's aim. . . ."[44] He summarizes the rationalism that the *Grammar* attacks as, "the unconscious assumption made by post Aristotelian skeptics, who from a denial of *a priori* knowledge concluded the irrationality of certitude. Thus was implicitly set up the 'pretentious axiom' that science is the criterion of certitude."[45] It is precisely this axiom that Newman attacked on behalf of all the "real knowledge" available to the non-scientist, the common "person in the street":

> There is a certain dramatic fitness that Newman, of whom Mark Pattison said "All the grand developments of human reason from Aristotle down to Hegel was a closed book to him," should point out to the rationalists that their superiority was based upon a mere assumption, that the "plain man" was not so much a puppet after all. It has been the contention that this assumption is contradicted by our natural procedure. Science anyway is but a luxury of a few, certitude a prerogative of man, and wisdom the obligatory complement of his being. To make science the criterion of certitude despite its limitations, is wantonly to tempt man (who, Newman somewhere says, does not wish to know the truth) to give up the quest for wisdom, to make it possible for him to be complacently agnostic in the high name of reason, when reason hardly countenances his criterion. He will deny the existence of God because the proofs do not convince him and then accept the first theory to hand to explain away the religions of the world (cf. Renan).[46]

In this developing judgment of the person under the influence of conscience, subjective and illegitimate influences are only *per accidens*, just as errors in sense perception are only *per accidens*. Lonergan defends Newman from the charge of subjectivism: "The same person both judges and wills; if you ask such a segregation of these two ac-

[43]Ibid., 311.
[44]"True Judgment and Science," 5.
[45]Ibid., 6.
[46]Ibid.

tivities that all the world may be assured there has been no confusion of their functions, you ask too much: God made man differently and His Providence is the guarantee of nature. Finally the power of logic to correct subjective influence is easily over estimated."[47] In his later years Lonergan will put it this way:

> Ojectivity is reached through the self-transcendence of the concrete existing subject, and the fundamental forms of self-transcendence are intellectual, moral and religious conversion. To attempt to ensure objectivity apart from self-transcendence only generates illusion.[48]

In a footnote to this quote Lonergan states that the basic statement on this issue is found in chapters eight and nine of Newman's *Grammar of Assent*, from which he quotes the famous line: "Logic makes but a sorry rhetoric with the multitude; first shoot round corners and you may not despair of converting by a syllogism."[49]

Many years later Lonergan will relate Newman's teaching on notional and real assent to his own theory of intellectual, moral, and religious conversion.[50] In "True Judgment and Science" he quotes Henri Bremond whose *Mystery of Newman* he had evidently read:

> I meet everywhere with nothing but demonstrations and demonstrators. Each of them promises to conduct their enquiry according to the rules, each parades the logical outfit of his time. It is not the miserable and passionate man—no it is the pure reason which speaks and it wishes to meet only with reason. . . . But to the majority of those who have taken in hand the examination of any question, and who plume themselves on their exact and pure reasoning the truth could say: "You do not know how to demonstrate me and in any case you would find it very difficult to do, if you already did not very fortunately possess me."[51]

---

[47]Ibid. Lonergan refers to the *Grammar of Assent*, 412.

[48]*Method in Theology*, 338.

[49]*Grammar of Assent*, 94, quoted there from Newman's earlier writing, *Discussions and Arguments on Various Subjects*.

[50]Cf. *Method in Theology*, 251, on having only a notional apprehension of conversion. Also, 169: "H. G. Gadamer has contended that one really grasps the meaning of a text only when one brings its implications to bear on contemporary living. This, of course, is paralleled by Reinhold Niebuhr's insistence that history is understood in the effort to change it. I have no intention of disputing such views, for they seem to me straightforward applications of Newman's distinction between notional and real apprehension."

[51]Henri Bremond, *The Mystery of Newman* (London: Williams and Norgate, 1907) 87. Ironically, in spite of Lonergan's apparent enthusiasm, Bremond is not always regarded as an authentic interpreter of Newman. Cf.Charles Stephen Dessain, "Newman's Philosophy and Theology," *Victorian Prose* (New York: Modern Language Association of America, 1973) 166–69.

We should note that in "True Judgment and Science" there is a definite ambiguity in clearly articulating all the aspects of our human knowing. As we noted in the previous article on "The Syllogism," Lonergan picks up from Newman the empiricist strain. For example, he writes that real apprehension is "not of reality as it is in itself— such is had only by God," and he refers to Newman's words in the *Grammar of Assent:* "We are accustomed, indeed, and rightly, to speak of the Creator Himself as incomprehensible; and, indeed, He is so by an incommunicable attribute; but in a certain sense each of His creatures is incomprehensible to us also, in the sense that no one has a perfect understanding of them but He. We recognize and appropriate aspects of them, and logic is useful to us in registering these aspects and what they imply; but it does not give us to know even one individual being."[52]

What in this view saves our knowledge of objective reality is the ineradicable tendency inherent in, and natural to the mind, to spontaneously think of sensible things as existing objectively and on their own.[53] This tendency Newman vindicates in the second half of the *Grammar of Assent* under the doctrine of the illative sense, and he amplified it in specifying the unconditional character of the act of assent. In its defense the early Lonergan in "True Judgment and Science," wrote: "To sum up the argument, 'nature does not fail us in necessaries,' a criterion of evidence is necessary. Science, the syllogistic method, shows itself to be inadequate and unfair (i.e. not the natural criterion) in its preliminary clearing the field by methodic doubt or suspension of judgment, the confinement of attention to the abstractly self-evident, in its emptying out the content of our knowledge and its barren definitions of the things the full meaning of which we are only more or less aware."[54]

The only adequate criterion of truth is the mind itself in its fullest exercise: "The alternative criterion is the mind itself 'far higher, wider, more subtle, than logical inference' which can use all our knowledge, evaluate evidence in the concrete, and remain in harmony with natu-

---

[52]*Grammar of Assent*, 283.

[53]Sillem, *The Philosophical Notebook of John Henry Newman*, vol. 1, 188. This too, according to J. M. Cameron, is characteristic of empiricism: "Now it is equally characteristic of empiricism . . . that self-scrutiny should be held to disclose powerful and ordinarily irresistible impulses to believe certain hypotheses; and that the felt energy of these impulses should in all matters of practice overcome, and rightly overcome, the uncertainties that belong to these hypotheses so long as they are treated as making claims to be rationally demonstrable." Cameron, *The Night Battle*, 226.

[54]"True Judgment and Science," 5.

ral procedure, neither *a priori* doubting everything or accepting anything.''[55]

4. Lonergan's Early Nominalism

In a letter he wrote to an older friend and fellow Jesuit, Henry Smeaton, in 1927, not long after he arrived at Heythrop, Lonergan remarked:
''I am afraid I must lapse into philosophy. I have been stung with that
monomania now and then but am little scholastic though as far as I
know a good Catholic. Still modern logic is fair. The theory of knowledge is what is going to interest me most of all. I have read Aristotle
his *Peri Psuches* and am of strong nominalist tendency.''[56] His ''lapse''
into philosophy finds him ''little scholastic'' though, he hopes, ''a good
Catholic.'' Reminiscent of Newman of whom it also could be said, he
was ''little scholastic?'' Still, he is following up his study of Aristotelian
logic with a study of the ancient philosopher's theory of mind.

In a letter to his provincial some years later Lonergan said, ''I left
Heythrop a votary of Newman's and a nominalist.''[57] Many years later
he related an incident that took place in 1930 as he was leaving
Heythrop to finish his external degree in London. He was speaking
to his superior, Father Bolland, about his future. He thought he might
be slated to teach either mathematics or classics, the subjects he was
doing in London—even though philosophy was at that time his ''fine
frenzy.''

> I was bidding Fr. Joseph Bolland farewell, listed for him the subjects I
> was doing at London, and asked him which was the one I should con-
> centrate on. He replied that I should keep in mind that superiors might
> want me to teach philosophy or theology. I answered that there was no
> question of that since I was a nominalist. He in turn said, ''Oh! No one
> remains a nominalist very long.'' It was, in current parlance, a quite
> ''cool'' reply from a high member of the establishment. . .[58]

One senses in Lonergan's remarks about Father Bolland, indeed
one of his ''Suarezian'' teachers, the presence of a man with practical
wisdom. Confronted by a creative and independent young man, the

[55]Ibid.

[56]Letter of June 20, 1927. Quoted with permission of the trustees of the Lonergan
Research Institute, Toronto.

[57]Letter to Provincial, January 22, 1935. Quoted with permission of the Lonergan Research Institute, Toronto.

[58]*Second Collection*, 263–64; also cf. transcripts by Nicholas Graham of discussions from
the Lonergan Workshop at Boston College, June 14, 1978, where Lonergan says, ''In
most places you would have been 'back-bogged' for saying you were a nominalist.''

older man goes with him. He does not try to refute. He just shows him the paths his thought can follow, with a relaxed conviction that clarity will come. Lonergan goes on to say that his nominalism did disappear; but it might behoove us now to dwell on what Lonergan might have meant by his early nominalism.

From his several references to himself as a nominalist, it is obvious that Lonergan thought of the meaning of the term as quite evident. Traditionally nominalism had been ascribed to the medieval philosopher William of Ockham and his followers. Ockham's thesis was that, since only individual things really exist, universal concepts are only names (*flatus vocis*) used to speak of individual things. Traditionally opposed to nominalism were various types of scholastic "realism" which vindicated the realistic character of universal concepts, and indeed, tended to build a whole philosophy around the importance of such concepts.

It was especially English empiricist philosophy that inherited the mantle of medieval nominalism. In the eighteenth century Thomas Hobbes emphasized the experiential character of human knowing in opposition to the "bewitchment" engendered by universal concepts. Such concepts only resulted from the process of association of various sensitive experiences. Later on, David Hume made it clear that if an idea was a picture formed by sensation or imagination, then it could be the picture only of something individual. In the middle of the nineteenth century the person who took up the nominalist banner was John Stuart Mill; and it was Mill who, as William Mathews has shown, had the greatest effect on the tradition of modern logic which so interested Lonergan.[59] It was Mill who prepared the way for the logic Lonergan studied in London.

Thus, nominalism was an accepted school of philosophical categorization during Lonergan's student days in Heythrop. It is mentioned in the various textbooks that he used. The categorization is always on the basis of the school's doctrine on universal ideas. Thus, Joseph's *An Introduction to Logic* presents three schools of thought on universal ideas: nominalism, realism, and conceptualism. He quotes James Mill, the father of John Stuart Mill, as representative of the nominalist position. For James Mill it is obvious and certain that

> men were led to class solely for the purpose of economizing in the use of names. Could the purposes of naming and discourse have been as conveniently managed by a name for every individual, the names of

[59]Unpublished article by William Mathews, "On Lonergan and John Stuart Mill." Quoted with permission.

classes, and the idea of classification, would never have existed. But as the limits of the human memory did not enable men to retain beyond a very limited number of names; and even if it had, as it would have required a most inconvenient portion of time, to run over in discourse as many names of individuals, and of individual qualities, as there is occasion to refer to in discourse, it was necessary to have contrivances of abridgement; that is, to employ names which marked equally a number of individuals, with all their separate properties; and enabled us to speak of multitudes at once.[60]

According to the categories of one of the scholastic texts Lonergan was familiar with, Father Joyce's *Principles of Logic*, there are three main philosophical schools in relation to "the controversy on universals." He asks, what is this "human nature" which is one and yet stands in the same relation to every member of the class—which though it is one, belongs at the same time to many members?

Various answers have been given to this question. We may hold (1) that this common nature is something real. Those who give this answer are termed *Realists*. We may say (2) that the common nature is merely a thought in the mind without objective counterpart in the real order. The adherents of this doctrine are known as *Conceptualists*. Or we may say (3) that the only common element is the name, given to a variety of objects because of some real or fancied resemblance. This view is that of the *Nominalists*.

In a footnote, Joyce notes: "Nominalism has been the traditional doctrine of the English sensationalist school from the days of Hobbes. It finds its most notable representative in Mill."[61] Joyce goes on to espouse what he calls a *"Moderate Realism"* which maintains that the mind abstracts from things concepts of their natures and it is those natures which are truly found in all the individuals of a class. Opposed to such moderate realism is the *"Exaggerated Realism"* of a Plato who held the objective existence in the real order of universal natures. Joyce complains that English writers often attribute this view to the Scholastics.

Now in understanding what Lonergan might have meant by his early nominalism it is important to realize that Newman himself had been accused of nominalism—and Lonergan was aware of that. In "True Judgment and Science," Lonergan refers to an article written in the *Dublin Review* of October, 1905, by F. Aveling accusing New-

---

[60]James Mill, *Analysis of the Human Mind, vol. 1* (London: 1869) 260; quoted in H.W.B. Joseph, *An Introduction to Logic*, 31.
[61]George Hayward Joyce, *Principles of Logic* (London: 1920) 132–33.

man of nominalism. In that article Aveling speaks of the troubling feeling he had reading the *Grammar of Assent*, a feeling he finally attributes to the absence of a central staple of scholastic philosophy, the emphasis on universal concepts. "I need hardly remind my readers of the enormous importance which this theory of universals—'the most fundamental point in the whole range of metaphysics'—assumes in the scholastic system of philosophy. The position it holds is, in many ways, a quite unique one. It is not only one of the central pivots of the whole philosophy; it is also, to a very marked extent, the cause which occasioned the real rise and progress of scholasticism."[62]

Aveling states that Newman's emphasis on experience translates into sense experience and thus constitutes his philosophy as a "sensism." Consequently, without the scholastic emphasis on universal concepts which are mental and metaphysical abstractions of the forms of things, there is no intellectual knowledge and no argument for the immateriality and immortality of the human soul. "Incidentally, both Nominalism and Conceptualism reduce man to a species of glorified brute animal and destroy the force of the only possible arguments that a saner form of scholasticism had to urge in favour of the immateriality, and consequent immortality, of the human soul."[63]

Newman possessed a copy of one of Joseph Kleutgen's works *La Philosophie Scholastique*, and he had marked the first volume at a section noting the two extremes in solving the problem of universal concepts and had noted: "Formalism inconceivably absurd to the modern mind; i.e., Occam. Nominalism highly plausible."[64]

In any case, Lonergan was aware of the imputation that Newman was a nominalist, and ironically in the light of his own self-definition as a nominalist, in "True Judgment and Science," he defends Newman from that attribution.

---

[62]F. Aveling, "Universals and the 'Illative Sense,'" *Dublin Review* 137 (October 1905) 255–56. (Lonergan spells the author's name "Areling.") Cf. also Aveling's reference to a review in *The Tablet* of March 25, 1899, regarding the *Grammar of Assent:* "In *The Tablet* a critic writes that the work in no way represents the current and immemorial teaching of Catholic philosophical schools."

[63]Ibid., 263.

[64]Cf. Sillem, *The Philosophical Notebook of John Henry Newman*, vol. 1, 240. Cf. also Newman, *The Theological Papers of John Henry Newman on Faith and Certainty*, 56: "A very difficult question arises whether the subject of ideas comes directly into the province of Logic. Or, in other words, whether names of terms stand for ideas or for things. It will be said that ideas and things go together, and therefore the question is unimportant—but there is the case in which there is, or is imagined, an idea without a thing, that is, the case of Universals—Accordingly those then on the side of Things against Ideas, say that there are *not* universal ideas; and a controversy ensues which is nothing else than

That the distinction between notional and real apprehension has a foundation in fact is beyond doubt. . . . It seems . . . to be one of degree and not coincident with the scholastic distinction of intellectual and possible apprehension inasmuch as its differentiae are quantity of content, direction of attention, and the presence or absences of a sense of reality or value. I am not aware of the impossibility [of] a distinction being made upon such grounds between different apprehensions of the same object. The imputation of nominalism may be thus explained away, especially as Newman was not a professional philosopher and intellectual apprehensions are a theory and not an experience.[65]

How then to understand Lonergan's early claim of nominalism? Perhaps we can understand Lonergan's early self-definition in the light of the following considerations:

1) His profound attraction to Newman and the latter's empirical method of philosophizing; and Newman was his "fundamental mentor."

2) His recognition of the importance of imagination in human understanding: the need for schematic images, etc.

3) Like Newman, his English philosophical tendency to phenomenalism.

4) His interest in understanding how words, terms, and language in general "work" in our human knowing. His interest in modern logic was an expression of this interest.

5) His conviction that the conceptual realism that was the prevalent scholastic theory of knowledge was an unreal account of human understanding.

As we noted, the prevailing scholasticism saw knowledge as basically the mental abstraction of universal concepts from things. A similar view of knowledge was presented in Lonergan's Suarezian philosophy textbooks. Later he would charcterize this type of realism as "naive." He would speak of it as "an incoherent realism, half animal and half human, that poses as a half-way house between materi-

---

a portion of the old scholastic controversy, between the Nominalists, Realists and Conceptionists." Of this controversy Newman says: "It is usual with Catholic writers to take the part of Universals—and in consequence to take the part of Ideas against Things. My own long habit has been the same—and it is difficult for me for that reason to do otherwise, but I confess the onus probandi is with those who maintain Universals, and it is difficult to prove their necessity—and taking that question away, it certainly does seem more simple and natural to say the words stand for things."

[65]"True Judgment and Science," 5.

alism and idealism."[66] For the young Lonergan, if this was realism, then he was not a realist. He could only accept a theory of mind that involved the grasp of relationships in schematic patterns or images and, with Newman, the ability of the illative sense to make judgments that were not formally "logical."

In addition, it should be noted that nominalism attributed a tremendous amount of weight to language, and of course, the analysis of language could be said to be the outstanding characteristic of twentieth century philosophy. Lonergan was on to this in the 1920s. If this emphasis meant being a nominalist, then he was a nominalist.

At about the time that Lonergan was reading Newman, the German Jesuit Erich Przywara gave a very interesting interpretation of Newman's empiricist leanings in his essay "St. Augustine and the Modern World." I do not know if Lonergan ever read this particular article, but a few years later Lonergan writes very positively of Przywara as a Catholic philosopher.[67] In his article Przywara points out three elements of the empiricist tradition. One is a stress on the visible world of sense. A second emphasis is on the importance of practice or action to the detriment of theory. And a third emphasis is on "the boundaries which confine the individual consciousness and render doubtful the existence of a world in itself common to all; this however, leads to that peculiar solipsism which may be regarded as the epistemological version of "my house is my castle." In this respect Berkeley is not the antithesis of Locke and Hume, but their inner and necessary fulfillment."[68]

Not only does Newman emphasize the priority of real apprehension over notional, but the latter "threatens to fade into a background of unsubstantial wraiths." Moreover, Newman's emphasis on "decision" in the *Grammar of Assent* merely continues an earlier emphasis—to the detriment of "theoretical" or "notional" inference. Finally, "that through the entire body of Newman's writings flow powerful currents whose source is Berkeley everyone knows who has felt the pendulum swing in his words whenever he speaks of the outer world."[69]

[66]*Insight*, 22 (xxviii).

[67]Cf. Lonergan's letter to his provincial of January 22, 1935.

[68]Erich Przywara, "St. Augustine and the Modern World," *A Monument to St. Augustine* (New York: Meridian Books, 1957; 1st ed. 1930) 281. Cf. Newman's distinction, in a letter to his sister in May 1834, between matter and its sensible phenomena: "To what extent Berkeley denied the existence of the external world I am not aware; nor do I mean to go so far myself (far from it) as to deny the existence of matter, though I should deny that *what we saw* was more than accidents of it, and say that space perhaps is but a condition of the objects of sense, not a reality."

[69]Przywara, *A Monument to St. Augustine*, 282.

In one of his later writings, Lonergan would note that Berkeley's "esse est percipi," the very existence of something is its being perceived, is the empiricist principle that moves easily into idealism.[70] Elsewhere he remarks on the concept of the "thing-in-itself" in Kant's idealism: "Because we have access only to objects sensibly presented, we are confined to a merely phenomenal world. 'Things themselves' become a merely limiting concept, a *Grenzbegriff,* by which we designate what we cannot know."[71] Hence, there is in the early Lonergan, as we will note later in this essay, an example of some of that "oscillation" he would later describe between empiricism and idealism—before arriving at a critical realism.

On the other hand, there is in Newman, as in the early Lonergan, that which overcomes all these tendencies: and that is his "surrender" to the transcendent God present in conscience and in history. It seems to me that Lonergan's later thought more than vindicates the inherently "realistic" thrust of Newman's work, not just by appealing to his deep spirituality, but more concretely, by emphasizing Newman's doctrine of assent, by which we posit the real existence of things, and his doctrine of the illative sense, by which we grasp the fulfillment of the conditions for making such assents.

As Lonergan was later to note, Newman's language was a floating one; it was not systematic. Still, he was striving to express the facts of human consciousness in a way peculiar to modern culture. Newman helped to make possible Lonergan's later achievement. In one of his later writings Lonergan quotes Newman approvingly in his distinction between the creative genius whose language about newly discovered realities is not yet settled and others who complete the verbal clarification: "It is the second-rate men, though most useful in their place, who prove, reconcile, finish, and explain."[72]

5. Conclusion

Newman is not cited a great deal in Lonergan's later writings. It is rather, it seems, Newman's method that is important: the focus on the concrete, the interior, the facts of consciousness, as of primary importance, as distinct from what philosophers or scientists "say" about knowledge. This principle became in Lonergan's writings the notion of self-appropriation. It is on the basis of our knowledge and appropri-

[70]*Second Collection,* 219.

[71]Ibid., 242. Cf. unpublished *Method in Theology* notes from 1962, 37. Available at the Lonergan Research Institute, Toronto.

[72]*Grammar of Assent,* 374. Lonergan adds that Newman writes "not without a touch of exaggeration." *Verbum,* 17.

ation of our own mental processes that we can come to express with accuracy who we are as human beings. And this brings us to what is perhaps the central effect Newman had on Lonergan. In Newman, Lonergan found someone who was highly respected, able to dialogue with those outside of the Church as well as those within, a man of "imperial intellect," able to converse with the world at large, taking the world on its own terms; and still, a spiritual person and a faithful Catholic.

In his later years Lonergan would always speak of his philosophy professors at Heythrop as "extremely honest" in their presentations.[73] I always wondered why he would characterize his teachers in this way, until it occurred to me that by this he was indicating precisely what he received from them. Not their philosophy; but their honesty. They taught him to face issues squarely, and if in his particular case that meant a radical disagreement with the scholastic tradition, so be it. He had to be honest. Still, as he said in his early letter to Henry Smeaton, "I think I am a good Catholic."

It is perhaps significant that one of the first things Lonergan did when he was sent to study in Rome in 1933 was to write a thirty-thousand-word essay on Newman which he gave to the American professor of the history of philosophy at the Gregorian, Leo W. Keeler, S.J., to critique. The essay in its entirety has since been lost, but the Lonergan archives in Toronto contain some fragments that might be from that lost essay. At least internally they seem to cohere with Lonergan's interests in the early 1930s. In these fragments there are several references to Newman, including the following on the *Grammar of Assent:*

> The essential morality of assent is the supreme contention of the *Grammar of Assent.* Assent is moral in its prerequisite of moral living, in its appeal to men of good will, in the seriousness with which it is to be regarded, in its reaction upon our views of what right morality is, in its being an *actus humanus,* in its norm—a real apprehension of human nature. We are to determine our assents not merely by the artificial standards of logic, a mere common measure of minds, but by the light that God gives us, by our judgment, by our good sense, by our *phronesis,* by the facts as we know them to be. The right assent is not according to rule but by the act of a living mind. It has no criterion, no guarantee external to itself. It is to be made with all due circumspection, with careful investigation and examination, as the nature of the case demands and circumstances permit.[74]

[73]Cf. for example, *Second Collection,* 263. The same remark can be found elsewhere.
[74]Page 36 of the fragments of what may be the lost essay on assent. Lonergan Research Institute, Toronto.

In these fragments, Lonergan uses Newman's own conversion to Catholicism to illustrate the relation between intellectual assent and actual moral and religious living. "The conversion of Newman offers a striking illustration of this problem of light and assent. For a considerable time before his actual conversion, Newman was intellectually satisfied of the truth of Catholicism; he did not yet assent; he feared that this light of his intellect was a false light that had come upon him in punishment for his sins; he did not assent but he prayed. The kindly light had indeed led him on, led him where he never expected to be brought; it led him to an extremity that terrified him; he wrestled, as Jacob with the angel."

Chapter Three

Stewart's Plato

1. A Theory of Intellect

In the summer of 1930, after finishing his degree in London, Lonergan returned to Canada and was assigned to teach at Loyola College, Montreal. In spite of numerous duties, he was able to do some reading and among the books he read was a book on Plato by an Oxford don by the name of John Alexander Stewart. It was Plato's influence, mediated by Stewart's work, that began to move him away from nominalism. In 1971 Lonergan wrote:

> As Fr. Bolland had predicted, my nominalism vanished when I read J.A.Stewart's *Plato's Doctrine of Ideas*. In writing this paper I recalled that I had been greatly influenced by a book on Plato's ideas by some Oxford don. I had forgotten his name and the exact title of the book, so I went down to the library, patiently worked through the cards listing books on Plato and, finally, when I got to "S" found my man. I got the book out of the stacks, took it to my room, and found it fascinating reading. It contained much that later I was to work out for myself in a somewhat different context, but at the time it was a great release. My nominalism had been in opposition, not to intelligence or understanding, but to the central role ascribed to universal concepts.[1]

Certain themes in Stewart's book resonated with what Lonergan had learned from Newman. The first of these was the theme of focussing on present personal experience. Stewart felt that many commentators had missed Plato's point in his theory of Ideas because they had not asked the basic question: what human and psychological experience was Plato talking about? They had tended to make Plato's ideas seem fantastic because they had not related them to the facts of present human psychology. Only in this way could the origins of his Plato's theory be discovered.

> The cardinal question is not asked: What has present-day psychology to tell us about the variety of experience which expresses itself in the

[1]*Second Collection*, 264–65.

41

doctrine of Ideas? The doctrine is treated as if it were a 'past event' in the 'history of philosophy' for determining the true nature of which there is such and such documentary evidence which, if only marshalled in the right way, is in itself conclusive.[2]

To the exegetes of Plato Stewart asks: " 'But,' we ask, *'What are the Ideas?'* What were Plato and these other people talking about? Surely about the right way of expressing some experience which they all had in common, and we ourselves still have. Tell us in the language, vernacular or philosophical, of today what that experience is."[3]

The young Lonergan must have responded to such frankness. It resonates with Newman's emphasis on discerning the concrete events of personal consciousness, on concentrating on things and not just on ideas, on facts instead of notions. Throughout his life this was a common theme: "What in the world are we talking about?"

For Stewart, Plato was both a scientist and an artist. Aristotle, however, because of a lack of appreciation for the aesthetic side of Plato, also seriously underestimated the scientific side. As a result he handed on to posterity a simple-minded interpretation of Plato's Ideas as "separate things."

> The doctrine of Ideas, expressing this double experience, has accordingly its two sides, the methodological and the aesthetic. The former side Aristotle misunderstands, and to the latter is entirely blind. If the Ideas are "separate things," as Aristotle maintains, then the doctrine of Ideas can have no methodological significance; for methodology must assume that science works with "concepts," which are not themselves "things" but general points of view from which things, i.e. sensible things—the only "separate things" known to science—are regarded.[4]

In some fragments from the Lonergan archives that appear to be from the early 1930s, Lonergan makes reference to Stewart's book and critiques Aristotle's mis-conception of Plato.

> Plato in speaking of the idea as separate or separable . . . may very well have been no more than referring to the idea as such, the abstract idea separate and distinct and entirely different from the pure presentation which it informs. The intellectual place (*noetos topos*) may be no more than a metaphor for what we with other metaphors describe as the intellectual order, the intellectual level, the intellectual plane.[5]

[2]J. A. Stewart, *Plato's Doctrine of Ideas* (Oxford: 1909) 1.
[3]Ibid., 2.
[4]Ibid., 3.
[5]Fragments of what may be the lost essay on assent from the early 1930s: Lonergan's page number 13. Archives of the Lonergan Research Center, Toronto.

In these early fragments Lonergan speaks of upholding "the theory of intellection as an immanent act" as opposed to the scholastic theory of understanding as "spiritual apprehension." Here he finds the root of Aristotle's mis-conception of Plato.

> If one tries to think of the spiritual apprehension as separate, one gets the ridiculous Aristotelian interpretation of Plato as holding "universalia a parte rei." The very argument Aristotle was against [in] Plato is used in one of Plato's dialogues by Parmenides against "young" Socrates. I.e., Socrates got over that notion in his youth. Cf. *Plato's Theory of Ideas* by Stewart.[6]

Stewart gives an interpretation of Plato's ideas in terms of methodology:

> Explained on these lines, the *eidei,* so far as methodology is concerned, are points of view from which the man of science regards his data. They are the right points of view, and, as such, have the "permanence" of phenomena; but only so in the sense that they are the "explanations" as distinguished from the "phenomena explained." They are not "separate *things*". . . . If we dismiss from our minds the prejudice raised by Aristotle's criticism, we find nothing in the Dialogues of Plato to countenance the view that the Ideas, so far as they have methodological significance, are "known" as statically existent: they are "known" only as dynamically existent—only as performing their function of making *sensibilia* intelligible. It is as true of Kant's categories that without sense they are empty. The Ideas, so far as their methodological significance is concerned, are nothing more than concepts-in-use—the instruments by employing which human understanding performs its work of interpreting the world—this sensible world, not another world beyond.[7]

For Lonergan, at last, this was an account of concepts that related them to the dynamisms of the human mind. They are "points of view" from which the sensible world is interpreted. They structure human questioning in its dynamic search for an understanding of this world. According to Stewart, Plato maintains this view of the function of the Ideas, or forms, throughout the whole series of his dialogues, but especially in his earliest dialogues. There his object is to find the forms of the moral virtues, that is, to *explain* the moral virtues by exhibiting each in its special context. Each form, such as justice, temperance, etc., is assigned its special place and use in the social system, the system of the "Good." Sense, imagination and desultory thinking, express-

---

[6]Ibid.
[7]Stewart, *Plato's Doctrine of Ideas,* 3.

ing themselves in rhetoric, present the virtues separately, taking no account of the system in which they inhere.

On the other hand, there is the process of "remembering," *anamnesis*, that enables a person to arrive at the natures of things.

> *Anamnesis*, described as *aitias logismos*, connected thinking, stirred by dialectic, works out the special context of each virtue and the relations of that context to other contexts viewed as parts, along with it, of the whole system. "Context grasped," "scientific point of view taken," "*eidos* discovered"—these are equivalent expressions. The *eidos* is not an impression of sense passively received; it is a product of the mind's activity, an instrument constructed by the mind whereby it "makes nature," "moulds environment," so as to serve the purposes of human life.[8]

In the early dialogues Socrates is a figure who keeps asking questions and seeking the definitions of things. "What is justice?" "What is virtue?" Socrates' dialectical method inevitably brings his listeners to moments of confusion and perplexity, and to sometimes admitting that they do not know what they thought they knew. The Platonic Socrates does not succeed at arriving at a fully systematic viewpoint, but his point is to enlighten people about what they do not know.[9] Gradually, there emerges Plato's doctrine of Ideas: "The concept in question is no longer made to depend precariously on the few particulars observed, but is determined, shaped all round as it were, by the system which includes it: in the light of that system we come to see it for what it is, and are finally convinced that it 'cannot be otherwise': it has become *independent* of the few particulars the observation of which first suggested it."[10]

Plato's early dialogue, the *Meno*, which Lonergan later refers to on several occasions, includes the doctrine or myth of *anamnesis*: the doctrine that true knowledge is not received from without, but rather recollected from within. In the dialogue Socrates illustrates this doctrine to Meno by calling over a slave-boy and asking him the answer to a geometrical question, how to double a four-foot square. The boy at first thinks he knows the answer, that is, by doubling the sides of the square or by adding one foot to the sides. But both solutions are shown to be false, and finally confused, the boy admits that he does not know what he thought was "obvious." Then gradually, under the guidance of Socrates' questioning and by diagramming the diagonal

---

[8]Ibid., 6–7.

[9]*Caring About Meaning*, 24, "Socrates introduced definitions, and people who ask for definitions usually are crazy."

[10]Stewart, *Plato's Doctrine of Ideas*, 18.

of the four-foot square and constructing a square on that basis, the slave-boy "recollects" the answer. Through such questioning one moves beyond the knowledge of particulars (*doxa* or opinion) to scientific knowledge (*episteme*) which gives the "Idea," the causal context. Lonergan succinctly summarizes this contextual background needed to define.

> Definitions haven't got a precise meaning unless you have a fundamental set of terms and relations with the terms fixing the relations and the relations fixing the terms and the whole lot verified. Then you can have definitions that mean something. Any deductivist system has to have that to start.[11]

This, of course, is an explanation of Stewart's Plato that Lonergan gave many years later after reading the book. As he summarized his debt, through Stewart, to Plato: "from Stewart I learnt that Plato was a methodologist, that his ideas were what the scientist seeks to discover, that the scientific or philosophic process towards discovery was one of question and answer."[12]

To be a methodologist is to know how to question. It was Plato that taught Lonergan that every question, when properly formulated, implies the shadowy anticipation of its answer. Otherwise, we would never recognize an answer as *the* answer. We would never be able to say, "That's it! That's what I've been looking for!" Without the prior question the slave-boy in the *Meno* would never have *seen* the answer in the properly aligned diagram. "I believed in intelligence and I thought concepts were overrated. When I found in Stewart's *Plato's Doctrine of Ideas* that an idea, for Plato, was like Descartes' equation for the circle, I was home. You get the equation of the circle just by understanding."[13]

Concepts then are rooted in "grasping the intelligible in the sensible," as Lonergan would later put it. Stewart found this in Plato:

> The unity of the Idea . . . consists in its being a single point of view from which the phenomena are regarded, a single point of view taken of that which otherwise is undetermined. . . . Understanding this, we find it easy to dispose of the difficulty about the unity of the Idea being broken up among the particulars: "the Idea of the circle as defined by its equation in the general form, is not itself properly speaking a curve."[14]

---

[11]*Caring About Meaning*, 24.

[12]*Second Collection*, 264.

[13]*Caring About Meaning*, 44.

[14]Stewart, *Plato's Doctrine of Ideas*, 93. On the circle cf. 57 and 74; also 95: "It is only on the basis of mathematically exact determination of X by the appropriate A that empirical science is possible."

Lonergan was indebted to Stewart for a sense of the "heuristic" character of human understanding: the dynamism of the intellectual search for the unknown.[15] In between the concepts, on the one hand, and the sensible data on the other, there is the pre-conceptual dynamism of questioning and understanding.

> Aristotle and Thomas held that you abstracted from phantasm the *eidos*, the *species*, the idea. And my first clue into the idea was when I was reading a book by an Oxford don by the name of J. A. Stewart who in 1905 had written on Plato's myths and in 1909 on Plato's doctrine of ideas. And he explained the doctrine of ideas by contending that for Plato an idea was something like the Cartesian formula for a circle, i.e. $(x^2 + y^2) = r^2$ and that exemplified an act of understanding to me, and the idea was getting what's in behind the formula for the circle. So you have something in between the concept and the datum or phantasm. And that is the sort of thing that you can't hold and be a naive realist. . . .[16]

In the fragments that seem to be from an early essay that Lonergan wrote during this time, there are several references to Plato. In these fragments the young Lonergan is aiming at articulating "the theory of intellect" that he later claimed he got from Plato.

> Plato's expression of the ultimate identity of intelligence and reality is in the myth of recollection (*anamnesis*). Socrates is using his heuristic method upon a slave, who first tends merely to guess but under the pressure of Socrates' questions elicits the acts of understanding necessary for grasping the geometical theorem under discussion. The procedure here . . . is simply a recognition of the fact that understanding is an immanent act, that the teacher cannot understand in public, so to speak, that the best way to get the pupils to understand is by asking them leading questions. The point is not that the slave knew geometry in a prenatal state (for which no evidence is given) but that the slave was able to understand geometry, i.e. to know what was presented, what could not be presented. Strip the imagery off Plato's myth of *anamnesis* and we are left with an assertion of the ultimate identity of intelligence and reality.[17]

Absent from Stewart's book is any sense of nominalism and empiricist phenomenalism. Concepts are rooted in understanding which is itself the release to human questioning. Such concepts, as they de-

[15]"The reality of the intelligible *A* is constituted by the fact that it performs its function of making the *X* of the sensible world intelligible in the formula *X* is *A*." Ibid., 85.

[16]Transcript by Nicholas Graham of discussion from Lonergan Workshop, Boston College, June 19, 1979. Available at Lonergan Research Institute, Toronto.

[17]Fragments of what may be the lost essay on assent at Lonergan Research Institute, Toronto: Lonergan's page number 9.

velop with the development of human understanding, structure questioning which is itself heuristic: the mind's dynamic anticipation of understanding the natures of things.

We might add that Stewart sees the second dimension of Plato's Ideas, the more contemplative dimension, as not strictly scientific, but as giving rise to art and religion.

> For that experience the "idea" is not a "point of view" taken by the mind in "discourse," but a "real presence" confronting "contemplation" . . . The "eternal Idea" is revealed in some welcome, some familiar or beautiful, object of sense—literally *in* the object of sense: not as another object which the object of sense "resembles," but as that very object of sense itself transfigured, become a wonder. It is not *a* skylark that Shelley hears and sees, but *the* Skylark.[18]

Here again a theme is sounded that can be found in Lonergan's early writings: grasping an intelligibility in a singular sensible or imaginative example. Lonergan later noted: "My apprehension, at that time, was not that precise. It was something vaguer that made me devote my free time to reading Plato's early dialogues."[19]

2. A Critique of Culture

Lonergan never felt that Plato had all the answers. Nevertheless, he thought Plato was the perfect introduction to philosophy, to questioning our human questioning. "My idea of Plato is that he is the perfect introduction to philosophy. I don't think he has the answers but certainly he can build up interest and start one into serious questions."[20] From some of his early writings we can surmise that during the early 1930s Lonergan read Plato's *Meno,* the *Sophists,* the *Gorgias,* and *The Republic.*[21] As he said years later, "In the early thirties I began to delight in Plato, especially the early dialogues."[22] What will become evident in Lonergan's unpublished writings from the mid-thirties is that Plato gave Lonergan the sense of the normativeness of intelligence in its own right, a normativeness that in Plato becomes *the* means of

[18]Stewart, *Plato's Doctrine of Ideas,* 11.

[19]*Second Collection,* 264.

[20]*Caring About Meaning,* 49.

[21]Some years later, while a student in Rome in 1935, Lonergan wrote to his provincial that, among the few books he owned, there were four dialogues of Plato. There are also references to these early Platonic dialogues in his notes from the middle 1930s on the philosophy of history. Nevertheless, he did not at the time continue to read Plato. As he said: "I had other fish to fry." *Caring About Meaning,* 48.

[22]*Second Collection,* 38.

cultural critique. In those writings Lonergan states that in Plato philosophy emerged with the assertion of its social significance:

> "Towns and cities will not be happy till philosophers are kings" is the central position of Plato's *Republic,* and the *Republic* is the centre of the dialogues. To Plato, Pericles, the idol of Athenian aspirations, was an idiot; he built docks and brought the fruits of all lands to Athens . . . but he neglected the one thing necessary, the true happiness of the citizens. For did not the dialectic reveal that no man without self-contradiction could deny that suffering injustice was better than doing injustice, that pain was compatible with happiness, that shame, the interior contradiction, the lie in the soul of a man to himself, was incompatible with happiness.[23]

What was evident to Plato was that a higher control was needed in the governance of society and that higher control was virtue, and that virtue was to be known by human intelligence in its fullest exercise. "The achievement of Platonism lay in its power of criticism. The search for a definition of virtue in the earlier dialogues establishes that virtue is a certain something, the emergence of a new light upon experience. This discovery of the idea, of intelligible forms, gave not only dialectic but also the means of social criticism. For it enabled man to express not by symbol but by concept the divine."[24]

In the last years of his life Lonergan would point again to Plato as he recommended the commentaries of Eric Voegelin. For Voegelin, Plato's parable of the cave describes a person being forced against his or her will out of the shadows into the light. It reveals opposite principles at work in human life:

> On the one hand, opinion may lead through reason (*logos*) to the best (*ariston*), and its power is called self-restraint (*sophrosyne*); on the other hand, desire may drag us (*helkein*) towards pleasures and its rule is called excess (*hybris*). Or as Voegelin illustrates the matter, a young man may be drawn to philosophy but by social pressure be diverted to a life of pleasure or to success in politics. But if he follows the second pull, the meaning of his life is not settled for him. The first pull remains and is still experienced as part of his living. Following the second pull does not transform his being into a question-free fact, but into a questionable course. He will sense that the life he leads is not his "own and true life."[25]

---

[23]Unpublished philosophy of history notes, available at the Lonergan Research Institute, Toronto.

[24]Ibid.

[25]*Third Collection,* 190. Lonergan refers to Voegelin's "The Gospel and Culture," *Jesus and Man's Hope,* vol. 2, eds. Donald G. Miller and Dikran Y. Hadidian (Pittsburgh: Pittsburgh Theological Seminary, 1971) 59–101. Cf. *Caring About Meaning,* 22–23, on Voegelin:

Speaking of Voegelin's interpretation of Plato, Lonergan noted: "I had always been given the impression that Plato's dialogues were concerned with the pure intellect until I read Dr. Voegelin and learned that they were concerned with social decline, the break-up of the Greek city-states. It was human reasonableness trying to deal with an objective social, political mess."[26]

With the reading of Stewart and Plato something major was going on in Lonergan. He later spoke of it as "a great release." Nevertheless, even though in later years Lonergan attributed to Stewart and Plato his break with nominalism, in a letter he wrote to his provincial in 1935 he claimed that after reading Plato his nominalism was still intact. "I got interested in Plato during regency and came to understand him; this left my nominalism quite intact but gave a theory of intellect as well."[27] In other words, there would seem to have been an inner conflict in Lonergan at this time: that is, a growing and more factual awareness of the dynamics of human consciousness along with an underlying philosophical position—nominalism?—in conflict with that developing understanding.[28] After reading Plato it was only natural that Lonergan would go on to reading the most famous of Christian Platonists, St. Augustine. "I read St. Augustine's earlier works during the summer before theology and found him to be psychologically exact."[29] It was through Augustine that Lonergan's definitive break with nominalism took place, and from Augustine that he then made his way to the intellectualism of Aristotle and Aquinas.

"He is a moral man, and he certainly presents conscience, using Plato to do it—in *The Laws*, the puppeteer. The pull of the golden cord doesn't force you; you have to agree, make the decision. But the jerk of the steel chain, that's what upsets you. The viewpoint is Ignatius and it is the whole ascetic tradition of the discernment of spirits."

[26]Quoted in *The Question as Commitment: A Symposium*, ed. E. Cahn and C. Going (Montreal: The Thomas More Institute, 1977) 119.

[27]Letter to Provincial, Rev. Henry Keane, S.J., January 22, 1935.

[28]Newman speaks of such a conflict between his reason and his imagination regarding the Catholic church. His *Apologia* is a good example of the ongoing conflict between developing reason and an underlying imaginative vision: "Simultaneously with Milner I read Newton *On the Prophecies*, and in consequence became most firmly convinced that the Pope was the Antichrist predicted by St. Paul, and St. John. My imagination was stained by the effects of this doctrine up to the year 1843; it had been eliminated from my reason and judgment at an earlier date; but the thought remained upon me as a sort of false conscience. Hence came that conflict of mind, which so many have felt besides myself;—leading some men to make a compromise between the two ideas, so inconsistent with each other, driving others to beat out the one idea or other from their minds,—and ending in my own case, after many years of intellectual unrest, in the gradual decay and extinction of one of them,—I do not say in its violent death, for why should I have not murdered it sooner, if I murdered it at all." *Apologia pro vita sua*, 7.

[29]January 22, 1935, letter to Provincial.

Chapter Four

Augustine's Cassiciacum Dialogues

My apprehension, at that time, was not that precise. It was something vaguer that made me devote my free time to reading Plato's early dialogues . . . and then moving on to Augustine's early dialogues written at Cassiciacum near Milan. Augustine was so concerned with understanding, so unmindful of universal concepts, that I began a long period of trying to write an intelligible account of my convictions.[1]

1. An Intelligible Account of Conversion

In the summer of 1933 Lonergan was in Montreal finishing his regency, a period of teaching for young Jesuit scholastics, and preparing to begin the study of theology in the fall. In Augustine the focus of his reading became again, as in reading Newman, someone explicitly a Catholic Christian. In Augustine intellect and its activities are one part of a larger picture, the picture of Augustine's whole life: his moral struggles, his wrestling with the religious and philosophical currents of his time, his wrestling with God. Years later Lonergan would write of Augustine: "A convert from nature to spirit; a person that, by God's grace, made himself what he was; a subject that may be studied but, most of all, must be encountered in the outpouring of his self-revelation and self-communication."[2]

Lonergan specified the works of Augustine that he read in the summer of 1933 as the ones written at Cassiciacum in November, 386, perhaps the modern Cassiago near Lake Como, outside of Milan. These dialogues are the *De Beata Vita (The Happy Life)*, *Contra Academicos (Answer to Skeptics)*, the *De Ordine (Divine Providence and the Problem of Evil)*, and the *Soliloquiae (The Soliloquies)*.[3] The dialogues took place at a moun-

---

[1]*Second Collection*, 265. Cf. also *Caring About Meaning*, 22, 48; also *Understanding and Being*, 250, where Lonergan claims the order was from Newman to Augustine to Plato.

[2]*Verbum*, x.

[3]Quotations from these sources will be indicated in the text as following: *DBV (De Beata Vita)*, *CA (Contra Academicos)*, *DO (De Ordine)*, and *SOL (The Soliloquies)*. Unless otherwise noted, our references and translations will be from *The Fathers of the Church, Writings of Saint Augustine* 1, ed. Ludwig Schopp (New York: Cima Publishing Co., 1948).

tain villa lent to Augustine by a friend, Verecundus, where he had re-
tired with his mother, his brother, his son, and several pupils, after
the events of his conversion in August, 386. "You are faithful to your
promises, and you will repay Verecundus for his country house at Cassiciacum, where we rested in You from the world's troubles, with the
loveliness and eternal freshness of your paradise." (*Confessions*, 9, 3)

At the time, Augustine was experiencing some physical ailments,
perhaps brought on by the emotional upheaval of his conversion, and
at least one of the motives for the vacation was just physical rest. There
are a number of "homey" references to life at the villa in the beautiful
foothills of the Alps during these fall months of 386 and the coming
together of this small band of friends around Augustine: references
to taking care of the farm, the weather intermittently sunny and rainy,
watching a cock fight, Augustine waking in the middle of the night
and listening to the on-and-off flow of water in a drain clogged with
autumn leaves. In this context of rest, the "otium liberale" of creative
leisure that Augustine had so long desired, the group frequently con-
vened, indoors or outdoors weather permitting, with a scribe at hand,
to dialogue about the central issues of life:

> What is the good life? Does it consist in great possesions? But do not
> great possessions bring the fear of their own loss? Is "wisdom" the way
> to a happy life? a wisdom in which the lower levels of the human per-
> son are subordinated to the human mind? (*De Beata Vita*) . . . Does wis-
> dom consist in knowing the truth or only in seeking the truth? Can any
> truth be known with certitude? Is there *the Truth* that can enlighten us
> about what is truth? How come to a vision of such Truth? (*Contra
> Academicos*) . . . If God is good, how account for evil? Does evil, like
> the jagged edges of a single stone in a mosaic, fit into some larger plan,
> some larger order in the universe? (*De Ordine*)

Finally, in the *Soliloquies* the dialogue with others becomes a dialogue
of Augustine with his own mind and soul—and with God. These dialogues took place when Augustine was thirty-three years old.

The question can be raised why Lonergan chose to read precisely
these dialogues of Augustine; why not some of Augustine's later writings? Perhaps the answer can be found quite simply in Lonergan's
previous reading in Plato; these early Augustinian dialogues are patently "Platonic" in inspiration. In fact, they are so rationally argued
and philosophical that some critics have emphasized the discrepancy
between the highly religious and "incantatory" nature of the account
of Augustine's conversion in the *Confessions* and these highly

philosophical reflections.[4] Some have contended that his conversion of August, 386, was really a conversion to the Neo-Platonic philosophy which fills the dialogues, and not primarily to Catholic Christianity. For example, the incident of the "Tolle lege" in the garden in Milan, so central to the *Confessions*, is absent here.

Today it is generally conceded that the context of these philosophical reflections is indeed highly religious and Christian.[5] The religious and moral underpinnings gleam through the dialogues. There are references to "our priest," that is, Ambrose. There are Monica's very distinctly religious contributions to the dialogues, which Augustine highly approves. There are references to the incarnation, the Scriptures, invocations of the Trinity, the *sacra* and *mysteria* of Christian belief and worship. The fervent prayer at the beginning of the *Soliloquies* shows that the author of the *Confessions* is already present in these dialogues. Above all, there is explicit deference to the "authority" of faith. For Augustine at this point faith plays an essential role in coming to the "true and authentic philosophy."

Nevertheless, the general focus of these dialogues is philosophical; but the "philosophy" Augustine has in mind is a combination of the Platonic philosophy which had just recently opened his mind to Christianity and his newly appropriated Christian faith. Just emerging from his famous "conversion experience" described so movingly in the *Confessions*, in these dialogues Augustine is obviously trying to set his convictions into some kind of intelligible framework. Afraid perhaps of being carried away with the emotion of the moment, he is trying to consolidate the fruits of his conversion in rational terms.[6]

Consequently, both in his own mind, for his own self-understanding, and because he is still in contact with his Neo-Platonic

---

[4]Cf. Eugene TeSelle, *Augustine the Theologian* (New York: Herder and Herder, 1970) 39; cf. also 59–60. Also Peter Brown, *Augustine of Hippo* (Berkeley: University of California Press: 1969).

[5]Cf. TeSelle, *Augustine the Theologian*, 59–60.

[6]As Newman said in the *Apologia* when he became aware of some intimations of profound changes in his own future life: "I determined to be guided, not by my imagination, but by my reason." *Apologia pro vita sua*, 119. Newman needed time to determine "the logical value" of his experience and its bearing on his duty. Peter Brown speaks of the period of Augustine's dialogues this same way: "Seen in his works at Cassiciacum, this 'conversion' seems to have been an astonishingly tranquil process. . . . As [Augustine] wrote to Zenobius, some men deal with the wounds inflicted on them by the senses by 'cauterizing' them 'in solitude,' while others 'apply ointment to them' by means of the Liberal Arts (*De Ordine* 1, 1, 2). Plainly Augustine, surrounded by his relatives and pupils, his library in Cassiciacum well stocked with traditional textbooks, had chosen the more gentle treatment of the Liberal Arts." Brown, *Augustine of Hippo*, 113.

friends, Augustine's dialogues are couched in philosophic categories. To put it in terms of the later Lonergan, at this point Augustine was aiming at clearly expressing the intellectual conversion whose pivotal moment took place in the spring of 386, the intellectual conversion that opened the way for the religious and moral conversion of the following summer.

Our method here is not to provide an exhaustive account of each of these dialogues, but rather to highlight the themes that will later find their way into Lonergan's own writings. These themes are:

1) Conversion from corporeal thinking;
2) Refutation of skepticism;
3) Faith and understanding;
4) *Veritas:* from truths to the Truth.

These themes represent concrete understandings that occurred to Augustine in the course of his own journey; they facilitated concrete understandings in Lonergan's intellectual journey.

We might begin by noting that in the first completed Cassiciacum dialogue, the *De Beata Vita*, Augustine takes up the theme of a philosophical journey over the sea of life to the port of true philosophy. In his own case, he recalls the beginning of his own journey in his reading of Cicero's *Hortensius* at age nineteen. "From the age of nineteen, having read in the school of rhetoric that book of Cicero's called *Hortensius*, I was influenced by such a great love of philosophy that I considered devoting myself to it at once." (*DBV* 1, 4) What the *Hortensius* represented for Augustine, as he beautifully recounts in the *Confessions*, was that it inspired in him a disinterested search for the truth, a desire that remained beneath the surface of his life throughout all the years of his moral and philosophical wandering:

> Quite definitely it changed the direction of my mind. . . . Suddenly all the vanity I had hoped in I saw as worthless, and with an incredible intensity of desire I longed after inward wisdom. I had begun that journey upwards by which I was to return to You. . . . The one thing that delighted me in Cicero's exhortation was that I should love, and seek, and win, and hold, and embrace, not this or that philsophical school but Wisdom itself, whatever it might be. The book excited and inflamed me; in my ardour the only thing I found lacking was that the name of Christ was not there. For with my mother's milk my infant heart had drunk in, and still held deep down in it, that name according to your mercy, O Lord, the name of Your Son, my Saviour; and whatever lacked

> that name, no matter how learned and excellently written and true, could not win me wholly (*Confessions* 3, 4).[7]

Years later, in *Insight,* Lonergan would repeatedly write of "the pure, detached, disinterested desire to know." The desire for the truth evidenced in Augustine, irrespective of philosophical schools, must have struck a deep chord in the young Lonergan. In addition, as with Augustine and his reading of the *Hortensius* and later, "certain books of the Platonists" (*Confessions* 7, 9), Lonergan's philosophical journey had also been marked by certain books: Newman's *Grammar of Assent,* Joseph's *Introduction to Logic,* Stewart's *Plato's Doctrine of Ideas,* and now . . . Augustine's dialogues at Cassiciacum.

2. Conversion from Corporeal Thinking

> Yet I was not free of those intellectual mists which could confuse my course, and I confess that for quite a while I was led astray, with my eyes fixed on those stars that sink into the ocean (*DBV* 1, 4).

The reference is to Augustine's involvement in the fantastic myths of the Manichees from 374 to 383. This eastern cult held all kinds of imaginative tenets about the battle between the two principles of good and evil. These two principles, God and Satan, each had its own kingdom, the kingdom of light and the kingdom of darkness. Satan invaded the kingdom of light and did battle with the Primal Man, an emanation from the God of Light. In their battle Satan overcame the Primal Man and his "five elements" and these latter remain as scattered elements of light in the kingdom of darkness. Jesus personifies the light elements imprisoned in darkness and the whole of human history is concerned with the freeing of the light elements from the realm of darkness and restoring them to the kingdom of the light.

> A childish superstition deterred me from thorough investigation, and, as soon as I was more courageous, I threw off the darkness and learned to trust more in men that taught than in those that ordained obedience, having myself encountered persons to whom the very light, seen by their eyes, apparently was an object of highest and even divine veneration. I did not agree with them, but thought they were concealing in those veils some important secret which they would later divulge (*DBV* 1, 4).

Within the Manichean community a small body of the Elect engaged in certain ascetical practices so as to release more effectively the elements of light from the darkness. These consisted in such things as

---

[7]Our references to the *Confessions* will be from the translation by F. J. Sheed, *The Confessions of Saint Augustine, Books I–X* (New York: Sheed and Ward, 1942).

the eating of certain foods and the practice of celibacy. Augustine was not a member of the elect, but only one of the larger number of Hearers (*auditores*) among the Manichees for whom there were no such strict rules. They were encouraged to virtue, but if they did fall into sin, they were consoled by the teaching that they were not reponsible; sin was rather the work of the foreign power of evil at work within them. Augustine rejected the religion of the Manichees in 383 when he realized the unintelligible nature of these myths and was very unimpressed with the philosophic understanding of the Manichee leaders. Nevertheless, as Newman said of some of his own early reading, his imagination was "stained" by these doctrines for years to come.[8] "They cried out 'Truth, truth;' they were forever uttering the word to me, but the thing was nowhere in them" (*DBV* 3, 6).

According to the *Confessions*, the chief intellectual obstacle in Augustine's journey to Christianity—besides the moral obstacles so emphasized in the *Confessions*—was his need to imaginatively "picture" things which cannot strictly speaking be pictured, whether those things be God or even his own conscious self. It is a theme that Lonergan took up more than fifteen hundred years later in the introduction to *Insight*.

> St. Augustine of Hippo narrates that it took him years to make the discovery that the name "real" might have a different connotation from the name "body."[9]

This theme is present in the Cassiciacum dialogues in embryonic form. For example, what struck Augustine in listening to the sermons of St. Ambrose was the incorporeal character of God and the soul. "For I have noticed frequently in the sermons of our priest, and sometimes in yours, that, when speaking of God, no one should think of Him as something corporeal; nor yet of the soul, for of all things the soul is nearest to God" (*DBV* 1, 4; cf. *SOL* 2, 4, 6; 2, 17, 31). And again, in the *Contra Academicos:* "The populace is rather prone to rush into false opinions, and through familiarity with bodies, a person very readily—but very dangerously, as well—comes to believe that all things are corporeal" (3, 17, 38).

The *Confessions* bring out this theme much more forcefully and fully. Surely the young Lonergan was familiar with these passages. "Though I did not even then think of You under the shape of a human body, yet I could not but think of You as some corporeal substance, occupy-

---

[8] Cf. Newman, *Apologia pro vita sua*, 7.
[9] *Insight*, 15 (xx). Cf. 778–79 for the editors' note on this statement.

ing all space, whether infused in the world, or else diffused through infinite space beyond the world (*Confessions* 3, 1). . . . How far then is the reality of You from those empty imaginings of mine, imaginings of bodies which had no being whatever (3, 6). . . . When I desired to think of my God, I could not think of him save as a bodily maginitude—for it seemed to me that what was not such was nothing at all: this indeed was the principal and practically the sole cause of my inevitable error'' (5, 10).

Augustine even thought of evil as a type of bodily substance. ''By all this my ignorance was much troubled, and it seemed to me that I was coming to the truth when in fact I was going away from it. I did not know that evil has no being of its own but is only an absence of good, so that it simply is not. How indeed should I see this, when the sight of my eyes saw no deeper than bodies and the sight of my soul no deeper than the images of bodies? (3, 7). . . . In my ignorance I thought of evil not simply as some kind of substance, but actually as a bodily substance, because I had not learned to think of mind save as a more subtle body, extended in space'' (5, 10).

At one point Augustine set out to write a treatise *On the Beautiful and the Fitting* and in the course of this writing he faced the question of the character of his own mind and soul.

> I defined and distinguished the Beautiful as that which is of itself, the Fitting as that which is excellent in its relation of fitness to some other thing; and it was by corporeal examples that I supported my argument. I did consider the nature of the soul, but again the false view I had of spiritual things would not let me get at the truth—although by sheer force the truth was staring me in the face. I turned my throbbing mind from the incorporeal to line and colour and bulk, and because I did not see these things in my mind, I concluded that I could not see my mind (4, 15).

The philosophical issue, as he slowly began to realize, was the character of his own mind. ''My mind was in search of such images as the forms of my eye was accustomed to see; and I did not realize that the mental act by which I formed these images, was not itself a bodily image'' (7, 1).

As he had stated in the *De Beata Vita,* he learned from Ambrose not to interpret the Scriptures in a corporeal way. It was while listening to the homilies of Ambrose that some of Augustine's imaginative ways of thinking began to dissolve. For example, some of the Manichean objections to the anthropomorphisms of the Scriptures were themselves based on imaginary ways of thinking. ''If only I had been able to conceive of a substance that was spiritual, all their strong points would have been broken down and cast forth from my mind. But I could not" (5, 14).

Slowly Augustine began to believe in the reality of the unseen (what Lonergan later spoke of as the world "mediated by meaning"). It is a world mostly mediated to us by belief.

> I began to consider the countless things I believed which I had not seen, or which had happened with me not there—so many things in the history of nations, so many facts about places and cities, which I had never seen, so many things told me by friends, by doctors, by this man, by that man; and unless we accepted these things, we should do nothing at all in this life. Most strongly of all it struck me how firmly and unshakeably I believed that I was born of a particular father and mother, which I could not possibly know unless I believed it on the word of others (6, 5).

Augustine sensed the falsity in the Manichean position, but still held back from believing the Christian faith as he heard it expounded by Ambrose.

> Nothing of what he said struck me as false, although I did not as yet know whether what he said was true. I held back my heart from accepting anything, fearing that I might fall once more, whereas in fact the hanging in suspense was more deadly. I wanted to be as certain of things unseen as that seven and three make ten. For I had not reached the point of madness which denies that even this can be unknown; but I wanted to know other things as clearly as this, either such material things as were not present to my senses, or spiritual things which I did not know how to conceive save corporeally (6, 4).

What was happening, as Lonergan later pointed out, was a movement begun by Christians in other areas of the ancient world to think of God, not on the analogy of matter, but properly, on the analogy of spirit. "The point was picked up by Clement of Alexandria who taught that the anthropomorphisms of the bible were not to be taken literally and, thereby, started the century-long efforts of Christians to conceive God on the analogy of spirit rather than of matter."[10] But first, before satisfactorily addressing this problem, Augustine was forced to consider another issue: can we know anything for certain? Having been mistaken once in his Manichean beliefs, how could he be certain he would not be mistaken again?

---

[10]Bernard Lonergan, *Doctrinal Pluralism* (Milwaukee: Marquette University Press, 1971) 67–68. Cf. also *Method in Theology*, 307, 319, 329, 344.

3. Refutation of Skepticism

> After I had shaken them off and abandoned them, and especially after
> I had crossed this sea, the Academics for a long while steered my course
> amid the waves, while my helm had to meet every wind (*DBV* 1, 4).

After leaving the Manichees, Augustine faced another major obstacle on the way to truth and that was the skeptics' philosophy that
truth could not be attained. He himself had embraced this philosophy
between 383 and 386 and he felt deeply that many people, influenced
by skepticism, were threatened by a despair of attaining the truth. This
philosophy had a stultifying effect on the mind and was a great obstacle to faith. For the skeptics of Cicero's "New Academy" the truly
wise person will refuse to give assent to anything; for the wise person
merely seeks the truth. Lest this lead to a paralysis of action, the skeptics held that some things *resemble* the truth, that is, they are probable,
and probability is a sufficient basis for action in this world.

Augustine pointed to the inconsistencies in the Academics' position. For someone to know what "resembles the truth," that is, what
is probable, one must know some truth. Sometime later Augustine
would phrase his method for showing the implicit possibility, and indeed inevitablity, of knowing truth: "Everyone who knows that he
has doubts knows with certainty something that is true, namely, that
he doubts. He is certain, therefore, about *a* truth. Therefore everyone
who doubts whether there be such a thing as *the* truth has at least *a*
truth to set a limit to his doubt; and nothing can be true except truth
be in it. Accordingly, no one ought to have doubts about the existence
of *the* truth, even if doubts arise for him from every quarter."[11]

Augustine devotes a great portion of the Cassiciacum dialogues to
refuting the Academic position. His basic position, one he would develop later in the *De Trinitate*, is that there are certain ineluctable truths,
especially truths of the self and reason, that it is "self-contradictory"
to deny. Centuries later Bernard Lonergan would pay tribute to Augustine's basic methodology: "For Augustine, the mind's self-
knowledge was basic; it was the rock of certitude on which shattered
Academic doubt; it provided the ground from which one could argue
to the validity both of the senses of one's own body and, with the mediation of testimony, of the senses of the bodies of others."[12]

In the *Contra Academicos* Augustine vindicates the validity of the
senses. Against the classic argument of the delusion of the senses by

[11]*De vera religione*, 39, 73, *Augustine: Earlier Writings, The Library of Christian Classics*
6, John H. S. Burleigh, trans. (Philadelphia: Westminster Press, 1953).
[12]*Verbum*, xii.

the oar that appears bent in water, Augustine places the emphasis on the acting subject, even the subject as being deluded.[13] He admits the appearance of the delusion, while maintaining the truth of the fact that the acting subject sees or feels this or that. If there were reason to believe the senses were deceived, one would need to study the causes for the different appearances of things. "Therefore, as to what they see with regard to an oar in the water—is that true? It is absolutely true. In fact, since there is a special reason for the oar's appearing that way, I should rather accuse my eyes of deception if it appeared to be straight when it is dipped in water, for, in that case, they would not be seeing what they ought to see" (*CA* 3, 11, 26; cf. *SOL* 2, 6, 10).

The act of sensing itself, as an internal fact of the subject, remains certain and secure, and in its own manner true.

> "Nevertheless," says someone or other, "I am deceived if I give assent." Restrict your assent to the mere fact of your being convinced that it appears thus to you. Then there is no deception, for I do not see how even an Academic can refute a man who says: "I know that this appears white to me. I know that I am delighted by what I am hearing. I know that this smells pleasant to me. I know that this tastes sweet to me. I know that this feels cold to me." Tell me, rather, whether the oleaster leaves—for which a goat has a persistent appetite—are bitter *per se*. . . . I know not how the oleaster leaves may be for flocks and herds; as to myself, they are bitter. What more do you wish to know? Perhaps there is even some man for whom they are not bitter. . . . Have I said they are bitter for everyone? I have said they are bitter for me, but I do not say that they will always be so. . . . This is what I say: that when a man tastes something, he can in good faith swear that it is sweet to his palate or that it is not, and that by no Greek sophistry can he be beguiled out of this knowledge (*CA* 3, 11, 26).

Salvino Biolo, a commentator greatly influenced by Lonergan, has commented on the above passage. "Here it is a case of the acting subject affirming oneself as conscious of one's internal phenomena through the mediation of external objects, which are not themselves the primary focus of the interior testimony."[14] Biolo goes on to say that here in the *Contra Academicos* it is a question of the certain and irrefutable self-affirmation of the subject on the level of experience. The focus is on sensitive consciousness, affirmed however by conscious judgment.

---

[13]Somewhere in Lonergan's writings he refers to this classic example of the oar appearing bent in water; I have not been able to locate the reference.

[14]Salvino Biolo, *La Coscienza nel "De Trinitate" di S. Agostino* (Rome: Libreria Editrice dell'Università Gregoriana, 1969) 12. My translation.

In the *Soliloquies* Augustine argues to the immortality of the soul by an analysis of truth and its inherence in the human soul. He begins by engaging in a dialogue with his own Reason.

> R. Do you, who wish to know yourself, know that you exist?
> A. I know it.
> R. How do you know it?
> A. I do not know.
> R. Are you conscious of yourself as simple or composite?
> A. I do not know.
> R. Do you know that you are moved?
> A. I do not know.
> R. Do you know that you think?
> A. That I know. (2, 1)

Two basic facts are here held to be immune from doubt and ignorance: first, the human subject inevitably knows that he exists; and secondly, he knows that he thinks. Augustine brings out the *immediacy* of the "knowledge" that the concrete subject has of himself as existing and acting through the very fact that he thinks. As Biolo comments on this text:

> It is a self-affirmation lived, not reasoned to; it is an existential conscious-ness internal to the fact of being a person and being a thinker. Nothing is said of the nature of this knowledge. It seems to me that the sense implied in the text demands that typical "consciousness" that the think-ing subject has as a subject, that is, before formulating and objectifying oneself for one's interior thought. It is merely an intimate experience of oneself as a human being, which adds nothing entitatively to exis-tence and thought, but accompanies them from within as self-consciousness.[15]

Biolo traces this theme throughout Augustine's writings, especially its clearest expression in the *De Trinitate*. But there is another example of the same theme which I would like to mention here, since it comes soon after the Cassiciacum dialogues, the *De Libero Arbitrio*. Lonergan might have included this in his early reading, since it includes an em-phasis on *intelligere*, which he later remembered as so prominent in Augustine. In this work Augustine aims at proving the existence of God by beginning with the first evidences of the human spirit: one's personal existence, about which one cannot be mistaken, because ex-istence is the first condition of the possibility of error itself. Also, since the existence of his interlocutor, Evodius, is evident through the fact

[15]Ibid., 13–14.

that he actually lives, his living is also at the same time evident. The two facts are evidently true. The interlocutor clearly understands them. Therefore, Augustine moves to a third fact, the fact of understanding.

> A. Therefore, this third fact is likewise manifest, namely that you understand?
> E. Yes, it is evident (*De Libero Arbitrio* 2, 3, 7).

And thus there is touched upon the understanding, the most noble element in the human person, precisely because it implies the other two, and not vice versa. Augustine's interlocutor gives the reason: "For the one who understands both necessarily lives and exists." Biolo comments:

> This third fact, the intellectual act, enjoys a fundamental transparency, which illuminates also the other two, a transparency manifest to the subject precisely in the act of understanding: "it is evident you understand." The Holy Doctor thus professes in this text, concretely, in a manner implicit but clear, the luminous self-witness inherent in the person as actually understanding, and thus with indestructible certitude known to be both existing and living. It is the human intellectual consciousness which emerges and becomes evident to the interlocutor even as he exercises it, and which affirms itself as a distinct value different and superior for its nobility and dignity, not only from the inanimate world of stones, but also from the biological and psychological world of animals.[16]

The unifying science that concerns the self is philosophy and the result of refuting academic skepticism is a philsophical knowledge even more certain than numbers.

> I now say to both of you: Beware lest you think that you know anything except what you have learned at least in the manner in which you know that one *plus* two *plus* three *plus* four is ten. And, likewise, beware lest you think either that in philosophy you will not gain a thorough knowledge of the truth, or that truth can by no means become known in this manner. Believe me—or rather, believe Him who says: "Seek, and you shall find"—that knowledge is not to be despaired of, but that it will be even more manifest than those of numbers (*CA* 2, 9).

4. Faith and Understanding

In the Cassiciacum dialogues we see Augustine as an ardent lover of philosophy—for this is associated in his mind with wisdom and with

[16]Ibid., 15.

happiness. In his own case this search had first been delayed through his involvement with the Manichees and now, more recently, with Academic skepticism. Finally, at length, "I came into this land; here I have learned to know the North Star, to which I entrust myself" (*DBV* 1, 4). "This land" is the land of true philosophy which combines the best of the world's philosophy with Christian wisdom. He had come upon "certain books of the Platonists" and compared them with the authority of those who taught the Divine Mysteries.[17] It was this combination that so "inflamed" him that he was able to cast asunder all the anchors that kept him from sailing into the harbor of true philosophy. That philosophy was an amalgam of reason as expressed in the Platonic writings and of authority as embraced in the teachings of the Church.

It was especially in the sermons of "our priest," Ambrose of Milan, that the subject of such philosophy was broached: God and the soul, a preoccupation of the Platonic tradition. The study of the soul gives us knowledge of ourselves; that of God gives us knowledge of our origin, the Parent of the universe of whom reason can give no adequate knowledge since he is better known by not being known (*melius scitur nesciendo*) (*DO* 1, 18, 47). Later on in the dialogues Augustine will speak of such philosophy as "our true and solitary habitation . . . our sacred inner shrine" (*DO* 1, 3, 9).

In the *Contra Academicos* there is again an extravagant praise of philosophy whose two-fold paths of reason and authority are distinct, but not separate. His benefactor, Romanianus, had furnished him with certain books "packed with thought," (*libri quidem pleni*), which produced in him a marvelous effect: "They at once enkindled in me such a conflagration that I scarcely believe it of myself. What importance did I then attach to any honor? Was I affected by human pomp? by a craving for empty fame? or, in fine, by the bond and bondage of this mortal life?" (*CA* 2, 2, 5). Augustine describes his reaction to such books:

> Certainly, no one doubts that we are impelled toward knowledge by a twofold force: the force of authority and the force of reason. And I am resolved never to deviate in the least from the authority of Christ, for I find none more powerful. But, as to what is attainable by acute and accurate reasoning, such is my state of mind that I am impatient to grasp what truth is—to grasp it not only by belief, but also by comprehension. Meanwhile, I am confident that I shall find among the Platonists what is not in opposition to our Sacred Scriptures (*CA* 3, 20, 43).

[17]Cf. *Confessions*, 7, 9, 13.

The "true and authentic philosophy" Augustine has in mind in these dialogues is a combination of Christian faith and the philosophy of Plato mediated to him by the Neo-Platonic writings of Plotinus and perhaps Porphyry. Though this philosophy has gone through many mutations, still a single valid doctrine has filtered through. Speaking of Plato and his "re-appearance" in Plotinus, Augustine says: "Then Plato's countenance—which is the cleanest and brightest in philosophy—suddenly appeared, especially in Plotinus" (CA 31, 41–42). What Augustine obtained from the Neo-Platonic stream of philosophy was a unifying vision of God, the eternal Truth and Light, ever present to the human self, even when the latter's attention was directed toward the external world. According to Plotinus, the human soul, fallen from its pre-existent state—a doctrine later repudiated by Augustine—animates the human body by forming a portion of matter as an expression of its inward life, even while it is able, in principle, to remain "within itself" and "outside" all that is corporeal. (*Enneads* IV, 3, 9–10).[18] In this condition the soul becomes enslaved to the things of the body and, becoming fascinated with the brilliant reflections of the divine in the material world and, losing sight of itself, it "turns" toward them and "goes forth" from itself and "becomes present" not to itself but to the body (9, 12, 17). As Eugene TeSelle notes:

> Both of these aspects—the power of man's inward life over his bodily actions, and his enslavement by his own affections for the finite—were a matter of experience to Augustine; he could give unconditional assent when he read them in Plotinus or in Porphyry. He could say along with them but out of personal conviction, for himself, that the soul has gone outside itself (*progressus*) and is poured out (*a seipso fusus*) into the world of multiplicity, from which it needs to return to itself and thereby to God, who is present within the self. And he could say, again with them, that the way of return is through "fleeing sensible things altogether" (*SOL* 1, 14, 24; cf. *DO* 2, 11, 31), without thereby meaning to suggest that the soul must lose all relation to the body.[19]

Although Augustine had perhaps come across this Platonic schema only recently—he probably read the Platonic books in the beginning of the summer of 386—he had thoroughly interiorized it.[20] The anal-

---

[18]It is interesting to note that in a letter to his superior from Rome in 1935 Lonergan mentions that among the few books he possesses are selections of Plotinus' *Enneads*.

[19]TeSelle, *Augustine the Theologian*, 70.

[20]As Peter Brown says: "It was a reading that was so intense and thorough that the ideas of Plotinus were thoroughly absorbed, 'digested' and transformed by Augustine. . . . For Augustine . . . Plotinus and Porphyry are grafted almost imperceptibly into his writings as the ever present basis of his thought." *Augustine of Hippo*, 95.

ogy of spirit demanded a conversion in one's understanding of one's own spirit. After years of intellectual searching and wrestling with his own moral life, and after a sojourn in the gardens of the Academics, Augustine was able, with the help of the books of the Platonists, to make the beginnings of his own intellectual breakthrough.

In these dialogues Augustine emphasizes the possibilities of the knowledge of God even in this life; but when it comes to the *actual* human condition, that is a different story. Even when people catch some glimpse of the light shining inwardly upon them, they are unable to endure its splendor because of their impurity of mind; afraid to turn toward the light, they fall back into their accustomed patterns (*DBV* 4, 35; *CA* 1, 1, 3; 2, 2, 5; *SOL* 1, 6, 12). And in the case of most people, there is no awareness at all of the divine presence. In their concern with external things they have turned away from God and forgotten him.[21]

Consequently, in the present condition of humanity people need to be shown the way to return to God; and God in his "clemency" has made this way known (*DO* 2, 5, 6). "Human reason would never lead such souls to that intelligible world if the most high God had not vouchsafed—through clemency toward the whole human race—to send the authority of the divine intellect down even to a human body, and caused it to dwell therein, so that souls would be aroused not only by divine precepts but also by divine acts, and would thus be enabled to reflect on themselves and to gaze upon their fatherland, without any disputatious wranglings" (*CA* 3, 19, 42). It is here that the authority of faith finds its essential role in relation to reason.[22] Authority is the doorway that must be humbly entered; but it leads to the further treasures of rational knowledge, and this is the goal aimed at by revelation itself. Reason supplies arguments which aid the comprehension of the truths of revelation; and at the same time reason exercises the mind so that it will be capable of beholding spiritual things.

For Augustine this second practical goal is extremely important, reason's "anagogical" character, leading the mind toward the goal of immediate vision and accustoming it to the intelligible realm so that it will not be blinded by the light of eternity.

> Believe me, then, you will attain to these things when you will have given attention to learning, by which the mind, heretofore in no way fitted

---

[21]Cf. TeSelle, *Augustine the Theologian*, 68.

[22]Ibid., 74: "Augustine understands *auctoritas* not in the abstract sense that the word 'authority' has in modern political theory, but more in the classical Latin sense of authentic and authoritative *testimony* to or *disclosure* of something that is not directly known."

for a divine planting, is cleared and cultivated. Now these discourses, precious to us by reason of their association with your name rather than by the satisfaction of our own work, will, I am sure—especially if you will have the good will to co-operate and make yourself a part of this very order of which I am writing to you—sufficiently show you what is the nature of all this clearing and planting, and what mode of procedure it demands, and what it is that reason promises to those who study and are good (*DO* 1, 1, 4; *CA* 3, 9, 20; *SOL* 1, 13, 23; 2, 20, 34).

There is then a process that Augustine himself experienced of moving from being so wrapped up in the senses that he could not think except in representative images to another type of thinking, a type of thinking that is characterized by *veritas:* "the truth": "If anything is true, it is through truth that it is true (*SOL* 1, 15, 27). . . . Will anyone deny that that is Truth itself through which all branches of learning are true? . . . that by which all things are true is through itself and in itself the true Truth" (*SOL* 1, 11, 21). Such is the truth of the soul; such is the truth of God. And that is all that Augustine desires: *Noverim te; noverim me* (*SOL* 1, 2, 7; cf 2, 1, 1; also *DO* 2, 18, 47). It is the philosophic desire in his soul that has brought Augustine back to himself and to the courts of "true philosophy."

Divine authority, which is "true, reliable, and supreme," which transcends every human power, bids the human person not to be held down by the allurement of sensible things, but to fly to reason, for it tells him that he can acquire great things by the use of this power. And yet, whatever reason can attain is transmitted in a more hidden manner and with greater assurance (*secretius firmiusque*) "through those sacred teachings in which we are initiated and by which the life of those who are good is purified not by the intricacies of arguments, but by the authority of the Mysteries" (*DO* 2, 9, 27). Perhaps it is significant that, soon after reading Augustine, Lonergan wrote a thirty-five thousand word essay—now lost—on the nature of the act of faith. It was in reading Augustine that Lonergan was led to articulate the relationship between faith and human reason.

5. *Veritas:* **From Truths to the Truth**

Henry Chadwick in the introduction to his translation of the *Confessions* explains how the Neo-Platonic schema on personal conversion is part of a total vision of the return of the whole universe to the One.[23]

---

[23]Henry Chadwick, *Saint Augustine's Confessions* (New York: Oxford University Press: 1992) xxiv: "The last four books make explicit what is only hinted at in the autobiographical parts, namely that the story of the soul wandering away from God and then

The dialogue *De ordine* asks how a divine and beneficent Providence can be said to exercise a universal guidance and control when lack of harmony appears so evident both in the physical and the moral order? The difficulty, Augustine believes, is due to two causes: first, the scope of the human person's vision is so limited that he cannot discern the unity and perfection of the entire plan of the universe.

> If one were examining the details of an inlaid pavement, and if his searching eye could grasp no more than the outline of one little cube, he might censure the artificer for lacking skill of arrangement and order. On this account he might think the uniformity of the little stones disarranged, just because the drawn lines, harmonizing into one integral form of beauty, could not be seen and examined all at once. Something very similar to this is found in the case of uninstructed men, who, on account of their feeble mentality, are unable to grasp and to study the integral fittingness of things. They think the whole universe is disarranged if something is displeasing to them, just because that thing is maginified in their perception (*DO* 1, 1, 2).

Secondly, in the present condition of humanity the person finds himself so "immersed in sensible things" that it is no easy task for him to refuse to accept at face value the information received by way of the senses and to seek the truth within the sanctuary of one's mind.

> The chief cause of this error is that man does not know himself. Now, for acquiring this self-knowledge, he needs a constant habit of withdrawing from things of the senses and of concentrating his thought within himself, and holding it there. This they alone succeed in doing who definitely mark out in solitude the impressions of opinion which the course of daily life has made, or correct them by means of the liberal branches of learning. When the soul has returned to itself in this manner, it understands what is the beauty of the universe (*DO* 1, 1, 3).

---

in tears finding its way home through conversion is also the story of the entire created order. It is a favorite Neoplatonic theme, but also, as Romans 8 shows, not absent from the New Testament. The creation, made out of nothing, is involved in the perpetual change and flux of time. It falls into the abyss of formless chaos, but is brought to recognize in God the one source of order and rationality. Because it comes from God, it knows itself to be in need of returning to the source whence it came. So Augustine's personal quest and pilgrimage are the individual's experience in microcosm of what is true, on the grand scale, of the whole of creation. Augustine found his story especially symbolized in St. Luke's account of the parable of the prodigal son. But this parable also mirrors the evolutionary process of the world as understood by the Neoplatonic philosophers of the age.'' In that light one can understand how the last four books of the *Confessions* on memory, time, eternity, and creation are just the cosmic dimension of what is illustrated in an autobiographical way in the first nine books.''

This process is keenly reminiscent of a quote from Lonergan in an article from *Insight* published in 1958. He is speaking of the importance of moving from "our own little worlds" to the universe of being grasped by true judgment. This move requires a constant correction of our own private worlds. However, Lonergan notes, quoting Thomas Aquinas: "I am inclined to believe . . . that this constant and sedulous correction does not occur without a specifically philosophic conversion from the *homo sensibilibus immersus to homo maxime est mens hominis.*"[24]

For Augustine, very helpful in this journey of the soul's return to itself is the proper study of the liberal arts. In them reason is exercised and can establish its mastery over the senses. In the *De Ordine* Augustine establishes this by reflecting on the various disciplines, beginning even with those that directly concern the delights of the senses, such as cuisine, music, and architecture. Even in these studies there is a distinction between the delight *of* the senses and delight in reason's mastery *through* the senses. Reason becomes more aware of itself in the art of grammar wherein the proper use of words is considered. Higher again on the scale of the liberal arts is the study of numbers which have an "immortal" quality about them. Finally, there is dialectics, the "discipline of disciplines": "This science teaches both how to teach and how to learn. In it, reason itself exhibits itself, and reveals its own nature, its desires, its powers. It knows what knowledge is; by itself, it not only wishes to make men learned, but also can make them so" (*DO* 2, 13, 38).

In dialectics reason provides us with a revelation of itself: it discloses what it is, what it wishes, what power it has. Therefore it is the highest and most useful of the disciplines (*DO* 2, 13, 38). It could be said that dialectics is precisely the exigent discipline that Augustine is exhibiting in these dialogues: the Socratic quest exposing superficial views and moving the mind to "the Truth" whose influence on the human soul is, indeed, at the origin of the quest. Such a science of "right reasoning," of bringing everything to a synthetic grasp of a higher unity, has a mathematical quality to it and, indeed, Augustine makes this connection:

> No one ought to aspire to a knowledge of those matters without that twofold knowledge, so to speak—the knowledge of right reasoning and that of the power of numbers. And, if anyone thinks that this is indeed a great deal, let him master either numbers alone or only dialectics. But, if even this seems limitless, let him merely get a thorough understand-

[24]*Collection,* 148.

ing of what unity in numbers is, and what its import is—not yet in that supreme law and order of all things, but in the things that we think and do here and there every day (*DO* 18, 47).

As one reads these dialogues one cannot help but remember the long analyses in Lonergan's *Insight* of mathematical and scientific understanding. All point to the human importance of what Lonergan calls "the intellectual pattern of experience," that concentrated attention that pulls the mind out of distracting images and helps it attain to truth.

Augustine wrestles with the nature of various dimensions of imagination and its distinction from intellect. He notes, for example, that imagination can be misleading, pouring false colors and forms into the mind, so that even truth-seekers are misled. For like the fabled Proteus, who impersonates the truth, false images constantly strive "to deceive and delude us through the very senses which we use for the needs of this life" (*CA* 3, 6, 13). On the other hand, the mind can through the process of abstraction arrive at what is essential. "Thus, for example, thought depicts to itself and, so to speak, displays before the eyes squares of varying size. But that inner mind which desires to see the true rather turns aside, if it is able, toward that vantage whence it judges that they are all squares" (*SOL* 2, 20, 35).

In the same passage the distinction between imagination and intellect is captured, significantly enough, by geometric examples (one of them Lonergan's favorite, the circle).

A. What if someone tells us that the mind judges according to what it is wont to see with the eyes?
R. Why, then, does it judge, if, indeed, it is well instructed, that a true sphere of any size whatsoever is touched by a true plane at only one point? What thing of this kind does the eye ever see or can it see, when nothing like it can be pictured even by the imagery of thought? Do we not prove this whenever we describe by the mind's imagining the tiniest circle and draw lines from it to the center? For, when we have drawn two lines, between which one can hardly insert a needle, we are unable to draw, even in our imagination, other lines between them in such a way that they will reach the center without touching each other. Yet, reason asserts that lines without number can be drawn, and that, in these unbelievable narrow spaces, the lines can meet only in the center, so that in every space between the lines a circle can be described. Since the phantasy is incapable of doing this, and since it fails more than the eyes themselves—because it is through the eyes that the phantasy is imposed on the mind—it is evident that the phantasy is far different from the Truth, and, as long as it is seen, the Truth is not seen (*SOL* 2, 20, 35).

One position that made a particular impression on the young Lonergan was Augustine's emphasis on *intelligere*, understanding. Now it does not seem that this word occurs that often as such in these early dialogues of Augustine. In the *Soliloquies* he promises to discuss "understanding" in the future. Still, the reality is there: Augustine's emphasis on question and answer; the dialectical dialogue that goes on with others and, at its deepest level, with oneself; his high regard for dialectic's "tools" of definition, division and distinction (*SOL* 2, 11, 20ff.); his introspective account of the processes of human consciousness, etc. Eugene TeSelle summarizes Augustine's fluid terminology in these dialogues:

> Reason . . . can mean (a) the "eye" of the mind, (b) the mind's "looking" (*adspectus*), its attending to possible contents of knowledge without yet grasping them, (c) the mind's thinking (*ratiocinatio*), the activity of inquiry as it moves among the data, guided by the rules laid down in the science of dialectic, classifying and distinguishing things through definition and partition, separating them with disjunctive propositions and joining them through formal implication (*CA* 3; *De quantitate animae*, 25, 47; 26, 51-27, 52), and finally (d) the completion of the process either in an immediate vision (*intellectus*), a union of mind with that which is known (this is the Plotinian way of describing it) or, at a lower level, in a "grasping" of something with unshakeable conceptual knowledge ("*scientia*" [and this is the Stoic and Academic way of describing it]).[25]

There is a singularly interesting use of the term *intelligere* in the section where Augustine is speaking of the purification of the soul in order to see God. We will quote it in both Latin and English for it brings to mind a fundamental theorem concerning knowledge which Lonergan will later emphasize in studying Aquinas:

> Ipsa autem visio, intellectus est ille qui in anima est, qui conficitur ex intelligente et eo quod intelligitur; ut in oculis videre quod dicitur, ex eo sensu constat atque sensibile, quorum detracto quolibet, videri nihil potest.

> However, this vision itself is the understanding which is in the soul, brought forth by the one who understands and that which is understood: just as in the eyes, what is called "seeing" consists of the sense itself and the thing sensed, either of which being withdrawn, nothing can be seen (*SOL* 1, 6, 13).

One is reminded of Aquinas' axiom, owed to Aristotle and often alluded to by Lonergan: *sensibile in actu est sensus in actu, et intelligibile*

---

[25]TeSelle, *Augustine the Theologian*, 82–83.

in actu est intellectus in actu (the sense in act is the sensible in act; the intellect in act is the intelligible in act). This principle itself is opposed to the empiricist myth of the confrontation of the "blooming buzzing confusion" of sense data over against the sensing organ. On the contrary, sensation already structures and patterns its object in the very act of sensing. Intellect is primarily one with its object prior to sorting out the complexities of objectivity and subjectivity.

The above paragraph also reminds one of the section in the *De Ordine* where Augustine is pointing out the benefits to reason if it submits humbly to the dictates of the authority of faith: "When he has become docile through these precepts, then at length he will come to know: (a) how much wisdom is embodied in those very precepts that he has been observing before understanding; (b) what reason itself is, which he—now strong and capable after the cradle of authority— follows and comprehends; (c) what intellect (*intellectus*) is, in which all things are, or rather, which is itself the sum total of all things; (d) and what, beyond all things, is the source of all things" (*DO* 2, 9, 26).

For Augustine in these dialogues, the Truth—*veritas*—is that by which all things are true. The Truth is that which is the source of all truths and which illuminates the mind as to what is true. Ultimately, the Truth is the Word of God and the Light of God.

> Now consider, as far as it is required for the time being, something concerning God Himself drawn from that comparison of sensible things, which I will now teach you. God is, of course, intelligible, as those principles of the sciences also are intelligible, yet there is a great difference between them. The earth is visible and light is visible, but the earth cannot be seen unless it is brightened by light. So, likewise, for those things which are taught in the sciences and which everyone understands and acknowledges, without any cavil, to be most true—one must believe that they cannot be understood unless they are illumined by something else as by their own sun. Therefore, just as in this sun one may remark three certain things, namely, that it is, that it shines, and that it illumines, so also in that most hidden God whom you wish to know there are three things, namely, that He is, that He is known, and that He makes other things to be known (*SOL* 1, 8, 15).[26]

In the incantatory prayers at the beginning of the *Soliliquies* Augustine invokes God under the title of the true and intelligible Light.

> I call upon Thee, O God the Truth, in whom and by whom and through whom all those things are true which are true.

[26]For an exposition of the various usages of *veritas* in Augustine, see the monograph of Lonergan's Roman dissertation director, C. Boyer, *L'Idée de Vérité dans la philosophie de Saint Augustin* (Paris: 1941; original edition 1920).

O God, Intelligible Light, in whom and by whom and through whom all those things which have intelligible light have their intelligible light (*SOL* 1, 1, 3).

Later in his life Lonergan will refer to Augustine's doctrine of the inner and outer teacher to exemplify his own teaching on religious experience.[27] His specific reference will be to Augustine's *De Magistro*, written several years after the Cassiciacum dialogues, after Augustine's return to Africa.

Concerning universals of which we can have knowledge, we do not listen to anyone speaking and making sounds outside ourselves. We listen to Truth which presides over our minds within us, though of course we may be bidden to listen by someone using words. Our real Teacher is he who is so listened to, who is said to dwell in the inner man, namely Christ, that is, the unchangeable power and eternal wisdom of God (11, 38).[28] . . .

I have learned by your warning words, that by means of words a man is simply put on the alert in order that he may learn; also that very little of the thought of a speaker is made evident by his speaking. I have also learned that in order to know the truth of what is spoken, I must be taught by him who dwells within and gives counsel about words spoken externally in the ear (14, 46).[29]

5. Conclusion

Reading Augustine's dialogues was certainly a great consolation for the young Lonergan. Obviously, his personal journey was far different from Augustine's. Lonegran had never "wandered" far from the Catholic faith, as had Augustine. Still, he was a young man of quite independent views, one who, although a Jesuit scholastic, had defined himself as a "nominalist," because he could not accept the official scholastic philosophy of his day. Like Augustine, he had recently experienced a great "release" in reading Platonic philosophy. And like Augustine, his life—moral and religious—was connected with his thinking and his thinking was connected with his life. It behooved him to get things straight. "What on earth is this all about?" seemed to be his constant quest. He sought the truth—and this was one of the major Augustinian categories that was to influence him: *veritas*.

So many themes are present in these early dialogues of Augustine that it is not difficult to see how they prepared the way for Bernard

---

[27]*Third Collection*, 229.
[28]Burleigh, *Augustine: Earlier Writings*, 95.
[29]Ibid., 101.

Lonergan's own intellectual conversion. There is Augustine's honest desire for the truth, irrespective of philosophical schools. There is his obvious commitment to following out that desire, to submitting to the normative demands of reason, the intellectual pattern of experience that allows all relevant questions to arise. There is tremendous respect for liberal learning. There is Augustine's commitment to introspection, to coming to terms with the facts of his own consciousness and the inevitability of those facts. There is the dawning conversion to understanding God and the human spirit in terms of spirit and not in terms of matter. There is the transcendental *a priori* of Truth—*veritas*—that enables us to come to know any truth.

Augustine had a profound sense of the moral and religious implications of the pure desire to know. He knew the destructive force of human desires and their deleterious effect on human imagination and, consequently, human thought. As the years went on he would come to a greater awareness of the "reign of sin" that plunged human society into darkness and the absolute need for the liberating grace of Christ. In his unpublished writings on the philosophy of history from the mid-1930s Lonergan will refer to Augustine's doctrine that sin is from the human person, an unintelligible that has no "reason," and that infects all of human society. Everything else, all good thoughts, motives, and actions are ultimately rooted in God.[30]

Still, as Lonergan would later point out, Augustine's work was done in the world and language of common sense. In *Insight* he would even point out the remnants of a type of empiricism in Augustine's doctrine of illumination.

> For years, as he tells us, St. Augustine was unable to grasp that the real could be anything but a body. When with Neo-Platonist aid he got beyond that view, his name for reality was *veritas;* and for him truth was to be known, not by looking out, nor yet by looking within, but rather by looking above where in an immutable light men consult and contemplate the eternal reasons of things. It is disputed, of course, just how literally St. Augustine intended this inspection of the eternal to be understood. Aquinas insisted that the Uncreated Light grounds the truth of our judgments, not because we see the Light, but because our intellects are created participations of it.[31]

[30]Unpublished notes on the philosophy of history, available at the Lonergan Research Institute, Toronto.

[31]*Insight*, 437 (412); cf. 394 (370). Also *Verbum*, 73, where, after describing Augustine's position, Lonergan says: "The Platonism of this position is palpable, for its ultimate answer is not something that we are but something that we see; it supposes that knowledge essentially is not identity with the known but some spiritual contact or con-

But, as Lonergan would several times point out, Augustine's vocabulary, like Newman's, was in the world of common sense. Because he had no fixed technical language with which to express what he knew and struggled to express, his language floated. In a remarkable comparison with Aquinas Lonergan spoke of Augustine: "Augustine was not a technical theologian, a theoretical theologian. He was a person who knew the human soul in an extraordinary way. He knows more about consciousness than Thomas does. But he was not a technical theologian."[32]

In thinking of Augustine, then, it is well to remember, not just the remarkable religious conversion of August 386, but the quieter turning point in the spring of 386 when he read "certain books of the Platonists" and came to an intellectual conversion in his understanding of himself and of God.

It seems that something in this rang a bell in the soul of the twenty-nine-year-old Lonergan when he read these early Cassiciacum dialogues in the summer of 1933. In fact, as we mentioned previously, in *Insight* Lonergan uses Augustine's change of mind in 386 as a paradigm of the transformation that he is seeking to facilitate in the minds of "sufficiently cultured" readers of the twentieth century. Indeed, Lonergan once described intellectual conversion as meaning as much as Augustine meant when he spoke of *"veritas."*[33] From his later writings it seems evident that Lonergan intended to do just that. From now on his concerns, though always with the concrete processes of human consciousness, will also include the metaphysical dimensions opened up to him by Augustine's understanding of *veritas*.

---

frontation with the known." For the various possibilities of the meaning of Augustine's theory of illumination, cf. Eugene Portalié, *A Guide to the Thought of Saint Augustine* (Chicago: Henry Regnery Company, 1960) 109–14. This is the English translation of Portalié's article on Augustine published in the *Dictionnaire de Théologie Catholique*. In his notes on the philosophy of history from the mid-1930s Lonergan mentions Portalié's work.

[32]Interview with Bernard Lonergan in *Curiosity at the Center of One's Life* (Montreal: Thomas More Institute Papers, 1987) 403–04.

[33]"Method in Catholic Theology," *Method: Journal of Lonergan Studies* 10 (Spring 1992) 10–11.

Chapter Five

Growing Conviction

Augustine was so concerned with understanding, so unmindful of universal concepts, that I began a long period of trying to write an intelligible account of my convictions.[1]

Lonergan was sent to Rome to study theology in the fall of 1933. It was a great boon in his life, especially since his time teaching at Loyola College in Montreal had not been easy. As William Mathews wrote of this time in the early 1930s: "During his second year he had some kind of confrontation with the Rector, Thomas McMahon. He was a man who had the reputation of being something of a sergeant major, and of meddling in other people's work."[2] The nature of the confrontation is not clear. Nevertheless, Lonergan's departure to theology, which should have been in the summer of 1932, was delayed a year. In addition, two close friends had recently left the community.[3] It was obviously a very painful period for him, a period in which, nevertheless, he renewed his commitment to his Jesuit vocation. "I had regarded myself as one condemned to sacrifice his real interests and, in general, to be suspected and to get into trouble for things I could not help and could not explain."[4]

We might add a note here on Lonergan's personality. As we mentioned earlier, he was a quiet, retiring man whose interests were deeply intellectual. A Latin evaluation of him from sometime in the 1930s speaks of him as "indefatigabilis in labore." He was considered somewhat timid, and as is often the case with such folk, these characteristics can be misunderstood. Some felt he did not sufficiently consider the feelings of others. There was some suspicion of what was called,

---

[1]*Second Collection,* 265.

[2]William Mathews, "Lonergan's Apprenticeship," 14. Unpublished article, quoted with permission of the author.

[3]Frederick Crowe, "Obituary for Fr. Bernard J. F. Lonergan, S.J.," *Newsletter* of the Upper Canada Jesuit Province, 60 (May–June 1985) 15–18.

[4]Letter of January 22, 1935, to Provincial, Fr. Henry Keane, S.J., 3.

derogatively, "originality" in intellectual matters. Nevertheless, the same evaluation speaks of him as accepting humiliations well and making almost continual progress in the spiritual life. An evaluation in French speaks of him as " . . . a very good religious . . . a pleasing personality . . . one guesses at rather than sees his rich qualities . . . very suited to the intellectual apostolate, perhaps more as a writer than as a professor."[5]

In this light the request that he study theology in Rome was a tremendous elation for him. "At this juncture Fr. Hingston paid a flying visit to the Immaculate where I had begun my theology. I was to go to Rome. I was to do a biennium in philosophy. He put the question, Was I orthodox? I told him that I was but also that I thought a lot. I was beginning to go into detail and happened to ask if I was making myself clear. He said he considered I had already answered the question sufficiently."[6] In the same letter from which we have been quoting, a letter he wrote to his provincial, Lonergran expressed his joy at being sent to Rome. "It was a magnificent vote of confidence which, combined with the great encouragement I had had from Fr. Smeaton after years of painful introversion and with the words over the high altar in the church of St. Ignatius here 'Romae vobis propitius ero,' was consolation indeed."[7]

It was during this period of the summer and fall of 1933 that Lonergan began to write. In "Insight Revisited" he indicates that after reading Augustine, "I began a long period of trying to write an intelligible account of my convictions."[8] In other words, it is from this period of 1933 that he has such strong intellectual convictions that he is led to write. Plato had given him "a theory of intellect." We know from the letter he wrote to his provincial that after reading Augustine and finding him "psychologically exact," he put together a twenty-five thousand word essay on the nature of the act of faith and gave it to his friend Fr. Henry Smeaton, who had a reputation of being a brilliant Jesuit student. With what some might consider a touch of arrogance Lonergan later wrote, "It was a complete success. Fr. Smeaton admitted that the Catholic philosophers were content to serve theology as best they could without having any philosophic pretensions, that my

[5]Quoted from Crowe, "Obituary for Fr. Bernard J. F. Lonergan, S.J.," 18.
[6]Letter of January 22, 1935.
[7]Ibid. The words in Latin refer to the vision St. Ignatius experienced on his journey from Spain to Rome in the little town of LaStorta, outside of Rome, where the Lord spoke to him: "I will be good to you in Rome." The present writer was also ordained to the priesthood in the Church of St. Ignatius where Lonergan was ordained in 1936.
[8]*Second Collection*, 268.

views were far simpler and far more satisfactory, that there was no cornering me by appealing to any dogmatic decision."[9]

It seems that this particular effort to articulate his own convictions dates from the summer of 1933, before starting theology. Lonergan, along with the other Jesuit scholastics, spent the latter part of the summer at the Jesuit villa on Loyola Island, Kingston. "The area was marshy, the mosquitoes bad, so lights did not go on in the evening. But Bernie could be heard night after night typing through the twilight and into the dark—a trivial little fact that acquires enormous interest in the light of later information."[10]

1. "An Intelligible Account of My Convictions"

In addition to his essay on the nature of the act of faith, we know that after his arrival in Rome in 1933, Lonergan submitted to Fr. Leo W. Keeler, an American Jesuit teaching philosophy at the Gregorian, an essay on Newman, "a feeler of some thirty thousand words." "He did not grasp my main contention because I was not out to be unpleasantly plain-spoken. But he was quite impressed none the less."[11] These early essays on the nature of the act of faith and on Newman have as a whole been lost. Nevertheless, there are in the Lonergan archives in Toronto some thirteen pages of "fragments" of what seem to be parts of these early efforts to "write an intelligible account of my convictions."[12]

Keeler encouraged Lonergan to read Hume and other modern philosophers. In 1935 Lonergan wrote to his provincial, "What do I know of modern philosophy? I confess I never read a line of it but only such summaries as the history of philosophy gives and occasional

---

[9]Letter of January 22, 1935, 3.

[10]Crowe, "Obituary for Fr. Bernard J. F. Lonergan, S.J.," 16.

[11]Letter of January 22, 1935.

[12]Crowe writes of these as "fragments of what may have been the lost essay on assent." Cf. Fredrick E. Crowe, *Lonergan* (Collegeville, Minn.: The Liturgical Press, 1992) 34n. Internal elements in these fragments that seem to date them from the early 1930s are elements that reflect his concerns at that time, the same concerns articulated in his letter of January 22, 1935, to his provincial, Fr. Henry Keane. Those elements would be the following: the insistence on an "experimentum crucis" for any metaphysical theory; the argument against the idea of substance as "something there"; his reference to conflicting views on the nature of the act of faith during the Middle Ages; etc. Also, as we will show, the views expressed in these fragments reflect a definite stage in Lonergan's development; they do not reflect his later way of speaking: for example, his insistence on contrasting the transcendence of sensitive experience with intellect as "immanent act." Crowe also mentions Lonergan's somewhat negative assessment of Aristotle in these notes and his preference for Plato.

studies of particular authors. But I know something about it."[13] Nevertheless, in these fragments Lonergan addresses the basic philosophical issues of modern philosophy. He begins with David Hume. For Hume, human experience means the pure "presentations" of sense. Such presentations do not reveal intelligible categories, such as that of causality, for example. The category of causality is not apprehended in the presentations of sense; all we really apprehend is succession. As Lonergan wrote, "We do not see one man causing the death of another; what we see is the sword in the hand of one going through the body of the other."[14] On the other hand, "In reading Hume, Kant was awakened from his dogmatic slumbers; he granted Hume's contention that cause was not presented; more, he felt that substance and other terms did not represent what was presented in the strict sense, what was simply appearance, phenomenon. Then he went a step further; since these terms did not represent transcendent knowledge, they must be due to the understanding of what was presented, to a grasping of the *ratio intelligibilis* of the thing."[15] Consequently, Lonergan goes on to say, "the idea of substance has become the trial case, the 'experimentum crucis,' between the dogmatic and the critical schools."

What is meant by these two opposing schools? It seems obvious that by the "dogmatic" school Lonergan is thinking of the scholastic philosophers as he had known them. They are characterized by their doctrine of human understanding as some kind of "apprehension." On the other hand, the "critical school" seems to be his own understanding of human understanding in the light of modern philosophy. He goes on to distinguish these two approaches related to the idea of substance. "For if understanding is ultimately apprehensive, then 'substance,' what lies beneath or stands beneath the appearances, must be had by apprehension: this is the scholastic position. On the critical theory, the substance is known by an immanent activity and so is not apprehended but merely understood to be there; clearly this corresponds exactly with our knowledge of substance: we do not know what it is—as we would if we ever apprehended it; all we know is that it is there."[16]

Earlier in this essay we noted Erich Przywara's comment that English empiricism moves easily into Berkeley's perceptualism and eventually, into Kantian idealism. Later in his life Lonergan would recall

[13]Letter of January 22, 1935.
[14]Fragments, 7.
[15]Ibid.
[16]Ibid.

an early fear of falling into idealism, and these fragments indicate an initial sympathy with that tendency. Still, he seeks to distance himself from it.

> Of course, it does not follow that subscription to the main contention of Hume or the initial moment of Kant's thought implies either Hume's phenomenalism or the number of categories and antinomies—invented by Kant but hardly ever believed by anybody. Undoubtedly there are consequences to such subscription and acceptance; but what they are is to be decided not historically but logically. Meanwhile the evidence in favour of the critical view is not limited to the obscurity of the scholastics' spiritual apprehension, or to the correspondence between the critical theory of our knowledge of substance and what de facto we know about it. Verification of the hypothesis may be found all over philosophical inquiry.[17]

He goes on to point out what he considered the key to the Kantian error: it was a position he was to repeat through the years. "Kant suffered from the obsession that the only possible justification was some sort of spiritual apprehension of the thing-in-itself—a presentation and not a mere understanding of the object. Since such a presentation was not to be had. . .Kant decided that there could be no theoretical justification for the demand to understand. Metaphysics had to go by the boards; we have no right to understand; all that we have is a practical need of understanding, so as to be able to carry on the dull business of daily life."[18] In other words, Kant's basic error was the same as that of the naive realism of the scholastics: an understanding of understanding as some kind of "spiritual apprehension of the thing-in-itself."

Lonergan then goes on to provide the evidence for his "critical" theory of understanding, not as some type of "transcendent" apprehension, as scholastics would have it, but rather as "immanent act." For example, there is the very image of understanding as "light." Just as light does not add new features to the presented object, but only makes the features of the object actually visible, "so intelligence does not add new features to the sensible presentation, is not a superven-

---

[17]Ibid.

[18]Ibid., 9. In a note in the margin Lonergan wrote: "Distinguish 1) understanding that; 2) understanding what or how or why. 1) is a substitute for apprehension; 2) is *sui generis*. Kant's error seems a confusion of the two. This is the same error as the scholastics." We might note that there exists a number of pages of Lonergan's handwritten notes commenting on Kant's "Metaphysic of Costumi"; they seem to be a commentary on an Italian work either translating or commenting on Kant's critique of practical reasoning.

ing, spiritual apprehension, but only serves to make the sensible features intelligible, or understood, or interpreted. What else can be meant by the traditional phrase, 'intellectus agentis est illuminare phantasmata,' I have been unable to fathom.''[19]

Just as aesthetic pleasure accompanies apprehension and is preceded by curiosity, so understanding is preceded by wonder and is accompanied by its own peculiar subjective satisfaction. ''The intenser form of the pleasure, the joy, or still less grossly the light, of understanding are found in the student who has traced trains of influence in the drama of history, unraveled the mysteries of mathematics, or in philosophy catches unsuspected relations that link together into a harmony what else was but a bleak and insignificant plurality.''[20]

As opposed to the palpableness of apprehension, intellectual truth has for its characteristic trait, evidence. He relates evidence to total explanation.

> Evidence in itself is subjective; but evidence bears witness to truth, shows that the evident way of understanding is objectively the right way. We accept a theory, a way of understanding, as objectively the right way (i.e., as true) because it explains, illuminates, interprets, synthesizes, all the facts. The emphasis is on the fact of explanation; ''all the facts'' are important because, unless the facts are included, then the evidence of the theory will be destroyed when the incompatible fact receives attention. Then the explanation will not explain.[21]

Lonergan examines the Kantian synthetic *a priori* judgments. What is the source of the judgment that every contingent being must have a cause? Why must every contingent being have a cause? Precisely because otherwise its existence could not be understood; it would have no sufficient reason for its existence. It seems that the principle of sufficient reason is utterly central to Lonergan's thought at this point. It coheres with his repeated emphasis on understanding as explanation. ''There must be a sufficient reason, else we should be utterly unable to understand. We must be able to understand, else reality is not *per se intelligible*. The dispute over synthetic judgments is whether the decisive element comes from the presentation, from the subject transcending itself, or from the immanent activity of the subject, from the

[19]Ibid., 7.
[20]Ibid., 8.
[21]Ibid.

subject's demand to understand. It seems obvious that the latter is the case.''[22]

In a handwritten note on the margin of the above quote Lonergan emphasizes his point on the "transcendence" of sensitive knowledge as opposed to the "immanence" of understanding. Here he is arguing against the scholastic position of understanding as a "spiritual apprehension." *"Ens contingens:* the concept implies a cause, granted; but is the concept a compound of presentation-transcendent—and understanding-immanent? If it is such a compound, then the fact of the implication proves nothing to the point. The scholastic has to prove a spiritual apprehension; he doesn't and I don't think he can.''[23]

Unlike Kantian theory in which the apprehension of the object is according to the formal category of substance, Lonergan's analysis is "not formal but causal."

> The substance therefore is not only what unifies the different appearances of the object and makes it *ens per se*, a thing by itself distinct from other things; it is also the cause of the appearances. In other words, the appearances are the substance manifested to us sensibly. Hence there is no real distinction between the substance and the appearances; that is, there is no real distinction between substance and accidents as the scholastic theory requires. For example, the white of the object is not something objectively different from the object itself; white is what the object appears to be to the eye.[24] . . . Again, not only is the substance the cause of the appearances but also it is the explanation of its action and reaction. . . . We may remark that being the explanation of action includes being the explanation or cause of sensation (in so far as sensation is caused by the object perceived and not by the subject perceiving).[25]

The action and reaction of the substance is according to intelligible law and this follows from the intelligibility of reality. Such intelligible law is progressively discovered by developing human intelligence.

It is remarkable in these notes that there is a section prefiguring Lonergan's program in *Insight*, that is, a program of unifying all the sciences in a "science of sciences" based on developing understanding. "In so far as the critical metaphysic is a view or theory of reality, it is more pronouncedly positive and inductive; it takes advantage of all human understanding or science of the objective world and is, in

---

[22]Ibid., 8–9.

[23]Ibid., 9.

[24]Ibid., 23–24. Elsewhere he speaks of the scholastic theory of causality: "If on the scholastic theory it is impossible to deny the principle of causality, then it is too bad for the scholastic theory." Ibid., 28.

[25]Ibid., 24.

the theoretic order, a science of sciences. . . . Critical metaphysic takes the explanations arrived at in every field of science—physics, chemistry, biology, psychology, history, ethics, etc.—and frames a unified view of reality in its totality.''[26] Lonergan distinguishes the intelligibility of the object from the fact that the object exists and thus touches on the scholastic doctrine of the real distinction of essence and existence.

> The law of the object is distinct from the fact that the object exists. This distinctness is due to the nature of our knowledge. For the fact of existence is known by apprehension; the law of the object is known by understanding. Knowledge consists of a conjunction of presentation and understanding into one whole; the pure presentation of experience and the pure intellection (abstract idea) are the *entia quibus* of knowledge (human). This distinction the scholastic theory objectifies by a real distinction between essence and existence; it puts the composition, not in the mind, but in some very obscure way, in the object. Whether the critical metaphysician will assert such a real distinction or not, I shall discuss presently. But if he does, it will not be due to the distinction in the mind but only on the analogy of this distinction and as a theory to explain definite facts.[27]

These written fragments by Lonergan contain no further comments on the "real distinction," but since he had already denied the scholastic theory of the real distinction between substance and accident, and since he is at the very least ambiguous in his attitude toward it in the above quote, it is safe to say that at this time it is not a doctrine on which he has convictions.

There is then the critical problem: "What justification is there for the subject's demand to understand? Why may we suppose that evidence, a subjective experience, the illumination that comes of having things explained, should be an ear-mark of truth, that is, of the way things-in-themselves (so distinct from our minds) should be explained?''[28] Lonergan pays tribute to Hegel.

> Hegel indicated the germ of a solution by positing an identity of intelligence and reality. His interest in theory made him give the upper hand in this identity to intelligence; for him the world is the idea gaining consciousness of itself and unfolding itself according to thesis, antithesis and higher synthesis. This is all very nice for the theoretical side of things, however misty, but what happens to the practical? Feuerbach solved this by turning Hegel's house upside down. He asserted the identity of in-

[26]Ibid., 23.
[27]Ibid., 24.
[28]Ibid., 9.

telligence and reality but gave the upper hand to reality, in particular material reality.[29]

At this point Lonergan inserts a handwritten note about Marx's dialectical materialism necessitating Communism and the unity of theory and practice as the basis of Bolshevism. It is obvious that his interest in philosophy goes hand-in-hand with his interest in the contemporary historical situation. He indicates his own position. "The intelligibility of reality itself needs an explanation. The sole explanation is that there is an ultimate identity of intelligence and reality; i.e., that in virtue of which other things are must be not only a cause but also an intelligence."[30] He specifies the meaning of this identity of intelligence and reality:

> Now, though an identity of intelligence and reality is the solution, it does not follow that this identity need be verified in the actual world. A radical and fundamental identity is quite sufficient, the theist as opposed to the monist position. This sets up a pre-established harmony (I do not mean a psycho-physical parallelism) which makes the intellect of man apt to understand the right way, and so justifies the demand of the subject to understand, [and] gives a sufficient reason for the axiom "ens et intelligibile convertuntur."[31]

Referring to Newman, Lonergan then defines certitude: "Certitude is therefore an assent to an idea, to a theory, as the sole possible explanation of the facts."[32]

In a further page of these written fragments, Lonergan links this theory of "intellect as immanent act" with mystical experience. "The theory of intellection as immanent act fits in with a philosophy of mysticism; the mystical experience is *sui generis* because it is an experience, a transcendence, of the soul as soul and not merely as related to the body. The uniqueness of this experience is more readily understood, if our theory of ordinary knowledge does not postulate spiritual apprehensions."[33] At the same time, as in his early *Blandyke Papers*, there is in these notes an emphasis on the need for experience, imagination, the presentation, in order to understand. " . . . We have here an explanation of the need of phantasm, of diagrams in geometry, of ex-

---

[29]Ibid.

[30]Ibid., 33.

[31]Ibid., 9.

[32]Ibid., 33. He explains the meaning of Newman's "real apprehension": "If the apprehension is intimate enough and real enough then the idea that can be evident in it is the sole possible explanation." Ibid., 35.

[33]Ibid., 13.

periments in physics. Parallel to this is the need of illustration in oratory and exposition, of the importance of similitude, parable, analogy in gaining ideas of things unseen. The last brings us to the most profound example of the idea in the concrete, the Incarnation; in the words of St. John: *kai ho logos sarx egeneto.*"[34]

The ultimate aim of Lonergan's critical metaphysics is to consider human life, not only in its metaphysical character, but as it really is lived, with weakness but also tending toward a transcendent *telos.* As he quotes Augustine: *Fecisti nos ad te, Domine, et inquietum cor nostrum donec requiescat in te.*

In summary, we can make the following observations about Lonergan's position in these early fragments. As in his early *Blandyke Papers,* he is still distancing himself from the scholastic position which he again characterizes as treating of human understanding as some kind of spiritual "apprehension." His basic point in these notes is the absolutely unique character of the act of understanding and the radical identity of intellect and reality. It is obvious that he is on to something; and he knows he is. On the other hand, these notes are ambiguous about the sharp distinction he will later make between understanding and judgment. He speaks of the two components of knowledge as sensitive apprehension and the intellectual act of understanding. He characterizes the latter not only as light but also as evidence. He claims that "the fact of existence is known by apprehension."

Furthermore, he contrasts sensitive apprehension and understanding as transcendent and immanent. Later in life he will characterize these two acts as moments in the one self-transcending activity of the human person. But even in these fragments he is not entirely consistent in his use of these terms, for in speaking of mysticism he speaks of the "transcendence of the soul as soul and not merely as related to the body." Further still, this inconsistency over transcendence and immanence is apparent in his treatment of substance as "not apprehended but merely understood to be there." He says we do not know what substance is; "all we know is that it is there." At this point his understanding seems to presuppose spatial categories. I am reminded of what he later wrote of the idealist philosopher. "The idealist insists that human knowing always includes understanding as well as sense; but he retains the empiricist's notion of reality."[35] This underlying lack of clarity about the ultimate criterion of reality is also revealed in Lonergan's denial of the scholastic "real distinction" between substance and

---

[34]Ibid.
[35]*Method in Theology,* 238.

accident, as well as his down-playing, if not denying, the real distinction between essence and existence. This latter issue will be at the core of his intellectual conversion.

As I read these fragments from the early 1930s I am reminded of Lonergan's statement in *Insight,* that between a materialism and a critical realism "the halfway house is idealism."[36] He is on the way to a critical realism.

2. "An Analytic Concept of History"

In a letter from Rome to his provincial on January 22, 1935—a letter we will consider more fully later on—Lonergan indicated that he had applied his growing awareness to a philosophy of history. "As to application, I am certain (and I am not one who becomes certain easily) that I can put together a Thomistic metaphysic of history that will throw Hegel and Marx, despite the enormity of their influence on this very account, into the shade. I have a draft of this written as I have of everything else."[37] The claim is enormous: to overcome the philosophies of history represented by Hegel and Marx! He describes his thesis: "It takes the 'objective and inevitable laws' of economics, of psychology (environment, tradition) and of progress (material, intellectual; automatic up to a point, then either deliberate and planned or the end of a civilization) to find the higher synthesis of these laws in the mystical Body."

Some roots of this interest in a philosophy of history can be traced. From his time at Heythrop and a course by Fr. Lewis Watt, S.J., on ethics and economics, he had been interested in economics and social process. Watt introduced him to Marx and to what were considered the necessary and "iron laws" of economics. " 'It would have been sinful to interfere with the Irish famine; that was supply and demand!' So I was interested from that viewpoint. How can you get moral precepts that are based on the economy itself? That was my question?"[38] Also, during the early 1930s he had read Christopher Dawson's *The Age of the Gods,* which traced the move from primitive cultures to the great high civilizations. According to Lonergan, Dawson introduced him to "the anthropological notion of culture" as distinct from the "classicist" one. The classicist view held that there was only one culture and that was classical culture; all other cultures were "barbarians."

---

[36] *Insight,* 22 (xxviii).
[37] Letter of January 22, 1935.
[38] *Caring About Meaning,* 31. Cf. also 80–86, 225–26. Also Mathews, "Lonergan's Apprenticeship," 58f.

With the advent of historical scholarship in the nineteenth century, however, a new notion of culture had emerged, that is, the set of meanings and values that concretely inform a particular people at a particular time. It was the beginning of Lonergan's awareness of the distinction between classical and historical consciousness.

Also, during his theology courses in Rome one part of his Church history course dealt with political questions such as the relation of the Church to revolution, liberalism, nationalism, socialism and Bolshevism. It also dealt with the Church in America, Latin America, and Asia. William Mathews notes that this seems to have been one of the few courses in Rome for which Lonergan kept his lecture notes, an interesting indicator of personal interest.

There was also, of course, the great political ferment going on in Europe during this time of his own intellectual conversion and his breakthrough to understanding Thomas Aquinas' metaphysics. This combination of introspective cognitional theory and metaphysics gave him the tools with which to consider the ebb and flow, the progress and decline of human history.

Some unpublished papers, more than two hundred typed pages, were found in a file now located in the archives of the Lonergan Research Institute in Toronto. Eight of the papers belong to the 1930s and one is dated "Dominica in Albis 1935," that is, April 28, 1935. Some of the titles of the essays are the following: "Analytic Concept of History," "Sketch for a Metaphysic of Human Solidarity," "Analytic Concept of History, in Blurred Outline," "Essay in Fundamental Sociology," "Philosophy of History," "A Theory of History," "Outline of an Analytic Concept of History." There is also a paper entitled *"Pantôn Anakephalaiôsis"* with the accompanying first line: "Our aim is to outline the metaphysic of human solidarity that is more or less implicit in the epistles of St. Paul." From our point of view, the significance of these papers is that they are a reflection of the intellectual ferment that was going on within Lonergan during the early 1930s. It would seem that some of these papers were written before what he later called his own intellectual conversion, while others were written later.[39]

In speaking of cognitional process in these papers, Lonergan is not as clear as he will be in his later writings. Still, there is a focussing

---

[39]Cf. Michael Shute, *The Origins of Lonergan's Notion of the Dialectic of History* (Lanham, Md.: University Press of America, 1993). On the basis of internal evidence he divides the papers into two batches, an earlier group that include "Philosophy of History" and *"Pantôn Anakephalaiôsis,"* and a later that deal directly with the dialectic of history.

on the various levels of cognitional process, while at the same time a view of these levels in relationship to human action and human history. The language is not as stable as it will become. The papers consider human history from the viewpoint of intelligibility.

> . . . in the action of the individual there are three things: the physico-sensitive flow of change; the intellectual forms with respect to the phantasmal flux; the power of imposing the intellectual forms upon the flow of change, thus transforming behavior into rational conduct and speech into rational discourse. These three causes merge to constitute a single action.[40]

Human action for the most part is not initiation, but only control, the power of approval or inhibition. "What you can think about depends upon external experience. What you think about it depends upon the mentality you have imbibed from the environment of home, school, university, and the general influences of others."[41]

Human beings, then, are interconnected. From the viewpoint of matter, the human family consists in discrete individuals. But from the viewpoint of intelligibility and intelligible decisions, the human family is interconnected. We are dependent on the wise or foolish decisions of people in the past; we are connected by persuasion and by the intelligent or unintelligent decisions of others before us. "Thus the heritage of intellectual vacuity and social chaos given by the nineteenth century to the twentieth is the real reason why the twentieth century is such a mess."[42] To handle the issue there is need for a fundamental set of terms and relationships: "Hence nature explains why man is the kind of being that he is. History explains why men are doing what they are doing. Matter is the principle which makes the one human nature into a successive manifold of individuals operating the earlier upon the later according to the law of a pre-determined bracket of influence and a statistical uniformity within that bracket."[43]

Lonergan spells out what he calls "the analytic concept of history," as distinct from the synthetic concept. "Any human act of understanding is the apperceptive unity of a many. If the many in question is concrete and particular, we have a synthetic act of understanding. Example: Christopher Dawson's historical essays, Newman's illative sense. If the many is abstract and universal, we have the analytic act

---

[40]This is found in the set of notes entitled "Philosophy of History," 91. As Shute notes, "In 'Philosophy of History' . . . Lonergan does not clearly differentiate understanding and judgment as distinct conscious levels." Ibid., 161.

[41]"Philosophy of History," 91.

[42]Ibid., 93.

[43]Ibid.

of understanding."[44] As an example of an analytic act of understanding, he points to the metaphysician's understanding of limited being as a compound of essence and existence: such an analysis of a "many" is real but static. What is needed for an analysis of human history is a real but dynamic analysis. He proffers a scientific example: "The Newtonian astronomer's understanding of planetary motion as a resultant of different accelerations on a moving mass is an analytic concept based upon a real and dynamic multiplicity."[45]

Years later he commented on the significance of what he was writing about, though he dates the work somewhat later than the mid-1930s:

> It was about 1937–1938 that I became interested in a theoretical analysis of history. I worked out an analysis on the model of a threefold approximation. Newton's planetary theory had a first approximation in the first law of motion: bodies move in a straight line with constant velocity unless some force intervenes. There was a second approximation when the addition of the law of gravity between the sun and the planet yielded an elliptical orbit for the planet. A third approximation was reached when the influence of the gravity of the planets on one another is taken into account to reveal the perturbed ellipses in which the planets actually move. The point to this model is, of course, that in the intellectual construction of reality it is not any of the earlier stages of the construction but only the final product that actually exists. Planets do not move in straight lines nor in properly elliptical orbits, but these conceptions are needed to arrive at the perturbed ellipses in which they actually do move.[46]

The point is that several interlocking perspectives are needed to understand the concrete and dynamic. To analyze the concept of history Lonergan provides three basic "differentials": what he later called "vectors," for understanding the complexity of the ebb and flow of historical process: that is, progress, decline, and renaissance. He will change the names through the years to progress, decline, and redemption, but the basic schema will remain with him.

Thus, obscurantists to the contrary, there is such a thing as progress. "It is a matter of intellect. Intellect is understanding of sensible data. It is the guiding form, statistically effective, of human action transforming the sensible data of life. Finally, it is a fresh intellectual synthesis understanding the new situation created by the old intellectual

---

[44]This is found in the set of notes entitled "Analytic Concept of History in Blurred Outline," 1. Shute brings out that these essays on the "analytic" concept of history are probably from the later 1930s.

[45]Ibid.

[46]*Second Collection*, 271–72.

form and providing a statistically effective form for the next cycle of human action that will bring forth in reality the incompleteness of the later act of intellect by setting its new problems."[47] To the extent that human beings understand their situations, develop intelligent and reasonable policies, put these policies into effect, there will be progress.

The emergence of philosophy in Greece represents a significant moment in human progress. As we noted previously, Lonergan pays particular tribute to Platonism.

> The achievement of Platonism lay in its power of criticism. The search for a definition of virtue in the earlier dialogues establishes that virtue is an irreducible something, the emergence of a new light upon experience that cannot be brought back and expressed in terms of experience. This discovery of the idea, of intelligible forms, gave not only the dialectic but also the means of social criticism. For it enabled men to express not by a symbol but by a concept the divine.[48]

Although Lonergan does not clearly analyze the distinct role of judgment in these notes, he analyzes the notion of truth and its role in human history. Sense experience is always of "inexplicable multiplicity." Even consciousness of the self acting is "no more to be understood in itself as an existing *ens per se* than the difference between points can be explained by more points."[49] Consequently, we are forced to set up another metaphysical category and that is *contingence*. Contingence is the ultimate empirical in the order of consciousness just as matter is the ultimate empirical in the order of sense.

> Finally there is intellect and it has its form. This form is the truth of the intelligible. Whenever you understand, you go on to ask whether your understanding is true, for instance, whether the circle really is all that it is because it is the locus of points equidistant from a centre. And when you understand that it is, then you know the truth. . . . Now truth is true not in virtue of your knowing it. It is true in itself and the change merely happens in you in virtue of the contingence of your being. Thus, truth as an absolute, as something that is what it is in itself despite what you may happen to think and indifferent to what you happen to think, is the ultimate form of intellect.[50]

In the realm of human history, however, there is not just the thesis of progress, but the antithesis of human decline and sin. Where we

[47]Notes entitled "Philosophy of History," 94–95.
[48]Ibid., 101. This page seems to have been numbered by Lonergan—or someone else—106. It is the twelfth page in this set of notes.
[49]Ibid., 95.
[50]Ibid., 96.

would expect to find intelligibility, there is the surd.[51] Platonism as a philosophy was impotent to affect this human situation. It could not do away with the human cupidity and selfishness of individuals and groups. "Read Plato and you know the impotence of humanity to solve the problem created by the dialectic of sin. Plato saw the better and approved, but could do nothing; Aristotle wrote a practical ethic something that like Stoicism helped men to endure life but did not teach mankind to live it."[52] Eventually cupidity and selfishness discredit even the name of progress itself.

> There is the tendency to self-justification. The sinner hates his shame and his remorse, and cuts the Gordian knot by denying sin to be sin. If he is isolated in his sin, this attempt meets with little success and gives little satisfaction. But if the sinners are many, then the inner lie becomes an outward lie; the liars reinforce one another in their affirmations and fling their doubting consciences aside as superstition, the dark fears that attack man when he is alone. A society in this state is avid of excitement even if the excitement be only noise.[53]

As a result there is a sheer discrediting of human reason. The following words could easily have been written about our contemporary situation. "Philosophy takes on the soberer task of determining why philosophers are wrong, and mankind becomes a derelict ship its rudder broken. There rise the winds of doctrine."[54]

Finally, the third "differential" is "renaissance" or redemption. "Man disintegrated by matter can be united only by truth."[55] "Christ is the supernatural head of man, first in the order of nature, of voluntary membership of an intelligible unity in a society, of the personality of the *anthropos pneumatikos*, of grace."[56] . . . "It is in the Body of Christ that the Christian lives and moves, lives the life of a soul elevated to the supernatural order, moves in obedience to the *idee-force:* the intelligible or rather trans-intelligible form which by revelation is the Christian's dictate of reason."[57]

---

[51]This is a term that will be prominent in *Insight.* In these papers it is used to describe the deteriorating social situation. Cf. paper entitled "A Theory of History," 4.

[52]This quote is found in the paper entitled *Pantôn Anakephalaiôsis,* the fifth page in this set of notes. In his early writings Lonergan tends to be critical of Aristotle; this general evaluation will change as he studies Aquinas.

[53]This is found in the paper entitled "Outline of an Analytic Concept of History," 11.

[54]Ibid.

[55]*Pantôn Anakephalaiôsis,* 2.

[56]Ibid., 4.

[57]"Philosophy of History," the twenty-seventh page in this set of notes.

It seems to me that these notes on the philosophy of history evidence an awareness of what Lonergan will later call "the concrete universal," that is, the concrete demands of intelligibility in history. In order to have some grasp of that intelligibility, he constructs this "analytic concept of history," admittedly "abstract and universal," but with an amazing relevance to the concrete. In his later writings this fundamental schema, the product of his intellectual ferment in the 1930s, will be applied more concretely to history. Nevertheless, in spite of his interest in the concrete dynamics of history, his underlying focus will continue to be "the theory of knowledge." In this his developing understanding will be aided by certain Thomistic writers in the Jesuit community.

Chapter Six

Thomistic Influences

1. Peter Hoenen

After reading Plato and Augustine and beginning to write an account of his own convictions, Lonergan then went on to study the *Summa Theologiae* first hand and began to suspect that St. Thomas was "not nearly as bad as he is painted." His early scholastic studies had not left him with a good opinion of the *Doctor Angelicus.*

Perhaps the impetus to study Thomas first hand came from an article which he read in the *Gregorianum* of 1933 by Fr. Peter Hoenen, S.J., from Holland.[1] Hoenen, professor of philosophical cosmology at the Gregorian University and interested in science and mathematics, contended that there had been an oversight of the nature of the act of understanding in the scholastic tradition. In addition, what usually was presented as an account of Thomas' teaching on the understanding of first principles was really an account in the tradition of the medieval Oxford Franciscan John Duns Scotus.

> In 1933 I had been much struck by an article of Peter Hoenen's in *Gregorianum* arguing that intellect abstracted from phantasm not only terms but also the nexus between them. He held that that certainly was the view of Cajetan and probably of Aquinas. Later he returned to the topic, arguing first that Scholastic philosophy was in need of a theory of geometrical knowledge, and secondly producing various geometrical illustrations such as the Moebius strip that fitted in very well with his view that not only the terms but also nexus were abstracted from phantasm.[2]

From his studies on mathematics Hoenen was convinced that mathematical principles could not be derived, as generally scholastics

---

[1] Petrus Hoenen, "De origine primorum principiorum scientiae," *Gregorianum* 14 (1933) 153–84; cf. also "De philosophia scholastica cognitionis geometricae," 19 (1938) 498–514; and "De problemate necessitatis geometricae," 20 (1939) 19–54. An English translation of these articles—not very exact—can be found at the Lonergan Centers in Toronto and Dublin.

[2] *Caring About Meaning,* 266–67.

had held, from a mere analysis of the terms of those principles. The question was: what is the origin of an intellectual first principle such as: the whole is greater than the part? Traditional scholasticism had interpreted such knowledge as a comparison of concepts, such as "whole," "part," "greater than." On the contrary, Hoenen contended, first principles derived from an insight into the image, the "phantasm," and a grasp of the "nexus" or relationship between the terms in the phantasm. Experience, then, at least imaginative experience, was necessary for the abstraction of both universal ideas and universal principles. "We experience in singular instances the nexus between the subject and predicate and from this experience we attain to an intellectual grasp of the nature of this nexus. Consequently, without previous analysis the resultant knowledge, because it is derived from experience, will be immediate and, because it concerns the nature, universal and necessary."[3]

Hoenen presents quotes from Thomas de vio Cajetan, the sixteenth-century commentator on St. Thomas, giving his understanding of Aquinas and Aristotle on this point. According to Cajetan, Aristotle felt that even empirical science was a grasping of the universal in the particular. "Hence Aristotle in the same context adds the assertion that from the experimental knowledge of this and that herb there results the complex universal: every herb of this kind cures this kind of disease."[4] Hoenen summarizes Cajetan's summary of Aristotle on the process of abstraction:

> The intellect is only moved by that which is intelligible in act; but intelligible realities, as they are found in particular instances, are only intelligible in very remote potency because of an excess of materiality; in order that they may be gradually reduced to act, they are first brought to the exterior senses, then to the common sense, then to the cogitative faculty; then a frequent conversion and operation of the cogitative faculty is required in order that the realities may become close to intelligibility in act.[5]

An intellectual process is required then, whereby the presentations of sense and the representations of imagination are brought to the point at which understanding can grasp an intelligibility. Hoenen gives Cajetan's own understanding: "Then when the matter has been so disposed and reduced to such a degree of spirituality, it becomes, by the opera-

---

[3]Hoenen, "De origine primorum principiorum scientiae," *Gregorianum* 14. Our translation.

[4]Ibid., 7.

[5]Ibid.

tion of the agent intellect, truly universal and intelligible in act, and consequently moves the possible intellect to knowledge of itself."[6]

The opposite opinion, that of Duns Scotus, was simple: the agent intellect abstracts universal terms and concepts from experience and compares those terms and concepts. Some years later Lonergan would summarize the Scotist position:

> Scotus posits concepts first, then the apprehension of nexus between concepts. His *species intelligibilis* is what is meant immediately by external words; it is proved to exist because knowing presupposes its object and indeed its object as present; its production by agent intellect and phantasm is the first act of intellect, with knowing it as second act or inner word; it is not necessarily an accident inhering in the intellect but necessarily only a sufficiently present agent cooperating with intellect in producing the act of knowing; ordinarily it is the subordinate, but may be the principal, agent; sensitive knowledge is merely the occasion for scientific knowledge; as our inner word proceeds from the species, so the divine word proceeds from the divine essence. The Scotist rejection of insight into phantasm necessarily reduced the act of understanding to seeing a nexus between concepts; hence, while for Aquinas understanding precedes conceptualization which is rational, for Scotus, understanding is preceded by conceptualization which is a matter of metaphysical mechanics.[7]

This misunderstanding of the human process of knowing as some kind of "metaphysical mechanics" is a recurrent theme in Lonergan's writings. We already noted his statement in the *Blandyke Papers* where he opposes any "mechanical" theory of reasoning on the analogy of a slot machine: "Put in a penny, pull the trigger, and the transition to a box of matches is spontaneous, immediate and necessary." Elsewhere he will say our process of coming to know is not a kind of "metaphysical sausage machine, at one end slicing species off phantasm, and at the other popping out concepts."[8] And again, still later, our mind is not a "black box" in which there is sensitive "input" at one end and words emerge as "output" at the other end.[9] On the contrary, as Lonergan was increasingly to formulate it, our understanding is a conscious process of "grasping the intelligible in the sensible." And this fact about our human knowing can be grasped by concretely attending to our own human understanding in act.

---

[6]Ibid., 159.
[7]*Verbum*, 25n–26. Lonergan provides the references to Scotus' writings.
[8]Ibid., 34.
[9]*Third Collection*, 197.

Hoenen's article directed Lonergan to where this position could be found in St. Thomas Aquinas. In his commentary on Boethius' *De Trinitate* Thomas speaks of the first principles of the sciences, such as "every whole is greater than its parts":

> These principles, known by nature, become manifest to the human person by the light of the agent intellect, which is part of our nature; indeed, by this light, nothing becomes evident to us except in so far as, through it, the phantasms are rendered intelligible in act. For this is the act of the agent intellect, as is said in the *De Anima*. But the phantasms are derived from sensation; hence the starting point for the knowledge of these principles is sense and memory, as the Philosopher notes at the end of the *Posterior Analytics*.[10]

Human knowledge begins with sense and imagination, therefore, but it does so in the light of the agent intellect: that within us that can shed intelligible light on our experience. In the *De Veritate* Aquinas says:

> There pre-exist in us certain seeds of the sciences such as the first conceptions of the intellect, which are immediately known by the light of the agent intellect by means of the species abstracted from the sense impressions, whether they be complex, such as the first principles or incomplex, such as the notion of "being," and "one" and such like, which the intellect apprehends immediately. For from those universal principals flow all other principles as from certain seminal reasons.[11]

As in Lonergan's early *Blandyke Papers*, there is an insistence in Hoenen's interpretation of St. Thomas on focussing on the imaginative particular, the schema, as distinct from a focus on universal concepts. But there is also in Aquinas, as well, a metaphysical theory of intellect comprising such terms as the "agent intellect," the "possible intellect," "species," "abstraction," etc. What do all these terms mean? What is the origin of all these metaphysical terms that Lonergan had heard bandied about since his student days at Heythrop? That could well have been the young Lonergan's question at the time. Hoenen gave him some clues. For example, he quotes a Thomistic text that Lonergan himself will often quote through the years:

> Anyone can verify this in his own experience, that when he is trying to understand something, he forms some phantasms for himself by way of examples, and in these he as it were looks at what he wants to under-

[10]Thomas Aquinas, *In Boet. de Trin.*, 6, a. 4. Quoted in Hoenen, "De origine primorum principiorum scientiae," *Gregorianum* 14, 166.

[11]Quoted in Hoenen, "De origine primorum principiorum scientiae," *Gregorianum* 14, 166–67.

stand. It is for the same reason that when we want to have someone understand something, we offer him examples by means of which he may be able to form images for himself to aid his understanding.[12]

As Lonergan will later bring out, Aquinas is appealing to the reader's own inner experience, his or her own consciousness of themselves as sensing, imagining, understanding. As imagination is important in properly human knowing, so also is the act of understanding. "As we, without any discourse, know the principles *by a simple act of understanding*, so also the angels know all that they know; hence they are called intellectual beings; and the habit of the principles in us is called intellect.[13] . . . The intellect is so called because of its *inward penetration of the truth*; reason is so named because of its inquiry and discourse."[14]

In general, Lonergan has high praise for Hoenen. He later spoke of him as in the tradition of Thomistic writers for whom he came to have high respect, such as Rousselot and Peghaire.[15] He will have high praise for Hoenen's book *La théorie du jugement d'après S. Thomas d'A-quin.*[16] He will attribute to Hoenen the discovery of the eclipse of the act of understanding in the scholastic tradition due to the acceptance of Duns Scotus' theory of knowledge.[17] It was Hoenen who discovered the Scotist presuppositions in Kantian thought.[18] A point that Lonergan will later point out in regard to Hoenen's work, however, is that the latter's terminology—"abstracting the nexus from the phantasm"—is Scotist.

---

[12]Thomas Aquinas, *Summa Theologiae I*, 84, 7.

[13]Thomas Aquinas, *De Veritate*, 8, 15.

[14]Thomas Aquinas, *Summa Theologiae II–II*, 49, 5, 3.

[15]*Verbum*, 217–18.

[16] *Verbum*, 97. Hoenen's book was published in the series *Analecta Gregoriana* (Rome: 1946). It was translated into English, *Reality and Judgment According to St. Thomas* (Chicago: Henry Regnery Company, 1952).

[17]Cf. *Understanding and Being*, 19, 263, 356–58. It is significant to note that even the standard work on Trinitarian doctrine, that of Cardinal Billot, employed the Scotist analogy of sense knowledge; cf. *Understanding and Being*, 358n.

[18]*Caring About Meaning*, 11: "In Kant, understanding is the faculty of judgment. (But it is the faculty of making hypotheses.) Why did Kant get that idea? Because Scotus knew there is a metaphysical process that imprints the species on the possible intellect, you see. You take a look at the species, he thought, you compare two of them and you get a proposition. And you can say that this combination is possible or impossible or necessary and you get your judgments by comparing the concepts. That gave Kant the lead into analytic and synthetic propositions. There is a Scotist presupposition behind that. The man who pinned down this point about Scotus was Hoenen, in a 1934 [sic] series of articles in *Gregorianum.*"

But that terminology—that from phantasm are abstracted not only terms, concepts but also the nexus between concepts—you won't find either in Aristotle or Aquinas. That language is purely Scotist—terms with a nexus between them. You'll find that in Scotus, but you won't find it in Thomas. I've never run across Thomist texts of that type, as far as I can remember; that isn't his way of speaking. What he says is that what you abstract from phantasm is *species*—*species* is translating Aristotle's *eidos*. . . . If you want to say what's grasped by insight, you have Aristotle's expression: form, *to ti en einai*. It's not a matter simply of a nexus between terms; it's also that, but to describe it as a nexus between terms is a special case relevant to mathematics. Unity is another case—substantial unity. And if what is grasped by insight is form, what is expressed is related concepts. The presentation, the attention, has been so concentrated on the universal and the concept that the notion of the concept has permanence. But conscious intelligence is missing.[19]

2. The Keeler Review

It seems that upon his arrival in Rome, Lonergan was recognized as a gifted student. For he was asked by one of the young professors, the American Jesuit, Leo W. Keeler, to review his doctoral dissertation in the Jesuit publication, the *Gregorianum*. Keeler's dissertation was published in 1934 in the Gregorian series, the *Analecta Gregoriana*, under the title *The Problem of Error From Kant to Plato*.[20] Lonergan's review, in Latin, appears in the 1935 volume of the *Gregorianum*.[21] While Hoenen's article had highlighted the network of terms—experience, phantasm or imagination, agent intellect, a grasping or understanding of relationships in the phantasm—Keeler's book called attention to another term in cognitional process: that is, judgment.

While the book is an historical account of the problem of error in the history of philosophy, Lonergan's review focusses on the underlying issue: that is, the major acts in the process of knowing and their interrelationships. We will translate some of the key sections in Lonergan's Latin review.

First of all, the problem of error is none other than the problem of truth under another name and aspect. For if we are looking for the formal cause of knowledge, that cause cannot be just things themselves. For if this were the case, false knowledge could never be generated—unless perhaps things themselves were false. Consequently, since it is necessary

---

[19]*Understanding and Being*, 358.

[20]Leo W. Keeler, *The Problem of Error From Plato to Kant. A Historical and Critical Study*, Analecta Gregoriana VI (Rome: 1934).

[21]Petrus Hoenen, *Gregorianum* 16 (1935) 156–60.

to acknowledge that some other cause either can or often does intervene in the process of knowledge, the essence of human knowing is something other than a mere apprehension of terms and connections (*nexuum*). What and what kind of cause this is, when and how it intervenes—this is the problem of error properly so called. The exceptional difficulty of the problem can be seen in the following dilemma: it seems that some power, either cognitive or appetitive, must intervene in the knowing process. But if it is a cognitive power, there is a danger of losing certitude and the realistic character of knowledge. On the other hand, if it is an appetitive power that intervenes, then there is no way to explain why someone who errs always forcefully claims that his opinion is grounded in evidence.[22]

Here there re-appears a central theme in Lonergan's writings. It is a theme whose roots are found in Newman: that is, the *evidence* needed to make a judgment.

Lonergan, following Keeler, touches on some of the more modern opinions about the nature of error and finds them lacking. Descartes realized that there was a problem of error and so introduced epistemology or the science of the criteria of truth. However, by reducing judgment to will he contributed little to solving the problem. Nor can Hume's pure phenomenalism explain error—unless the phenomena contradict themselves. Nor can Kantianism explain error since "the immutable laws of mind" can only bring forth the same fruit, in no way any contradictions.

The ancients, however, gave some clues toward the solution to the problem. Plato, for example, in the *Sophists*, foreshadowed Aristotle's teaching about terms and propositions and even about the place that error has in judgment. "When that teaching had been fully developed and the syllogism invented, you would have thought that everything was ready for a diligent consideration of error. Aristotle, however, seems to have been deflected from that work, sometimes saying that mind (*nous*) was the cause of error and sometimes calling it infallible. In logic he affirmed that error was only an unformed syllogism, while in ethics he attributed the blame to the attractions of pleasure."[23]

Ensuing philosophers generally agreed that judgment was in some manner both free and voluntary; they were silent, however, on how this was possible; thus, the followers of the skeptic, Pyrrho, who taught that we should refrain from all assent; thus, the Stoics and Epicurus, who in the same way tried to explain error; thus, even St. Augustine himself, who tacitly assumed this opinion of his age.

[22]Ibid., 157. Our translation.
[23]Ibid., 158.

The problem of error was treated in the scholastic age in the context of the act of faith, and over this issue a fierce controversy raged in the fourteenth century. The Thomists and Scotists were considered too intellectualist, and the nominalists too voluntarist. Afterwards the "Augustinian Hermits" seemed to find some middle ground, but they did not put an end to the controversy.

> The question formerly raised by Scotus was raised again after the rebirth of philosophical studies in Spain: whether the mental process should be divided into both apprehension and judgment. To which question Suarez, among others, responded to the effect that judgment is the apprehension of the nexus; but this happens in such a way that in a false judgment a nexus that does not exist is apprehended—something which not even the will can command.[24]

We see here reappearing in Suarez Scotus' language of understanding as an apprehension of a nexus between terms, and judgment as a comparison of terms. Keeler puts the issue simply in the introduction to his work: "Moreover, this doctrine (that judgment consists solely in the *percipientia nexus*) cannot be carried over to false judgment, because when we err, we certainly do not perceive the nexus we affirm, that nexus being non-existent."[25] Lonergan, following Keeler, finds in Francisco Suarez no clear teaching on the acts of the mind. "Furthermore, when he deals with faith the *Eximius Doctor* seems to have forgotten his opinion on judgment and does not hesitate to affirm a certain assent distinct from the apprehension of the nexus. Nor should it be forgotten that the same contradiction had not yet been removed from scholastic doctrine: that one thing is said of judgment when it is a question of first principles and another when it is a question of faith or of error."[26]

In this light Father Keeler, according to Lonergan, seeks "more as an interpreter than a critic," to understand the mind of St. Thomas, so as to find in this great philosopher, not the perfect solution to the whole thing, but some indications that could be very useful for the solution.

> He especially tries to show that for St. Thomas the apprehension of a nexus is one thing, the act of assent is another; the former dwelling in the purely intelligible world, the latter affirming the objective existence of the intellectual content. From which distinction it can be deduced that

[24]Ibid., 159.
[25]Keeler, *The Problem of Error From Plato to Kant*, v–vi.
[26]Lonergan, *Gregorianum* 16, 159.

we err, not so much because we apprehend false things, but because we are too precipitous in assenting. Indeed, it is not in our power to refuse assent when the proper object of the intellect is present, but this happens in such a way that assent still remains distinct from knowledge of the nexus. On the other hand, when a proposition is present to the mind without full evidence, the way is open for the undue influence of the will. The author does not call this foundation the solution to the problem, since St. Thomas never directly treated of this great and difficult problem, but only touched on it occasionally when he was treating of other things.

A complexus of terms is appearing in the analysis of judgment: the prior need for evidence and for understanding the sufficiency of the evidence; the need not to be too "precipitous" in judging; the possibilities of the undue influence of imagination, desire and bad will on judgment.

Later on, in *Insight*, Lonergan will emphasize the need for "asking all the relevant questions" and for a grasp of all the evidence sufficient for the affirmation of a "virtually unconditioned": that is, a "conditioned" whose conditions de facto are understood to be fulfilled. It is interesting to note that in this review Lonergan uses the term "apprehension" to refer to intellectual activity—something he does not do in "the fragments" where apprehension seems to be limited to sensitive perception. At the same time, such intellectual apprehension is beginning to be sharply distinguished from assent.

Although Keeler's work is chiefly historical and not projected as a "solution" to the problem of error, it is evident in the review that the young Lonergan cannot resist mentioning the need for a serious critique of the following points of the Scotist-Suarezian school: first, the supposed complete dichotomy between the objective existence of the intellectual content either being apprehended or not apprehended, "for if it is apprehended, it is not evident why another further assent would be necessary, for by the apprehension itself there would be sufficient assent. On the other hand, if it is not apprehended, it does not appear how there could ever be rational assent."[27]

It is evident in this review that the young Lonergan is convinced that knowledge of existence does not take place through a simple apprehension or intuition. In fact, he speaks later of his need at this time to break with "intuitionism."[28] He also writes of the pain this break can entail:

[27]Ibid., 159–60.
[28]*Second Collection*, 265–69.

Fourteenth century Scholasticism discussed with considerable acumen the validity of an intuition of what exists and is present. Now you may or may not hold that valid perception is what constitutes human knowledge as objective. But at least in all probability you did at one time take a perceptualism for granted. And if, by some lucky chance, you succeeded in freeing yourself completely from that assumption, then your experience would have been quite similar to that of the prisoner who struggled might and main against his release from the darkness of Plato's cave.[29]

As part of this struggle, something can be discerned in Keeler's work which will reappear in Lonergan's later writings. In treating of Plato's *Theatetus*, Keeler notes Plato's emphasis on the discursive activity of the mind and the fact that knowledge cannot be reduced to simple apprehension. "Judgment is the mental act of affirming or denying, which concludes such interior discourse."[30]

Finally, Lonergan's review refers to the Suarezian insistence on the undue influence of the perverse will as the origin of error. In the Suarezian position the sole reason for the existence of the faculty or function of assent seems to be that, given an insufficient motive for affirming, the perverse and evil person would still judge erroneously. Lonergan replies: "But even if this were so, error would not yet be explained. You say that the will has an undue influence. But does it influence to such an extent that the one who thinks and believes false things does not also think that he holds such things, not precisely because of the influence of the will, but because of the objective evidence of things?"[31] Lonergan ends his review with a cryptic remark that prefigures his whole methodology: ". . . Nor, we suspect, could anyone investigate these problems who confused his own light of intelligence and reason with error."

In this review the stage seems to be set for the final act of Lonergan's journey to intellectual conversion. The issue is existence—and rational judgment seems to be the way.

---

[29]*Third Collection*, 193. In his footnote to this quote Lonergan notes: "The extreme views of Nicholas of Autrecourt are listed in Denziger & Schönmetzer, *Enchiridion*, nos. 1028–49. The distinction between divine power itself and divine power as ordered by divine wisdom opened the way to advancing that divine power itself could do anything that did not involve a contradiction. There followed questions of the type, Is there any contradiction in supposing that one can have an intuition of X as existing and present although X neither is present nor even exists?" Ibid., 200.

[30]Keeler, *The Problem of Error From Plato to Kant*, 19.

[31]Lonergan, *Gregorianum* 16, 160.

3. Joseph Maréchal

Shortly after arriving in Rome, Lonergan met a young Greek Jesuit by the name of Stephanos Stephanou with whom he struck up a friendship. The two prepared their exams at the Gregorian together. "Our aim was clarity and rigor—an aim all the more easily obtained, the less the theses really meant."[32] The remark reflects a dissatisfaction with the "unmethodical" approach involved in his Roman theological studies. As he remarks elsewhere, he realized that if theology studies were to be "anything more than a heap," he would have to write a book on method.[33]

Stephanou was an Athenian who had entered the Sicilian province of the Jesuits and had been sent to study philosophy at Louvain at a time when the thought of Fr. Joseph Maréchal held sway there. It was a time when "Maréchal taught psychology to the Jesuit students and the other professors at the scholasticate taught Maréchal."[34] Maréchal was a Belgian Jesuit who had a degree in experimental psychology and was very familiar with modern philosophical thought. His massive five-volume work *Le point de départ de la métaphysique* aimed at bridging the gap, indeed, the chasm, that separated the thought of St. Thomas from the Kantian idealism that dominated philosophy on the continent of Europe.[35] It was from Maréchal by way of his friend, Stephanou, that Lonergan was first introduced to a sympathetic account of Thomas Aquinas' thought: "My philosophical development was from Newman to Augustine, from Augustine to Plato, and then I was introduced to Thomism through a Greek, Stephanos Stephanou who had his philosophic formation under Maréchal. It was in talking with him that I came first to understand St. Thomas, and see that there was something there. After all, St. Thomas had insights, too! If he didn't have insights, he didn't mean anything."[36]

Maréchal felt that the basic thrust of Aquinas' thought could successfully complete the "transcendental turn to the subject" in modern philosophy initiated by Immanuel Kant. Kant had maintained that a "critique of knowledge," that is, a study of "the conditions of the

[32]*Second Collection*, 265.

[33]Transcript by Nicholas Graham of discussion, Lonergan Workshop, Boston College, June 19, 1979.

[34]*Second Collection*, 265; cf. *Caring About Meaning*, 46.

[35]Joseph Maréchal, *Le point de depart de la métaphysique*, vols. 1–5 (Bruxelles: L'Edition Universelle, 1944–1949). The first volume ("cahier") appeared as early as 1922. The famous fifth volume was published posthumously.

[36]*Understanding and Being*, 350. Keeler's work also refers very positively to Maréchal, *The Problem of Error From Plato to Kant*, 97.

possibility of knowledge," only revealed the forms and categories of human knowing, but in no way revealed the possibilities of objective knowledge. For Kant objective knowledge would be possible only on the basis of an intellectual intuition, and since he discerned no such intuition, the objectivity of human knowledge disintegrates. Maréchal disagreed. In his famous fifth volume, dedicated to a face-to-face confrontation between St. Thomas and Kant, Maréchal maintained that Kant became an idealist because he was not consistent in his own transcendental reflection on the *a priori* conditions of human knowledge. "Kant accounted for the mind's *a priori* unification of the object of its affirmation in terms of matter and form alone. Sensations, the forms of space and time, the schemata of imagination, and the categories were fitted together statically to form the purely immanent object of experience. In the account of knowledge given in *The Critique of Pure Reason* Kant forgot . . . that the mind's act of knowledge was not static. Knowing is an operation, a motion. Furthermore, a dynamic motion is a tendency toward an end."[37]

Maréchal maintained that a comprehensive and modern critique of knowledge revealed the objective dynamism of human knowledge, culminating in objective judgments of existence. In other words, as Lonergan would later put it, "authentic subjectivity leads to objectivity." The Catholic and Thomist need not fear the modern critique of knowledge, for such a critique, if adequate, could arrive at the basic Aristotelian and Thomistic metaphysical positions. At the time, this "turn to the subject" was a risky step in Catholic thought. Those who attempted it were often accused of sacrificing the objectivity of human knowledge. Nevertheless, it was a turn that Maréchal felt was absolutely necessary if Thomistic and Catholic thought was to arrive at a common method and frame of reference with modern thought. Without this turn, Catholic thinkers would not even be "speaking the same language" as the world around them. And that was clearly a position that Thomas Aquinas would not have countenanced.

Certainly, there was the danger of arriving at the same position as Kant and much of European thought after him, that is, a transcendental idealism. The fear was that by "turning within" one could never again emerge "without." There would be no possibility of escaping from the clutches of subjectivism. This was the basic reaction of the great medieval Catholic historian, Etienne Gilson, to this transcendental

[37]Gerald A. McCool, *Catholic Theology in the Nineteenth Century* (New York: Seabury Press, 1977) 256.

"turn within" in Catholic thought.[38] That was why "the problem of the bridge" loomed so large in modern scholasticism. It loomed large in my own philosophical training in the late 1950s: how do we get from "in here" to "out there?" I remember very vividly being told that the only answer is to dogmatically assert that our knowledge does cross over that bridge, that we do get from "in here" to "out there" and any analysis of our cognitional activities risks leaving us trapped "in here" in an idealism.

But the whole articulation of "the problem of the bridge" presupposes a confrontational and visual understanding of human knowledge. It was this view of knowing that could be discerned both in the medieval Scotist view and in modern idealism. As Lonergan would note in *Insight:* "Five hundred years separate Hegel from Scotus. As will appear from our discussion of the method of metaphysics, that notable interval of time was largely devoted to working out in a variety of manners the possibilities of the assumption that knowing consists in taking a look."[39]

The fact that Lonergan himself was aware of this danger of idealism is evident from his remarks about his "fear of idealism" in his early years. Asked in an interview about being "a little dazed" and seeking assurance that he was not an idealist during this period when he was arriving at his basic philosophical convictions as spelled out in *Insight,* Lonergan replied:

> Not when I was writing the book but when I was arriving at the conclusions I set forth in the book—in other words, when I got hold of the idea that knowledge is discursive. Why did Fichte, Schelling and Hegel write their enormous systems? Because for them the possibility of judgement was that you have to know everything about everything; that was the

---

[38]Cf. his *Réalisme thomiste et critique de connaissance* (Paris: Vrin, 1939); English translation: *Thomist Realism and the Critique of Knowledge* (San Francisco: Ignatius Press, 1986). Cf. also McCool, *Catholic Theology in the Nineteenth Century*, 253–55. Cf. Lonergan's critique of Gilson's position in "Metaphysics as Horizon," *Collection*, 188–204, where he lists the various places in which Gilson writes of "perceiving being." Previously, he had reviewed Gilson's *Being and Some Philosophers* in *Theological Studies* 11 (1950) 122–25; also in *The Ensign* (Montreal: May 28, 1949) 10.

[39]*Insight*, 396–97. Lonergan goes on to say: "The ultimate conclusion was that it did not and could not. If the reader himself does not accept that conclusion as definitive, certainly Hegel did. . . . For being as fact can be reached only insofar as the virtually unconditioned is reached; and as Kant had ignored that constitutive component of judgment, so Hegel neither rediscovered nor reestablished it. The only objective Hegel can offer the pure desire is a universe of all-inclusive concreteness that is devoid of the existential, the factual, the virtually unconditioned. There is no reason why such an objective should be named being. It is, as Hegel named it, an Absolute Idea."

only possible unconditioned. They didn't have the idea of the virtually unconditioned.[40]

In other words, through Maréchal, mediated through Stephanou, Lonergan learned that human knowledge is discursive, that is, incremental: it proceeds by acts of experiencing, understanding, and judging to limited knowledge of reality and then the cycle of knowing begins again to fill out perspectives or to rise to higher viewpoints. Unlike the Kantian, the idealist and the relativist traditions that felt that you had to know "everything about everything" in order to arrive at certain judgments, Maréchal pointed out the concrete activity of judging that posits the concrete existence of understood contents of thought.

> People talk about Maréchal. Maréchal was the one that effectively introduced in Catholic circles the notion that human knowledge is discursive and that you know when you affirm. An affirmation is a detail of the process, the third level. I was taught philosophy on an intuitive basis—naive realism—and I took refuge in Newman's *Grammar of Assent*. Later I read a book by J. A. Stewart, *Plato's Doctrine of Ideas*—it was a book that influenced me unconsciously a great deal. I discovered that, according to Stewart, Plato's ideas are what the scientist is trying to discover and what Plato is doing in the Dialogues is setting up a methodology.[41]

Lonergan never really immersed himself in the writings of Maréchal. It was, as he put it, "by osmosis," through his friend Stephanou, that the influence of Maréchal was mediated to him.[42] Lonergan pinpoints Maréchal's contribution through Stephanou very simply: "He told me that human knowledge was discursive, you know when you are saying something. In other words, human knowledge emerges when you arrive at judgment. And a judgment is not simply having a nexus between terms. Any hypothesis includes a nexus between terms. It is when you are positing the nexus between terms, when you are affirming or denying a nexus that you arrive at judgment. Of course, it is good scholasticism to say that truth formally is found only in the judgment. And that put me into a scholasticism."[43]

---

[40]*Caring About Meaning*, 110–11; cf also unpublished tapes of method seminar in 1962. Cf. *Insight*'s remarks on the "startling strangeness" experienced in arriving at these basic philosophical positions.

[41]*Philosophy of God and Theology* (Philadelphia: The Westminster Press, 1973) 62.

[42]*Second Collection*, 265.

[43]Transcripts by Nicholas Graham of discussions from Lonergan Workshop, June 19, 1979.

Connections back and forth across the history of philosophy are being understood in terms of the basic structure of human knowing as discursive: prepared for through acts of experiencing, questioning, imagining, understanding, conceiving—and consummated through the process of reflecting and judging. This will become yet clearer in Lonergan's further studies of Thomas Aquinas and in the statement of his own positions in *Insight*. Nevertheless, there is at this point another source of introduction to Aquinas' thought and that is the course he takes at the Gregorian in the fall and spring of 1935–1936 from Fr. Bernard Leeming on "The Incarnate Word."

Chapter Seven
Lonergan's Intellectual Conversion

In the Preface to *Insight,* Lonergan writes of the ideal detective story in which the reader is presented with all the clues yet fails to spot the criminal. "He may advert to each clue as it arises. He needs no further clues to solve the mystery. Yet he can remain in the dark for the simple reason that reaching the solution is not the mere apprehension of any clue, but a quite distinct activity of organizing intelligence that places the full set of clues in a unique explanatory perspective."[1]

Placing all the clues into "a unique explanatory perspective": this is what the early Lonergan was seeking, an *explanation* that would bring together all he had learned from mathematics and logic, from his reading of Newman, Plato, Augustine, Hoenen, and Maréchal, and most of all, from his own mind. As he would say in years to come, philosophy is not something in a book; it's in a mind.

But how did these elements fit together? How was his early emphasis on the schematic image connected with Hoenen's writings on grasping "first principles" in imaginative presentations? How did the heuristic character of intellect in J. A. Stewart's book on Plato relate to Augustine's doctrine of *veritas?* How was his insistence on understanding as "immanent act" related to Maréchal's emphasis on the discursive nature of human understanding? How was all this related to the scholastic insistence on the real distinction of essence and existence? What did these terms really *mean?* How were they all related to each other and to a whole explanatory viewpoint on human mentality and reality?

The whole process was not an easy one. By now he had been engaged in it for some years. It represented a personal problem. As he once put it: "An exact account of knowledge raises the epistemological problems in a real fashion, not merely in the sense of refuting adversaries, but also in the sense of solving personal problems—and not how I am going to help other people that are in difficulties, but how I'm going to help myself! The intrusion of epistemological problems

[1]*Insight,* 3.

106

in a real significant way is a disturbing event.''[2] That this whole issue represented a personal and ''existential'' issue for him is evident from a letter he wrote from Rome to his superior in Canada in January of 1935.

1. The Letter of 1935

In the introduction to *Insight,* Lonergan writes of the process of self-appropriation taking place, not publicly, but privately. The process takes place in the hiddenness of one's presence to oneself and one's growing knowledge of oneself. Nevertheless, as Lonergan goes on to say in the same introduction, though the act is private, both its antecedents and its consequents have their public manifestation.[3]

That this whole period of the mid-1930s was a period of enlightenment and powerful emotions is certainly evident from a letter Lonergan wrote from Rome to his Jesuit superior in Canada, Fr. Henry Keane, dated January 22, 1935. The letter is a remarkable testimony to the character and depth of the transformation that was taking place in him. What comes through in the letter are the clear and firmly held convictions of a relatively young man of thirty-one, a young man who, as he says, ''thought a lot.''

Lonergan begins the letter with some minor matters of Jesuit obedience: permission to continue smoking in spite of the high cost (twenty dollars a year!), to read works on the Index connected with his proposed future study of epistemology, to possess a typewriter and some books, and to study German the following summer at the villa for the German students. Then he gets down to the main issue: ''at which I have been poking about for expression for some time.''[4]

The issue is his own intellectual development and the quandary that development had placed him in on a practical level. He begins with a history of his philosophical development as we have recounted it: beginning with his early nominalism and then moving on to his study of Plato, St. Augustine, and St Thomas. In the letter he identifies the beginnings of his reading of St. Thomas with the time in Canada before coming to Rome. His consolation of studying in Rome is followed by the words: ''I can give you my present position in a few words. It is definite, definitive and something of a problem. The current interpretation of St. Thomas is a consistent misinterpretation.'' The words are indeed ''definitive.'' In the context of the times, they are

[2]*Understanding and Being,* 351.
[3]*Insight,* 13 (xix).
[4]Letter of January 22, 1935, 4.

a challenge. They represent a stance at variance with the reigning interpretation of St. Thomas. He goes on to present his convictions. "A metaphysic is just as symmetrical, just as all-inclusive, just as consistent, whether it is interpreted rightly or wrongly. The difference lies in the possibility of convincing expression, of making applications, of solving disputed questions. I can do all three in a way that no Thomist would dream possible. I can prove out of St. Thomas himself that the current interpretation is absolutely wrong."

The words can seem arrogant—especially in light of the fact that his own views had recently been influenced by certain Thomists, Hoenen and Maréchal among them, and within some months he will look on himself as a "Thomist" through his involvement with Bernard Leeming's course. In fact, he goes on to invoke the authority of Joseph Maréchal, even though the latter's view were frowned upon at the Gregorian:

> Not only can I prove it, but the issue has already been raised decisively though not completely or altogether satisfactorily by Fr. Maréchal whose views reign in our house in Louvain but are somewhat frowned upon here. The whole difficulty is to grasp Maréchal's point not in the abstract but in the concrete; because Fr. Maréchal is utterly in the abstract he is not understood. This may sound arbitrary so let me give the reason: the only argument raised against Maréchal is that it is "obvious" he is wrong; but in the abstract nothing is obvious either way since it is all a matter of argument and against Maréchal they cannot argue; when they say it is obvious he is wrong in interpreting St. Thomas, they mean no more than that they want an explanation that goes into the concrete.

Lonergan uses words here that he will repeat time and time again in the coming years: one of those words is "explanation": he is seeking the intrinsic causes of things, a systematic understanding. The other word is "concrete." It is not a question of deducing truths from abstract concepts or propositions; the issue is an understanding and explanation of facts. "That explanation I can give and I can prove and I can confirm from every view-point."

Strong words. Explanation of what? What is it that Lonergan can explain that is a *terra incognita* to contemporary Thomists? "In a word it is that, what the current Thomists call intellectual knowledge is really sense knowledge; of intellectual knowledge they have nothing to say; intellectual knowledge is, for example, the 'seeing the nexus' between subject and predicate in a universal judgment: this seeing a nexus is an operation they never explain." The issue is joined. The Scotist and Suarezian presupposition of intellectual knowledge as "seeing the nexus" between the concepts of a universal judgment is the basic misunderstanding in most philosophical thought.

In Lonergan's future writings he will maintain that this basic misinterpretation of intellectual knowledge as a type of "seeing" is the fundamental error in cognitional theory. It is at the root of the basic counter-positions in philosophy, whether in their naive realist, empiricist, or idealist forms. Let us call to mind his definition of intellectual conversion from thirty-seven years later. "Intellectual conversion is a radical clarification and, consequently, the elimination of an exceedingly stubborn and misleading myth concerning reality, objectivity, and knowledge. The myth is that knowing is like looking, that objectivity is seeing what is there to be seen and not seeing what is not there, and that the real is out there now to be looked at."[5]

The only way such a misinterpretation can be challenged is by examining the facts of consciousness. In his letter of 1935 Lonergan prefigures what he will later call his basic philosophical method of self-appropriation. This method will be at the basis of his understanding and explaining the real meaning of Thomas' thought. It is reminiscent of Stewart's interpretation of Plato: "What were Plato and these other people talking about? Surely about the right way of expressing some experience which they all had in common, and we ourselves still have."[6] As Lonergan put it in 1935: "The important thing about my views are that they are entirely a difference of interpretation. I do not say, Thomas said this and I say that. I say, Thomas said this; the current Thomists going into their own experience pick out this element to be what St Thomas is talking about; I go into my experience and find something entirely different to be what St. Thomas means."[7]

Lonergan speaks in the letter of using the same method in understanding of what is meant by "will." "I establish from introspective psychology that the 'will' is what Card. Billot wants the will to be to provide himself with an analogy for the Trinity. I prove what he asserts." A short time later, in his unpublished notes on the philosophy of history, he will describe himself: "But I am not speaking of the supernatural order; I am speaking as a psychologist of the school of St. Augustine and St. Thomas."[8]

How does this Augustinian and Thomistic psychologist propose to explain human intelligence? What is his basic approach? In the letter

[5]*Method in Theology*, 238.
[6]Stewart, *Plato's Doctrine of Ideas*, 2.
[7]Letter of January 22, 1935.
[8]In Lonergan's unpublished philosophy of history essay: *"Pantôn Anakephalaiôsis—* A Theory of Human Solidarity,"* 10.

Lonergan gives us a clue. "From an initial Cartesian 'cogito' I can work out a luminous and unmistakable meaning to intellectus agens et possibilis, abstractio, conversio to phantasm, etc., etc. The Thomists cannot even give a meaning to most of this."[9]

In Lonergan's later writings it is obvious that he was sympathetic with Rene Descartes' basic project of analyzing the basic facts of human consciousness, although it is also obvious that he disagreed with Descartes' method of universal doubt and his inadequate division of reality into *res cogitans* and *res extensa*.[10] In his letter Lonergan writes,

> At the same time I can deduce the Thomist metaphysic: universal individuated by matter; real distinction of essence and existence; the whole theory of act and potency.

The reference is to the arsenal of interlocking terms in the Aristotelian-Thomistic metaphysics. The reference to the real distinction of essence and existence is evidence that he is wrestling with the issue that he will later identify as mediating his own intellectual conversion.

He goes on in his letter to say that the validity of his "explanation," as with any theory, will be seen in its adequacy for explaining all the facts, in its ability to solve disputed questions, and in the fruitfulness of its applications. The basic facts to be explained are those of consciousness. In addition, his explanation can solve problems, such as the nature of the act of faith and the centuries' old theological problem, "de auxiliis," on the relation between divine grace and human freedom. This will be the subject of his doctoral dissertation a few years later. As he writes in his letter, "I have a complete solution to the arguments against Bellarmine's opinion in the *de Auxiliis* and not only is Bellarmine the only Doctor Ecclesiae who had an opinion on the precise issue but to defend Bellarmine you have to know what intelligibility is; indeed, if you know that, you are inclined to leave the question where St Thomas left it."

As to new applications which would demonstrate the fruitfulness of his ideas, Lonergan mentions one of his central preoccupations of this period, that is, the philosophy of history. "As to new applications, I am certain (and I am not one who becomes certain easily) that I can put together a Thomistic metaphysic of history that will throw Hegel and Marx, despite the enormity of their influence on this very account, into the shade. I have a draft of this already written as I have of every-

---

[9] Letter of January 22, 1935, 4.

[10] In *Method in Theology* he remarks favorably of Descartes' *Regulae ad directionem ingenii*, 261.

thing else.''[11] A Thomistic metaphysic that will throw Hegel and Marx into the shadow? Certainly a startling claim! No wonder he had trouble putting this letter together! And yet, ''I have a draft of this already written.'' We have already taken a look at those unpublished writings on the philosophy of history from the mid-thirties.

He gives two ''extrinsic'' arguments in favor of his views: one is the fact that the current Thomist profession not to understand St. Augustine on intelligence is in fact *eo ipso*, an admission that they do not know what Thomas means by intelligence, since Thomas professes to agree with Augustine at every turn. As for Lonergan, ''I am quite certain that I understand Augustine.'' On the other hand, there is no difficulty in conceiving a long tradition of misinterpretation of Thomas and Augustine on intellect. The conflicting views of the Middle Ages on such issues as the nature of the act of faith gave every opportunity to confuse understanding, or intelligible explanation, with demonstrability, that is, the mere absence of intelligibility in the contradictory proposition. In addition, there are examples of now firmly held positions which took centuries to establish.

Why did no one suspect there was something wrong before? Here Lonergan gives a brief conspectus of the history of philosophy, with the Scotist ''intuitionism'' becoming firmly established in the naive realism of the Suarezians—substance as ''something there.'' The same stream of intuitionism then filtered into secular philosophy with Kantian philosophy obviously needing to be completed by a critical Thomism.

> After Thomas there was Scotus, the nominalists, the conceptualists; then Suarez and the Spaniards with their naive realism (substance is the ''something there''); then the brilliant Jesuit pupil, Descartes, who was brought up on this stuff; then the antithesis of Spinoza and Hume; then Kant (and do you see any difference between Kant's need to go back to the causal origin of knowledge to know the thing-in-itself and, on the other hand, the Thomistic conversion to phantasm to know the singular; only singular things exist; therefore, existence is not in intellect alone; nor is it in intellect plus phantasm, since one can imagine what does not exist); then traditionalism, ontologism, Hermesian rationalism; finally, Pope Leo's ''Back to Thomas.'' I take him at his word. I also accept his ''vetera novis augere et perficere''; hence my excursion into the metaphysic of history.[12]

[11]Letter of January 22, 1935, 4–5.

[12]Some of these allusions to historic philosophical positions can be seen in Keeler's book. Certain expressions will even find their way into *Insight*: cf. the use of the term ''half-way house'' to speak of Platonic philosophy: ''This is just the Eleatic doctrine that

Lonergan's letter is not clear on "existence"; but he is obviously adopting a position different from what he had adopted in the "fragments" from the early 30s. There he seemed to hold that existence was perceived. Here he is convinced it is not.

Although Lonergan's interests extended far and wide into the philosophy of political history, nevertheless he will spend the next eleven years of his life researching what Thomas Aquinas really meant: first, on the doctrine of grace, the subject of his doctoral thesis in the latter part of the 1930s; then on Thomas' actual writings on intelligence in the 1940s. He truly took Leo XIII at his word and Leo's words, "vetera novis augere et perficere," became something of a motto for him in his future years: to build up and perfect what is old by means of the new.[13] The new was certainly Lonergan's new and "simpler" understanding of what St. Thomas meant by understanding. The new was also his interest in the philosophy of culture, of history and economics which had remained abiding interests through the 1930s. The new was also the new methods for studying all these issues: the new methods of science, the new methods of scholarship and philosophy.

What is remarkable in Lonergan's letter is that it all hangs together: the history of philosophy, the philosophy of history, and the philosophic understanding and misunderstanding of Christian theology. All are linked together by a common thread: the accurate or inaccurate account of human intelligence.

> The disputed question is the crucial experiment of a philosophic system; you have to explain everything except what you can prove to admit no explanation; otherwise you are not a philosopher or your system is inadequate. But this, the presupposition of all argument, is precisely what 99% of the people you would argue with neither grasp nor grant. They simply do not take philosophy seriously, they do not consider whether arguments are valid or not but simply what they prove, and when they prove what seems to them the wrong thing then you are a Bolshevist in character and a heretic in mentality.[14]

Nor can you explain everything by theology: you have to invoke philosophic understanding to understand the natural order of things.

there is no half-way house between 'what is' and blank nonentity"; *The Problem of Error from Plato to Kant*, 6. Cf. *Insight*, 22 (xxviii).

[13]Cf. *Insight*, 768–70 (747–48).

[14]Letter of January 22, 1935, 7. Cf. the phrase "experimentum crucis" in the fragments from the early 1930s, 7. Cf. also the introduction to *Insight* with overtones of this "crucial experiment": "The crucial issue is an experimental issue, and the experiment will be performed not publicly but privately"; 13 (xviii). Cf. also *Method in Theology*, 253: "Such an objectification of subjectivity is in the style of a crucial experiment."

And such philosophic understanding has to be, as he has said all along, comprehensive and explanatory. The Catholic philosopher must formally invoke the principle of sufficient reason for his explanations of the facts. He cannot, as has taken place too often in the past, merely show that opposed views involve contradictions. "The method is sheer make-believe but to attack a method is a grand scale operation calling for a few volumes."[15]

The "few volumes" will certainly be Lonergan's future works. He ends the letter with reflections on his own situation as a Jesuit: "I should add that I am substantially a Jesuit with no difficulties about obedience on this matter. Naturally I think this is my work but I know more luminously than anything else that I have nothing I have not received, that I know nothing in philosophy that I have not received through the Society."

Still, what is to be done? He has done his duty to the Truth and the Light by laying his capabilities before his superiors. It is up to them what happens next. Still, "I am no tragedian. I do care enormously about the good of the church." His basic intention in writing is to ask advice from his superiors:

> What on earth is to be done? I have done all that can be done in spare time and without special opportunities to have contact with those capable of guiding and directing me as well as to read the oceans of books that I would have to read were I to publish stuff that is really worthwhile. Briefly, this question is: shall the matter be left to providence to solve according to its own plan; or do you consider that providence intends to use my superiors as conscious agents in the furtherance of what it has already done?

It is difficult to imagine the response of his superior to this letter. Concern about the pretensions, possibly the "megalomania" of a bright young man? As far as I know, there is no record of the superior's response. The fact remains that Lonergan continued on the normal course of Jesuit studies, that he was chosen to teach, not just in Canada, but in the Society's prestigious Gregorian University in Rome. Perhaps most of all, the fact remains that he continued to write on his chosen project, the analysis of human understanding. All of these indications lead one to believe that the superior treated him as deftly and wisely as Father Bolland had when Lonergan told him in 1930 that he was a "nominalist."

[15]Letter of January 22, 1935, 8.

2. Bernard Leeming's Course on the Incarnate Word

Lonergan always attributed his basic intellectual conversion to the course he took in the Catholic doctrine on Christ in the fall and spring of 1935–1936 with the Jesuit, Bernard Leeming, S.J. (1893–1971). Of course, he brought his own questions to Leeming's course!

To Leeming, along with Maréchal, Lonergan attributes his first acceptance of the label "Thomist." "I had become a Thomist through the influence of Maréchal mediated to me by Stephanos Stephanou and through Bernard Leeming's lectures on the *unicum esse in Christo.*"[16] The whole of his previous development was "rounded out" by Leeming's course: that is, at this point all the intellectual influences from his early years come together.

> It was through Stephanou by some process of osmosis, rather than struggling with the five great *Cahiers*, that I learnt to speak of human knowledge as not intuitive but discursive with the decisive component in judgment. This view was confirmed by my familiarity with Augustine's key notion, *veritas*, and the whole was rounded out by Bernard Leeming's course on the Incarnate Word, which convinced me that there could not be a hypostatic union without a real distinction between essence and existence. This, of course, was all the more acceptable, since Aquinas' *esse* corresponded to Augustine's *veritas* and both harmonized with Maréchal's view of judgment.[17]

As someone once said to me, "Moments of enlightenment come during periods of enlightenment." That this was a period of enlightenment is certainly evident from the feeling-charged letter Lonergan wrote to his superior in January 1935. But "the whole" of his previous development was "rounded out" by this moment in Leeming's course, the moment he later remembered as the key moment in his own intellectual conversion.

The precise question that was being dwelt with in the course was the *unicum esse in Christo*, the one act of existence in Christ. What did this mean? What was this "unicum esse in Christo"? The basic theological issue came down to this: If, as Christian faith always held, Christ was both divine and human, what were these "two" in him? Furthermore, if we must maintain that there is an underlying and substantial unity in Christ, what is that "one" in him?

---

[16]*Caring About Meaning*, 276. Originally I had thought that Lonergan's letter to his provincial of January 22, 1935, came after the course with Fr. Leeming. But after consultation with Fr. Fred Crowe and Fr. Robert McNamara of the diocese of Rochester, it became evident that Fr. Leeming's course was given in the fall and spring of 1935–1936.

[17]*Second Collection*, 265.

At the time traditional European scholastic philosophers were engaged in a battle over the "real distinction" between essence and existence. Many traditional Thomists held the real distinction between these two principles of being, but others, especially Jesuits influenced by Suarez, denied the distinction and its presence in St. Thomas.[18] I remember Jesuits telling me that even during the 1950s, soon after entering the society, they were approached by other young Jesuits during recreation periods to ascertain their fundamental feelings on the "real distinction." Difficult as it may seem to believe to people today, it was a question which, at least for some, had an existential import! In an interview Lonergan gives an account of the relevance of the controversy.

> I was very interested in philosophy, but I [had] no use for the scholastic philosophers. I first discovered that Saint Thomas might have something to say when I was taught "De Verbo Incarnato" in Rome. Can you have one person who has two natures? The argument given me by a good Thomist, Father Bernard Leeming, was that if you have a real distinction between *esse* and essence, the *esse* can be the ground of the person and the essence too. If the *esse* is relevant to two essences, then you can have one person in two natures. On that basis I solved the problem of Christ's consciousness: one subject and two subjectivities. It wasn't the divine subjectivity that was crucified, but the human subjectivity; it was the human subjectivity that died and rose again, not the divine person.[19]

The theological problem was to maintain the full integrity of the humanity of Christ and at the same time to explain why such a full humanity is not that of another person besides the person of the Word of God. Francisco Suarez, who held the real identity of essence and existence, held that the personhood of Christ was merely a "substantial mode" added to the existing essence. To Suarez' position Leeming in his Christology textbook replied that it was not at all evident why a fully existing singular nature would not by that very fact be a *suppositum*, that is, a thing in itself. The Suarezian "mode," in this case the personhood of Christ, seems to be nothing other than an accidental property of something already fully constituted in itself.

Leeming chose to follow the opinion which he believed was that of St. Thomas, the opinion also of the Thomistic commentator, Capreolus (1380–1444). The latter held that the core of personhood is to have one's own existence in oneself. By the very fact that essence is united

---

[18]For an account of this controversy, cf. Helen James John, *The Thomist Spectrum* (New York: Fordham, 1966) 72ff.

[19]*Caring About Meaning*, 258.

with existence, there is the subsistence and "incommunicability" of personhood. Capreolus' opinion, Leeming felt, best maintains the integrity of the human nature of Christ, while also explaining the unity of Christ.

> It shows that Christ is one person, precisely because he has one *esse*, one act of existence; it shows that in which the human nature and the divine nature communicate: that is, in the *esse* of the Word; but it leaves the human nature entirely whole in its essence. Christ is one; truly the Son of God is human; truly this man is God; and in these sentences the word "is" is indeed a logical copula; but in our opinion it is much more than that: it is especially taken in a real sense and not just as a denotation.[20]

Leeming goes on in his notes to comment on the use of such philosophical distinctions in the understanding of a theological and religious doctrine.

> Someone might say that this opinion is grounded on a philosophical distinction that, if not uncertain, is at least denied by many, namely the real distinction between essence and existence. To which we reply: the revealed dogma evidently teaches a truth which can be called philosophical: namely, that a singular nature cannot be identified with personhood. We should, therefore, clarify our philosophical concepts in such a way that this truth remains uncontested. But, if among the philosophical systems that try to explain this truth, one is found to be more apt than the others to properly protect this truth, while the others are less apt, then this is obviously an argument in favor of that system.[21]

What the terms essence and existence add to Lonergan's philosophical vocabulary are the objective correlatives of the subjective acts he has been so intent on differentiating in his own consciousness. As he would later point out, Aristotle had basically pointed to two types of questions that the human spirit asks: questions of the type, "What is it?" or "Why is it so?" and questions of the type, "Is it?" or "Is it so?" The first type of question cannot be answered by a "Yes" or a "No." This type of question heads toward an understanding of the nature of something, eventually, its essence. On the other hand, the second type of question can only be answered by a "Yes" or a "No"— or "I don't know." It aims at judgment, the determination of existence.

What Lonergan was coming to see, the core of his own intellectual breakthrough, was that the entire Aristotelian metaphysical system of Aquinas was really the objective "heuristic' framework for the acts he

---

[20]Bernard Leeming, *Adnotationes de Verbo Incarnato* (Rome: 1936) 124. Our translation.
[21]Ibid., 124–25.

had all along been so intent on coming to know. One dimension of that metaphysical system was the *real distinction* between essence and existence. Later on he would define a distinction as real if it is true that (1) P is not Q; (2) P is real; and (3) Q is real. A real distinction is asserted on the level of judgment, not on any previous level of consciousness, certainly not by a prior imagined "look."[22] Such real distinctions are major or minor. Major real distinctions are between things. Minor real distinctions are between the elements or constituents of proportionate being, such as between essence and existence.

In his Latin Christology notes, written during the 1950s, Lonergan uses the distinction between soul and body as an example of a minor real distinction between constitutive principles of a person.[23] He then shows from Church doctrines the effort to express this kind of a distinction in understanding the humanity and divinity of the one person of Christ. It is not just a mental distinction, a *distinctio rationis*. It is a real distinction, though a minor real distinction: not between two things, but between two principles in the one person of Christ. Of course, because it is a case of understanding the humanity and divinity of the Son of God, all these terms have to be understood analogously.

Certainly, such a distinction puts a great weight on words. But so does modern science. And so do all the doctrines of the Church. They reflect the understandings and judgments of the human family. They mediate our knowledge of reality. As he would later point out in the article "The Origins of Christian Realism," the ability to make such distinctions is rooted in the fact that we are human beings. We exist, not just in the infant's world of immediacy, but in the far vaster world mediated by meaning.[24]

An empiricist or a naive realist confuses the criteria for knowing the world mediated by meaning with the criteria for the world of immediacy. The latter is known by merely feeling and touching and seeing. The idealist knows there is more to human knowing than what the empiricist or naive realist assert, but he conceives that "more" in sensitive terms and so concludes that our knowing cannot be objective. The critical realist asserts that objective human knowing takes place, not just by experience, but by experience completed by human understanding and correct judgment.

The Thomistic metaphysical terms used by the Christian community to interpret its belief are "heuristic" categories correlative to human

---

[22]Cf. *Insight*, 513–14 (488–90).

[23]*De Verbo Incarnato*, 172; cf. 146 ff.

[24]*Second Collection*, 241.

understanding and judgment. Just as the scientist uses technical terms to penetrate to the constituents of physical reality, so the theologian uses terms like "nature," "person," "essence," "existence," to understand the realities of Christian faith. They aid our human understanding. While later developments put persons and natures in many further contexts, the context of the ancient Council of Chalcedon needs no more than these heuristic concepts.

> What is a person or hypostasis? It is in the Trinity what there are three of and in the Incarnation what there is one of. What is a nature? In the Trinity it is what there is one of and in the Incarnation what there are two of.[25]

Though such a heuristic understanding seems incredibly "simple," still it can be a tremendously rich method of focussing our thinking within the framework of the judgments of faith. It is similar to the methods of the scientists that enable them to focus on unseen realities far beyond the realm of immediate experience.

It was in relationship to this course in 1935–1936 with Bernard Leeming on Christology that Lonergan first uses the term "intellectual conversion" to identify the intellectual transition he was undergoing.

> So there was considerable room for development after Aristotle and you get it in St. Thomas when he distinguishes existence from essence and makes them really distinct; and to make them distinct really you have to have something equivalent to an intellectual conversion even if you don't know what is meant by an intellectual conversion. I had the intellectual conversion myself when in doing theology I saw that you can't have one person in two natures in Christ unless there is a real distinction between the natures and something else that is one. But that is the long way around.[26]

Lonergan spoke of his intellectual breakthrough as taking "the long way around," since it came by way of his theology course on Thomistic Christology. He implies that there could be a short way around—perhaps by reading his *Insight?*

In the same interview Lonergan gives a pithy description of the ultimate psychological and intellectual basis for the Thomistic real distinction between essence and existence. "I once gave a talk to psychiatrists at Halifax General Hospital and at the end of the talk one of the doctors said to me, 'Our patients have all kinds of insights; the trouble is they're wrong!' Well that is the basis of the distinction be-

---

[25]Ibid., 259.
[26]Transcript by Nicholas Graham of discussions at Lonergan Workshop, June 13, 1978.

tween essence and existence. They have hold of an essence, but it isn't true.''[27]

Before going on, let us note a line from his 1972 *Method in Theology* where he explicitly speaks of faith in the Word of God as a possible source of intellectual conversion.

> Finally, among the values discerned by the eye of love is the value of believing the truths taught by the religious tradition, and in such tradition and belief are the seeds of intellectual conversion. For the word, spoken and heard, proceeds from and penetrates to all four levels of intentional consciousness. Its content is not just a content of experience but a content of experience and understanding and judging and deciding. The analogy of sight yields the cognitional myth. But fidelity to the word engages the whole man.[28]

In the mid-1930s it seems obvious that Lonergan has explicitly recognized "the cognitional myth" that conceives of intellectual activities in sensible terms. But if, as in his own case, intellectual conversion is promoted by faith in the Word of God, still in itself it regards coming to know the intrinsic character of our own human intelligence and the relationship of that intelligence to reality.

[27]Ibid.
[28]*Method in Theology,* 243.

Part Two

Early Expressions
of Intellectual Conversion

" . . . intellectual conversion alone is not enough. It has to be made explicit . . . "

Method in Theology, 318

Chapter Eight

Grace and Freedom in Saint Thomas

On July 25, 1936, Lonergan was ordained to the priesthood in the Church of Saint Ignatius in Rome. The following year, upon the conclusion of his theological studies, he was sent to Amiens in France for the Jesuit "tertianship," a year of ascetical training and study. In his article, "Insight Revisited," he recounts an incident that took place during that tertianship year.

> I did my tertianship in France at Amiens, but the moment memorable for the present account occurred after Easter when we were sent to Paris to the *Ecole sociale populaire* at Vanves to listen for a week to four leaders of the *mouvements spécialisés* of Catholic Action then in full swing. The founder of the school and still its Rector, Père Desbuquois, had built the school in the teeth of great opposition, and had obtained the money to pay the workmen in the same last-minute style as that narrated by Teresa of Avila in her accounts of her foundations. He was a man I felt I must consult, for I had little hope of explaining to superiors what I wished to do and of persuading them to allow me to do it. So I obtained an appointment, and when the time came, I asked him how one reconciled obedience and initiative in the Society. He looked me over and said: "Go ahead and do it. If superiors do not stop you, that is obedience. If they do stop you, stop and that is obedience." The advice is hardly very exciting today but at the time it was a great relief.[1]

Apparently Père Desbuquois' advice represented for Lonergan a tremendous encouragement to follow out his own interests and convictions. And so, in the fall of 1938 he returned to the Gregorian in Rome for graduate studies. Originally slated for further studies in philosophy, when the time came, the mandate was changed to theology. A letter from the Rector of the Gregorian to his Provincial in Canada is of particular interest to his future English-speaking students in theology: "Fr. Lonergan has left a splendid record behind him here; and we shall be happy to see him back for further studies. I would suggest—supposing his own preferences are not too strong for one field

[1]*Second Collection,* 265–66.

rather than the other—that he devote himself to Theology. In that Faculty there are hundreds of English-speaking students, who will be needing his help in the future."[2]

Lonergan chose as his dissertation director Fr. Charles Boyer, S.J. During his time in France he had asked someone who would be a good director in Rome and had been told: Boyer. Why? "He's intelligent." And the grounds for that view? "He's able to change, as he did on the question of the real distinction between essence and existence."[3]

Throughout his life Lonergan's own intellectual conversion found expression in his reflections on methodology: the intellectually creative ways of asking and answering questions. Commenting on his earlier theological studies Lonergan noted: "I did my theology in Rome where we had a different professor for most of the treatises and so had the opportunity of seeing all the ways in which theology could be approached and taught. One could grasp that we were being given the parts but if we wanted more than a heap we would have to write a book on the subject of method. . . ."[4]

In his January 1935 letter to his superior he had criticized Catholic philosophers for their "make-believe" methodology and their unwillingness to seek explanation. "It is because the Catholic philosopher does not formally appeal to the principle of sufficient reason even when as a matter of fact that is what he is doing; he always tends to express his thought in the form of a demonstration by arguing that opposed views involve a contradiction. The method is sheer make-believe but to attack a method is a grand scale operation calling for a few volumes."[5]

The "few volumes" eventually did appear during the next four decades, but he was aware at this early time of the need for reflection on method, not only in general, but specifically in terms of modern science and historical scholarship.

Regarding the latter area, as we mentioned earlier, in the early 1930s Christopher Dawson's *The Age of the Gods* had convinced him of the importance of historical consciousness: developing a sense of "what

---

[2]Letter to the Provincial of the Vice-Province of Upper Canada (Henry Keane), written from the Gregorian University, Rome, July 20, 1938 (Lonergan Archives, Toronto). The North American College had begun to send its students to the Gregorian in 1930. Previously they had attended the College of the Propagation of the Faith.

[3]From a conversation of Frederick Crowe with Prof. Fred Lawrence, reported in *Method: Journal of Lonergan Studies* 3 (October 1985) 6.

[4]Unpublished discussion notes, transcribed by Nicholas Graham, from Lonergan Workshop, Boston College, June 19, 1979.

[5]Letter to Provincial, January 22, 1935.

was going forward'' in a particular culture. During the first part of the twentieth century such historical consciousness and scholarship was beginning to penetrate into various areas of Catholic thought: the study of the Fathers of the Church, primitive Church history, and even the area of Scripture studies. In all of these areas this new historical awareness was having the effect of modifying and enlarging previous conceptions. Since Leo XIII's *Aeterni Patris* it was having this effect on the study of Thomas Aquinas.[6]

To build on those past achievements and to contribute his own methodical insights and perspectives was the aim of Lonergan's doctoral dissertation. As we saw, his previous writings on the philosophy of history are erudite and with a contemporary relevance, especially in light of events in Europe at the time. Still, as Frederick Crowe has pointed out, at this point in his life, at the age of thirty-four, Lonergan would "turn aside from these bright dreams of youth to spend eleven years in apprenticeship to St. Thomas."[7]

1. The Theorem of the Supernatural

Lonergan chose as his topic the idea of operative grace, *gratia operans*, in St. Thomas. Years later his dissertation would be published under the title *Grace and Freedom: Operative Grace in the Thought of St. Thomas Aquinas*. The topic found its origins in Augustine's conflict with

---

[6]Since it required understanding an author in the context of his times and not according to some author's polemical or controversial aims, such historical study threatened facile interpretations.

> When the study of Aquinas was enjoined on all students of philosophy and theology, what was envisaged was the assimilation of the basic tenets of Thomistic thought. But the first concern of historical scholarship is not to set forth and convince readers or hearers of the profundity of an author's thought, the breadth of his vision, the universal relevance of his conclusions. That sort of thing may be allowed to pad a preface or to fill out a conclusion. But the heart of the matter is elsewhere. It is a long journey through variant readings, shifts in vocabulary, enriching perspectives—all duly documented—that establish as definitively as can be expected what the great man thought on some minor topic within the horizon of his time and place and with no great relevance to other times and places. Only from a long series of such dissertations can the full picture be constructed—a picture as accurate as it is intricate, broad indeed but with endless detail, rich in implications for other times if only one has the time to sort them out, discern the precise import of each, and infer exactly what does and does not follow.

From an unpublished lecture, "The Scope of Renewal," The Larkin-Stuart lectures at Trinity College in the University of Toronto, November 15, 1973, 2.

[7]Frederick E. Crowe, "Lonergan and Thomas Aquinas: An Overview," unpublished paper given at the Lonergan Workshop, Boston College, June 1990.

the Pelagians: How does God's grace act in the human person? How does God, in the words of Ezekiel, pluck out our heart of stone and place within us a heart of flesh—particularly if our heart basically wants to remain in its stony condition? Such is the work of operative grace: And what about our human freedom? If our human freedom is to be taken seriously, does that make God dependent on our actions? How does the grace of God "cooperate" with our human freedom?

This problem had vexed the Medieval theologians who reflected on Augustine's works. One problem, as Lonergan expressed it, was to explain why everything was not grace. After all, what is there that is not a free gift of God?[8] The problem also vexed the Renaissance theologians after Thomas. They basically came down on two sides of the problem: the Dominican followers of Banez held for a physical predetermination in the free action of the will. On the other side, the Jesuit followers of Molina posited a mediating type of knowledge in God (a *scientia media*) which enabled God to know future free actions and what human beings "would do" in certain situations. This latter position, Lonergan remarked, was what his Suarezian teacher at Heythrop, Fr. Bolland, had held.

Lonergan soon concluded that both of the traditional explanations were insufficient. Both failed to set aside their initial interests and concerns to enter into the world and concerns of Aquinas. Noting his growing awareness of historical method, Lonergan noted: "My own experience of this change was in writing my doctoral dissertation. I had been brought up a Molinist. I was studying St. Thomas' thought on *Gratia Operans*, a study later published in *Theological Studies*, 1941–1942. Within a month or so it was completely evident to me that Molinism had no contribution to make to an understanding of Aquinas."[9]

In the original introduction to his dissertation, Lonergan set out his methodological principles. Among these was the very form of speculative development itself. Such a scheme "is capable of synthesizing any possible set of historical data irrespective of their place and time, just as the science of mathematics constructs a generic scheme capable of synthesizing any possible set of quantitative phenomena."[10] Instead of either reading into the text hypotheses out of contemporary concerns or, on the other hand, like a "jelly-fish," just enumerating end-

[8]Lonergan gives a very clear summary of his dissertation in *Caring About Meaning*, 91–93.

[9]*Method in Theology*, 163.

[10]"The *Gratia Operans* Dissertation: Preface and Introduction," *Method: Journal of Lonergan Studies* 3 (October 1985) 11.

less texts, the historian of ideas employs a "pincer" movement that moves from the speculative understanding of the most general ideas of a development to a concrete understanding of the developments manifested in the texts.

The core of the solution to understanding Aquinas' thought on grace is found in the "theorem" of the supernatural order. A theorem is a technical term with an exact philosophic definition whose implications are consistently faced and worked out within a total system of thought.[11] It differs from a common sense term as the scientific term "acceleration" differs from the common term "going faster." The system of thought within which this theorem is to be understood is Aquinas' whole theology. Aquinas himself took over this theorem of the supernatural from Philip, the Chancellor of the University of Paris. It implied the validity of the term "nature."

> What Philip the Chancellor systematically posited was not the supernatural character of grace, for that was already known and acknowledged, but the validity of a line of reference termed nature. In the long term and in the concrete the real alternatives remain charity and cupidity, the elect and the *massa damnata*. But the whole problem lies in the abstract, in human thinking: the fallacy in early thought had been an unconscious confusion of the metaphysical abstraction, nature, with concrete data which do not quite correspond; Philip's achievement was the creation of a mental perspective, the introduction of a set of coordinates, that eliminated the basic fallacy and its attendant host of anomalies.[12]

Thomas took over Philip's achievement as the central core of his own massive theological *Summae.* Within the context of his belief in the creative and redemptive action of God, Aquinas came to affirm the reality and consistency of "secondary causes," the reality and integrity of the world of natural creation. Commenting on his meaning some years later Lonergan noted: "It was urged that we have to drop the words 'nature,' 'natural,' that we should be content to speak with Scripture and the Fathers of God's grace and man's sinfulness. Now I have no doubt that such words as 'nature' and 'natural' . . . can be abused. But I also have no doubt that if we are not only going to speak about God's grace and man's sinfulness but also we are going to say what precisely we mean by such speaking, then we are going to have to find some third term over and above grace and sin."[13]

---

[11]Ibid., 19.

[12]*Grace and Freedom*, 16.

[13]*Second Collection*, "Natural Knowledge of God," 131; there he refers to *Grace and Freedom*, 2–19.

For the grace of God to be understood precisely as grace, as a free gift to one who cannot claim it as his right; and for sin to be understood as sin, as falling short of what one really is; then a middle term between sin and grace must be introduced. Medieval theology, particularly in Aquinas, introduced such a term in the word "nature." Such was a revolution in the world of theory, the first of several that Lonergan studied during his lifetime.

> Still this assertion of dogmatic continuity must not obscure the existence of a "Copernican revolution" in theory: the center of the whole issue shifted violently; certain developments were released at once; others followed in a series of intervals, change implying further change, till the genius of St. Thomas Aquinas mastered the situation.[14]

In his dissertation Lonergan's intellectual conversion found expression in the discovery of the radically *systematic* character of Aquinas' thought on grace and the supernatural. The elements of this system are understood in their relationships to each other and not in common sense categories. In this area Aquinas adopts and transposes Aristotle's systematic metaphysics for his own theological ends.

In all of this the undertow of Aristotelian philosophy is felt. Treating of the Church's appeal to reason in his notes on the philosophy of history, Lonergan had noted: "The purely scientific character of the appeal to reason as well as the definition of the limits of that appeal was more than emphasized by the audacity of St. Thomas of Aquin who based his thought on Aristotle precisely because Aristotle was the most scientific."[15]

In the introduction to his dissertation Lonergan pays tribute to the centrality of Aristotle in the history of philosophy. "Philosophy as *philosophia perennis* is man's apprehension of the eternal and immutable. Like all limited being, it is potentiality and achievement, *dunamis* and *energeia*, potency and act. Its potency is the love of wisdom: it is detachment, orientation, inspiration. Its act is the triumph of the reason systematically revealing the light of the eternal in the light of common day. For all time the potency is represented by Plato, the act by

---

[14]*Grace and Freedom*, 16.

[15]Philosophy of history notes, "Sketch for a Metaphysic of Human Solidarity." Lonergan had mentioned in a letter to his friend, Henry Smeaton, reading the *De Anima* when he was in England in 1926. Certainly from those days in England and his work on H.W.B. Joseph's book, he was familiar with Aristotelian logic. In addition, there are remarks in his 1935 letter to his provincial and in his notes on the philosophy of history on the inadequacy of Aristotelian ethics.

Aristotle."[16] Later Lonergan would use a culinary image to speak of the relationship of Plato to Aristotle: "Nobody would be able to read Aristotle if he hadn't studied Plato. . . . You have to have the hors d'oeuvres before you start eating the meal."[17]

Plato, inspired by Socrates, set the questions for philosophy: what is the real as opposed to the merely apparent? true knowledge as opposed to opinion? What does it mean to know something? As Lonergan would often point out, Plato's Socrates sought universal definitions: what is the meaning of justice? He sought a definition that refers to every instance of justice and only to justice. Neither he nor the Athenians were able to come up with such a definition. But the difference between them was that he knew that he did not know, but they, thinking they knew, did not know. His was a *docta ignorantia*, a learned ignorance. He revealed to his fellow citizens the confusion in their own minds and the Delphic oracle deemed him the wisest of all because he knew that he did not know.

To Plato's questions Aristotle brought science and system. He could supply those definitions by means of his theoretical framework in which the terms fixed the relationships and the relationships fixed the terms and both were grasped in a synthetic unity by the human mind. It was Aristotle's whole metaphysical "system" that, by way of the Arabs, had entered into the medieval university and was the cultural "coin of the realm" in which philosophical and theological issues were joined. Through the Arab philosophers Aristotelian categories had penetrated the medieval universities.

> The Thomists were quoting Aristotle in the same way they were quoting Augustine, except that they quoted Aristotle more frequently. (Anyone quoted was for them a "Father of the Church.") But Aristotle was serving quite a different purpose than Augustine. He was supplying them with the means of having a coherent set of solutions when they were solving questions. He was supplying them with what is called a conceptuality, a *Begrifflichkeit*—in other words, a set of terms and relations where the terms fix the relations and the relations fix the terms and the whole set is verifiable.[18]

[16]"The *Gratia Operans* Dissertation: Preface and Introduction," *Method*, 26. In his later years he mentions what he considered the central sections of Aristotle: "There is a Swiss who claims that eighty percent of the 'works of Aristotle' are not by Aristotle. I know who the great man was—the fellow who wrote the seventh and eighth books of the Metaphysics and the third book of the *De Anima*." *Caring About Meaning*, 21. Frederick Crowe informs me that the man referred to was Joseph Zucher, *Aristotles' Werk und Geist* (Paderborn: 1952).

[17]*Caring About Meaning*, 50.

[18]Ibid., 120; cf. "Questionnaire on Philosophy," *Method* 2 (October 1984) 13.

So Aquinas employed Aristotle's whole conceptual framework with its interlocking terms and relationships to flesh out the whole order of nature. Aristotle's interlocking network of terms: matter and form, substance and accident, habits and acts, etc., are used by Aquinas to solve all kinds of problems that had baffled previous theologians and writers. The value of such a system was that it was theoretical: it presented a basic set of terms and principles with which to handle a multitude of problems. It was, to use the word Lonergan loved, "methodical." Aquinas transposed such method into the medieval context of the *questio*, the technique of systematically asking and answering questions. Speaking of Aquinas' *Contra Gentiles*, Lonergan says: "If one reads a series of successive chapters, one finds the same arguments recurring over and over in ever slightly different forms; what was going forward when the *Contra Gentiles* was being written, was the differentiation of operations and their conjunction in ever fresh combinations."[19]

This will basically be the underlying form of Lonergan's own method. But our point here is that in order for Lonergan to have understood Aquinas, it was necessary for him to have already broken through personally into an explicit understanding of what years later he will call "the world of theory."

> If man's practical bent is to be liberated from magic and turned toward the development of science, if his critical bent is to be liberated from myth and turned towards the development of philosophy, if his religious concern is to renounce aberrations and accept purification, then all three will be served by a differentiation of consciousness, a recognition of a world of theory. In such a world things are conceived and known, not in their relations to our sensory apparatus or to our needs and desires, but in the relations constituted by their uniform interactions with one another. . . . This differentiation of consciousness is illustrated by the Platonic contrast of the phenomenal and the noumenal worlds, of Aristotle's distinction and correlation of what is first for us and what is first absolutely, of Aquinas' hymns and his systematic theology. . . .[20]

2. The Transcendence of Imaginative Thinking

Besides the pervasive evidence of Lonergan's "systematic" understanding of Aquinas that made it possible for him to understand both the development of Christian thought up to Aquinas and the development within Aquinas' own understanding, perhaps the most evident

---

[19]*Method in Theology*, 30.
[20]Ibid., 258.

instance of Lonergan's own intellectual conversion can be discerned in the sections dealing with Aquinas' understanding of divine transcendence and human liberty. According to Lonergan Aquinas had at hand the tools, such as a theory of human liberty, with which it was possible to show actual grace as both operative and cooperative.

> The free act emerges from, and is conditioned by, created antecedents over which freedom has no direct control. It follows that it is possible for God to manipulate these antecedents and through such manipulation to exercise a control over free acts themselves. . . . Indeed, both above and below, both right and left, the free choice has determinants over which it exercises no control. God directly controls the orientation of the will to ends; indirectly he controls the situations which intellect apprehends and in which will has to choose; indirectly he also controls both the higher determinants of intellectual attitude or mental pattern and the lower determinants of mood and temperament; finally, each choice is free only *hic et nunc,* for no man can decide today what he is to will tomorrow. There is no end of room for God to work on the free choice without violating it, to govern above its self-governance, to set the stage and guide the reactions and give each character its personal role in the drama of life.[21]

Still, none of these created antecedents can be rigorous determinants of the person's free choice: God alone has the property of transcendence. As Augustine's major intellectual break-through was from a corporeal way of thinking about the divine, so Lonergan articulated the same breakthrough systematically in *Gratia Operans.*

> It is only in the logico-metaphysical simultaneity of the atemporal present that God's knowledge is infallible, his will irresistible, his action efficacious. He exercises control through the created antecedents—true enough; but that is not the infallible, the irresistible, the efficacious, which has its ground not in the creature but in the uncreated, which has its moment not in time but in the cooperation of eternal uncreated action with created and temporal action. Again, the antecedents *per se* always incline to the right and good. But the consequent act may be good or it may be sinful: if it is good, all the credit is God's, and the creature is only his instrument; but if it is evil, then inasmuch as it is sin as such, it is a surd. . .and so in the causal order a first for which the sinner alone is responsible.[22]

Furthermore, God acts in human lives, both providentially and through actual grace. But such action does not involve any change in

---

[21]*Grace and Freedom,* 115–16.
[22]Ibid.

God. In fact, the projection of such change onto the divine involves a "picture thinking," a projection of human common sense categories onto the transcendent action of God. It is similar to the intellectual error from which Augustine had to break on the way to his own religious conversion.

In this regard Lonergan considers the objection that if God knows every event infallibly, if he wills it irresistibly, if he effects it with absolute efficacy, then every event must be necessary and none can be contingent. To this objection Lonergan, following St. Thomas, replies: "The first fallacy lies in a misconception of time. To a temporal being our four-dimensional universe has three sections: past, present and future. To an eternal 'now' this division is meaningless. On this point St. Thomas never had the slightest doubt: he was always above our pre-Einsteinian illusions that still are maintained by our cosmology manuals; strenuously and consistently he maintained that all events are present to God."[23] He adds in a footnote, "before time" is "an illusory figment of the imagination."

The second fallacy lies in supposing God's knowledge of the creature or his activity are some reality in God that would not be there if He had not created. Yet,

> God is immutable. He is entitatively identical whether he creates or does not create. His knowledge or will or production of the created universe adds only a *relatio rationis* to the *actus purus*. They are predications by extrinsic denomination. Further, it is to be observed that a fallacy on this point is closely connected with fallacious ideas of time. For there can be no predication by extrinsic denomination without the actuality of the extrinsic denominator: else the *adaequatio veritatis* is not satisfied. Accordingly, to assert that God knows this creature or event, that he wills it, that he effects it, is also *ipso facto* to assert that the creature or event actually is.[24]

To assert that God acts in time is not to project any real change onto God. It is to assert that the assertion "God acts in time" is true.[25] Fi-

---

[23]Ibid., 103–04.

[24]Ibid., 104.

[25]The same doctrine is found in Lonergan's Latin notes from 1946–1947, *De ente supernaturale*, 53–69. Cf. especially 58: "Obiecerat quispiam: Deus aeternaliter scit et vult quodcumque scit et vult. Sed denominans extrinsecum est temporale. Aut ergo ante existentiam extrinsece denominantis Deus et nescit et non vult, aut tunc non fit praedicatio per denominationem extrinsecam. Et in utroque casu claudicat solutio data." To which Lonergan responds: "Difficultas oritur ex imaginatione. Imaginatur enim aeternitas esse tempus quoddam infinitum, contemporaneum cum tempore quamdiu habetur tempus, et sine contemporaneo antequam habeatur tempus. Huic difficultate ex imaginatione

nally, Lonergan points to another and more basic fallacy often present in conceiving the divine action.

> It fails to grasp that God is not some datum to be explained, that he is absolute explanation, pure intelligibility in himself, and the first cause and last end of everything else. Accordingly, attempts are made to explain God, to explain the attributes that are identical with God, to reconcile the predicates that have their ontological ground in the absolute simplicity of God. The result is a pseudo-profundity ending in insoluble problems, such as: How can God know the contingent? How can his *concursus* make him omnipotent without destroying human liberty? and so forth. So much for the fallacies that befog the issue and lead down blind alleys.[26]

I am reminded of an interview Lonergan gave in 1970 in which he was asked about "critically grounding" a religion. His response links religion with intellectual conversion.

> I put the question the other night. A person was demanding that I critically ground this religion and he was talking to Professor So and So and I went up to him and said, "Would you require Professor So and So to critically ground the love he has for his wife and children?" Being in love is a fact, and it's what you are, it's existential. And your living flows from it. It's the first principle, as long as it lasts. It has its causes and its occasions and its conditions and all the rest of it. But while it's there it's the first principle and it's the source of all one's desires and fears, all the good one can see, and so on. And critically grounding knowledge isn't finding the ground for knowledge. It's already there. Being critical means eliminating the ordinary nonsense, the systematically misleading images and so on; the mythical account. Every scientific or philosophic breakthrough is the elimination of some myth in the pejorative sense; the flat earth, right on. But if you are in love it doesn't need any justification. It's the justification beyond anything else. Just as you don't explain God, God is the ultimate explanation.[27]

On being asked: "Might not one then be deceived?" Lonergan replied:

> One can be deceiving himself. If one is deceiving oneself one is not in love. One is mistaking something for love. Love is something that proves

---

per alias imagines respondet sanctus Thomas, maxime in *Summa* quae novittis intenditur." Also cf. the notes from 1949–1950, *De scientia atque voluntate Dei: Supplementum schematicum.*

   [26]*Grace and Freedom,* 105. For a critique of "process philosophy" in the light of these principles, cf. David B. Burrell, "Does Process Theology Rest on a Mistake," *Theological Studies* 43 (March 1982) 125–35.

   [27]*Second Collection,* 229–30.

itself. "By their fruits you shall know them," and "in fear and trembling work out your salvation" and all the rest of it. Love isn't cocksure, either.

Chapter Nine

Verbum: Word and Idea in Saint Thomas

1. The Appeal to Interiority

Throughout his life Lonergan's major intellectual interest was the nature of human knowing. Eventually that interest would find expression in *Insight* and *Method in Theology.* But first he sought to research Aquinas' own cognitional theory. This he did in a series of articles published in *Theological Studies* between 1946 and 1949, eventually published in one volume under the title *Verbum: Word and Idea in Aquinas.* Remembering Augustine, he says: "He was talking about *intelligere* [understanding] all the time, you see. Later, after I had finished my dissertation on *gratia operans,* I remembered that Thomas too talks a lot about *intelligere* and he hasn't much to say about universals! So I went to work on that."[1]

He began this work in the early 1940s, after he had returned from Europe, published his dissertation and was teaching theology at L'Immaculée-Conception, the Jesuit scholasticate in Montreal. Lonergan's continuing research on Aquinas confirmed his conviction that the latter's philosophy was grounded in self-awareness. St. Thomas was too accurate in his metaphysical theory not to have been a superb psychologist. Lonergan shows that Aquinas' metaphysics of the human person is rooted in Thomas' knowledge of the human person, beginning with his knowledge of himself. That self-knowledge was the basis of Aquinas' development of the traditional psychological analogy in the theological understanding of the Trinity.

> The contention of this paper will be that Aquinas was speaking of understanding and that an interpretation in terms of general metaphysics misses the point; to follow Aquinas here, one must practice introspective rational psychology; without that, one no more can know the created image of the Blessed Trinity, as Aquinas conceived it, than a blind man can know colors.[2]

[1] *Caring About Meaning,* 27.
[2] *Verbum,* 11.

2. Understanding Understanding

Conjoined to Lonergan's deepening study of Aquinas was a deepening appropriation of Aristotelian psychology. For example, as we noted previously, Aristotle pointed out that there are two types of questions: "What is it?" or "Why is it so?" and "Is it?" or "Is it so?" Questions of the first type can not be answered by a "Yes" or "No." Questions of the second type can only be answered by a "Yes" or a "No," or a "Probably yes" or "Probably no."[3] Through the years Lonergan will emphasize that these two types of questions reflect two different levels of consciousness: the level of intelligence with its central act of understanding; and the level of reflection with its expression in judgment.

To focus on the first type of question, questions of the type, "What is this?" can be transposed to the type, "Why is this so?" by understanding them to be about the "form" of a thing.[4] In this Aristotle was clarifying the nature of the insight toward which questioning moves.

> What do you mean by "What?" asks Aristotle in the last chapter of the seventh book of the *Metaphysics*. What does "What is it?" (*ti esti*) mean? He says it means "Why is it?" (*dia ti*). "What is an eclipse ?" means "Why is the moon darkened in this fashion?" How do you change "What is a man?" into a "Why?" Ask: why is this flesh and bones a man? It is because of the soul, the form. The form is the insight. In the eighth book he says: of course, in material things, the answer to "what?" is form and common matter; in this man, it is form and particular matter. That is the Aristotelian essentialism. But Augustine spoke of *veritas* and corresponding to *veritas*, Thomas added on *esse*.[5]

All of this corresponds to what Lonergan says elsewhere about the course of his own intellectual conversion: from Plato to Augustine to Thomas. But to understand Aquinas, he had to understand Aristotle. And Aristotle had it right on insight into the phantasm. The following extensive quote from *Verbum* pinpoints one debt of Aquinas to Aristotle as well as the distinction between Aristotle, Aquinas, and Lonergan on the one hand, and other schools of philosophy on the other.

> . . . Why was Aquinas able to affirm that intellect penetrates to the inwardness of things? Only because Aristotle had made his point, against the old naturalists and with some help from number-loving Pythagoreans and defining Platonists (Met. A), that what is known by intellect is a partial constituent of the realities first known by sense. For the materi-

---

[3] Aristotle, *Posterior Analytics*, II, 2, 89b, 36ff.

[4] In fact, the title page of *Insight* bears in Greek Aristotle's words from the third book of *De Anima*: "grasping the intelligible form in the sensible phantasms."

[5] *Caring About Meaning*, 21. Cf. *Verbum*, 12 ff.

alist, the real is what he knows before he understands or thinks: it is the sensitively integrated object that is reality for a dog; it is the sure and firm-set earth on which I tread, which is so reassuring to the sense of reality; and on that showing intellect does not penetrate to the inwardness of things but is a merely subjective, if highly useful, principle of activity. To the Pythagoreans the discovery of harmonic ratios revealed that numbers and their proportions, though primarily ideas, nonetheless have a role in making things what they are; and for Aristotle the ratio of two to one was the form of the diapason. Socratic interest in definition reinforced this tendency, but the Platonist sought the reality known by thought, not in this world, but in another. Aristotle's basic thesis was the objective reality of what is known by understanding: it was a common sense position inasmuch as common sense always assumes that to be so; but it was not a common sense position inasmuch as common sense would be able to enunciate it or even to know with any degree of accuracy just what it means and implies. . . . When, then, Aristotle calls the soul a *logos* he is stating his highly original position, not indeed with the full accuracy which his thought alone made possible, but in a generic fashion which suited his immediate purpose; and it is that generic issue that remains the capital issue, for the denial of soul today is really the denial of the intelligible, the denial that understanding, knowing a cause, is knowing anything real.[6]

But Lonergan's fundamental interest was not Aristotle, but Aquinas. The latter's Aristotelian metaphysics did not hang in mid-air. Lonergan's interest in the dynamism of consciousness led him to ask how that dynamism is present in Aquinas. The first point is that, according to Aquinas, the act of human understanding takes place with regard to images, phantasms. As he says, describing the act of insight: "Anyone can experience in himself that when he tries to understand something, he forms for himself some images as examples in which he can, as it were, grasp what he is trying to understand."[7]

One is reminded of Fr. Peter Hoenen's article in the *Gregorianum* which Lonergan read in the early 1930s. Images when exposed to the light of intelligence become intelligible. The agent intellect, our human questioning, the wonder that Aristotle placed at the origin of all science and philosophy, moves images from the potentially to the actually intelligible.

> Thus, pure reverie, in which image succeeds image in the inner human cinema with never a care for the why or wherefore, illustrate the intel-

---

[6]*Verbum*, 20–21. Webster's defines the diapason as "the entire compass of tones."

[7]"Quilibet in se ipso experiri potest, quod quando aliquis conatur aliquid intelligere, format sibi aliqua phantasmata per modum exemplorum, in quibus quasi inspiciat quod intelligere studet." *Summa Theologiae I*, 84, 7.

> ligible in potency. But let active intelligence intervene: there is a care
> for the why and wherefore; there is wonder and inquiry; there is the
> alertness of the scientist or technician, the mathematician or philosopher,
> for whom the imagined object no longer is merely given but also
> something-to-be-understood. . . . Further, this illumination of the im-
> agined object, this reception of it within the field of intellectual light,
> has the characteristic of being abstractive; for it is not the imagined ob-
> ject in all its respects that is regarded as a something-to-be-understood;
> no one spontaneously endeavors to understand why "here" is "here"
> and why "now" is not "then;" effort is confined to grasping natures,
> just as explanation is always in terms of the character of person, the na-
> ture of things, the circumstances of events, but never in terms of their
> being then and there.[8]

In both Aristotle and Thomas, then, Lonergan found an awareness
of the inner act of understanding that grasps in sensible imagery the
ratio of things whence it is able to pivot and express in concepts the
content of that act of understanding. The point is present in Aristotle
where the key to his understanding of the function of syllogisms is
the act of grasping the intelligible form in the properly disposed or
configured imagery. All this takes place prior to words, even the "inner words" that are concepts. Concepts and definitions proceed from
acts of insight. "Because the act of understanding—the *intelligere
proprie*—is prior to, and cause of, conceptualization, any attempt to fix
the act of understanding, except by way of introspective description,
involves its own partial failure; for any such attempt is expression, and
expression is no longer understanding and already concept."[9] Thus,
one of Lonergan's perennial examples, the definition of a circle is a
set of interrelated concepts rooted in an insight into an image.

> A plane curve that possesses neither bumps nor dents, of perfectly uni-
> form curvature, cannot be had if not all radii are equal but must be had
> if all radii are equal; one sees the curve, the radii, their equality, the pres-
> ence or absence of bumps or dents by one's eyes or imagination; one
> cannot know them in any other way, for there is only one abstract ra-
> dius, and it does not move; but the impossibility or necessity of per-
> fectly uniform curvature is known by intellect alone in the act of insight
> into the phantasm.[10]

In *Verbum,* after working through the evidence from Aquinas, Lonergan set out the characteristics that distinguish our human process of
knowing from any other processes in the natural world. In the first

---

[8]*Verbum,* 174–75. For an excellent exposition of the "passive" character of the act
of understanding, cf. Patrick H. Byrne, "The Thomist Sources of Lonergan's Dynamic
World-View," *The Thomist* 46 (1982) 108–45.

[9]Ibid., 25.

[10]Ibid., 27–28.

place, the intelligibility of the natural processes of the universe is passive and potential; it is not the conscious active intelligibility of dynamic intelligence. It is not the stuff of conscious intelligence itself. Secondly, the intelligibility of natural processes is expressed in the intelligibility of some specific law or correlation; it is not the intelligibility of the very idea of intelligible law. Intelligence defies formulation in any specific law and the principles of logic are themselves rooted in intelligence. Thirdly, the intelligibility of natural processes is imposed from without. On the other hand, it is of the very nature of the procession of "the inner word" from the act of understanding to be actively intelligent. Intelligence in act does not follow laws imposed from without, but rather it is the ground of the intelligibility of law; it is constitutive and, as it were, creative of law.[11]

Intelligence always involves some abstraction: several circles of differing size involve the same intelligibility. The abstractive character of intelligence means grasping what is significant as significant and leaving aside the insignificant because it is known to be insignificant.

> The Aristotelian and Thomist theory of abstraction is not exclusively metaphysical; basically, it is psychological, that is, derived from the character of acts of understanding. On the other hand, it is in the self-possession of understanding as the ground of possible conceptualization that one may best discern what is meant by saying that the self-expression of understanding is an *emanatio intelligibilis,* a procession from knowledge as knowledge, and because of knowledge as knowledge.[12]

3. Understanding Judgment

This latter character of knowledge, which makes it possible not only for something to be known but known to be known, is most fully present in what Lonergan would later call the third level of consciousness, the level of judgment. Not only is understanding a constitutive increment in the process of human knowing, but Lonergan found in Aristotle, Augustine, Aquinas, and Newman the materials for distinguishing clearly between direct understanding and a further constitutive activity in human knowing, the activity of judging. Such judgment itself proceeds from an act of understanding, this time a reflective act of understanding that answers to a reflective questioning: Is it? Is it so? That is, Is my direct understanding correct?

[11]Ibid., 33–34.

[12]Ibid., 42. Cf. *Insight,* 55 (30): "Properly, then, abstraction is not a matter of apprehending a sensible or imaginative *Gestalt.* . . . Properly, to abstract is to grasp the essential and to disregard the incidental, to see what is significant and to set aside the irrelevant, to recognize the important as important and the negligible as negligible."

> Again, both acts of understanding have their instrumental or material causes, but the direct act has this cause in the schematic image or phantasm, while the reflective act reviews not only imagination but also sense experience, and direct acts of understanding, and definitions, to find in all taken together the sufficient ground or evidence for a judgment. Hence, while the direct act of understanding generates in definition the expression of the intelligibility of a phantasm, the reflective act generates in judgment the expression of consciously possessed truth through which reality is both known and known to be known.[13]

According to Lonergan, for St. Thomas our human knowing is not some kind of automatic and unconscious "metaphysical sausage machine," slicing off concepts in a mechanical way. Rather, it is, first of all, intelligence consciously and luminously seeking the intelligibility of things. The action of human understanding in response to human questions for intelligence is a grasping in the data of sense or imagination the patterns of relationships, the "forms" of things; and upon such a grasp, human understanding pivots and expresses to itself in inner words—concepts—the intelligibility it has grasped. But "bright ideas are a dime a dozen" and consequently there is evident in Aquinas, more clearly than in Aristotle, the centrality of the third level of consciousness, the level of judging. This is the level on which existence, *esse*, is attained. Judgment is not a mere composition or division of concepts. It is an *absolute positing* of such a mental synthesis as true or false and as such mediating reality.

Such an operation is conscious. Just as the Platonic Socrates in the *Meno* asked how the young boy could recognize an answer as an answer, Aquinas saw in the very nature of human intelligence the response to that question. For since our spirits are *quodammodo omnia*, somehow open to all things, there is within us, in our very ability to question, the notion of being: the notion of what any answer will have to live up to in order to qualify as *the* answer—in order to be *known* as the answer. Speaking of the metaphysical concept of being, Lonergan remarks:

> I think much less ink would be spilt on the concept of *ens* [being], were more attention paid to its origin in the act of understanding. Tell any bumpkin a plausible tale and he will remark, "Well now that may be so." He is not perhaps exercising consciously the virtue of wisdom which has the function of knowing the "ratio entis et non entis." But his understanding has expressed itself as grasp of possible being. Intelligibility is the ground of possibility, and possibility is the possibility of being;

---

[13]*Verbum*, 47–48. Cf. Newman in the *Grammar of Assent*, 188f., on "complex assent" in which we not only know, but know that we know.

equally, unintelligibility is the ground of impossibility, and impossibility means impossibility of being. To affirm actual being, more than a plausible tale is wanted; for experience, though it is not as such the source of the concept of being . . . still it is the condition of the transition from the affirmation of the possibility to the affirmation of the actuality of being. Hence, the first operation of intellect regards quiddities, but the second, judgment, regards *esse,* the *actus essendi.*[14]

In addition—again reminiscent of Hoenen—the metaphysical principles of being, of unity, of identity and non-contradiction, etc., all flow from the conscious nature of our intelligence and reason. Such intellectual light can be known by intellectual light.

> There is, then, a manner in which the light of our souls enters within the range of introspective observation. The most conspicuous instance seems to be our grasp of first principles. Scientific conclusions are accepted because they are implied by first principles; but the assent to first principles has to have its motive too, for assent is rational; and that motive is the light that naturally is within us. Again, the light of agent intellect is said to manifest first principles, to make them evident. In that light the whole of science virtually is ours from the very start. Just as conclusions are convincing because principles are convincing, so our intellectual light derives its efficacy from the *prima lux* which is God.[15]

It is particularly in judgment that the human spirit effects the self-transcendence to reality and being. "Inasmuch as the act of understanding grasps its own conditions as the understanding of this sort of thing, it abstracts from the irrelevant and expresses itself in a definition of essence. But inasmuch as the understanding grasps its own transcendence-in-immanence, its quality of intellectual light as a participation of the divine and uncreated Light, it expresses itself in judgment, in a positing of truth, in the affirmation or negation of reality."[16] Reflective understanding, prior to judgment, involves the grasp of "the native infinity of intellect," the *potens omnia facere et fieri* by which the human intellect is open to all of being. There is no intrinsic limit to our human questioning.

> The native infinity of intellect as intellect is a datum of rational consciousness. It appears in that restless spirit of inquiry, that endless search for causes which, Aquinas argued, can rest and end only in a supernatural vision of God. It appears in the absolute exigence of reflective thought which will assent only if the possibility of the contradictory proposition

[14]Ibid., 43–44.
[15]Ibid., 80.
[16]Ibid., 83.

is excluded. Just as Thomist thought is an ontology of knowledge inasmuch as intellectual light is referred to its origin in uncreated Light, so too it is more than an embryonic epistemology inasmuch as intellectual light reflectively grasps its own nature and the commensuration of that nature to the universe of reality.[17]

4. Our "Native Tendency to Extroversion"

Lonergan's research on Aquinas in the *Verbum* articles represents the consolidation of his own intellectual conversion. For these articles evidence a clear articulation of the two incommensurate criteria of reality present in our human consciousness. These criteria of the real are the fundamentally determining factors in the distinction between the perennial schools of philosophy: materialism, idealism, and realism.

> A useful preliminary is to note that animals know, not mere phenomena, but things: dogs know their masters, bones, other dogs, and not merely the appearances of these things. Now this sensitive integration of sensible data also exists in the human animal and even in the human philosopher. Take it as knowledge of reality , and there results the secular contrast between the solid sense of reality and the bloodless categories of the mind. Accept the sense of reality as criterion of reality, and you are a materialist, sensist, positivist, pragmatist, sentamentalist, and so on, as you please. Accept reason as a criterion but retain the sense of reality as what gives meaning to the term "real," and you are an idealist; for like the sense of reality, the reality defined by it is non-rational. In so far as I grasp it, the Thomist position is the clear-headed third position: reason is the criterion and, as well, it is reason—not the sense of reality—that gives meaning to the term "real." The real is what is and "what is," is known in the rational act, judgment.[18]

Parenthetically, it was Augustine's move from conceiving the divine as some kind of body to realizing that the real transcends imagination that illustrates the presence and influence of these two incommensurate criteria of the real.

Materialism, idealism, and naive forms of realism all see knowledge as primarily confrontational. How do we get from "in here" to "out there"? But for Aristotle and Aquinas knowledge is primarily by identity: *sensibile in actu est sensus in actu, et intelligibile in actu est intellectus in actu.*[19] Knowledge is primarily union and only secondarily does the human mind, through understanding and accurate judgment, come

[17]Ibid., 86–87.
[18]Ibid., 7.
[19]Cf. ibid., 72.

to distinguish the trees from the forest in the being it grasps—and by which it is grasped.

> The critical problem . . . is not a problem of moving from within outwards, of moving from a subject to an object outside the subject. It is a problem of moving from above downwards, of moving from an infinite potentiality commensurate with the universe towards a rational apprehension that seizes the difference of subject and object in essentially the same way it seizes any other real distinction. Thus realism is immediate, not because it is naive and unreasoned and blindly affirmed, but because we know the real before we know such a difference within the real as the difference between subject and object.[20]

Lonergan contrasts the Aristotelian-Thomistic view of knowledge primarily by identity with the confrontationism of materialism and even Platonic dualism. So also does he point out the distinction between the Aristotelian-Thomistic position and the ultimate Augustinian "vision of eternal truth." "For it is the light of the intellect that replaces the Augustinian vision of eternal truth; and regularly one reads that we know, we understand, we judge all things by a created light within us which is a participation, a resultant, a similitude, an impression of the first and eternal light and truth."[21] Still Aquinas owes a great deal to Augustinian introspection.

> From Augustinian speculation on the procession of the inner word, he was led to distinguish far more sharply than Aristotle did between intelligence in act and its products of definition and judgment. But his greater debt was to Augustinian theory of judgment with its appeal to eternal reasons; Aquinas transposed this appeal into his own *participatio creata lucis increatae* to secure for the Aristotelian theory of knowing by identity the possibility of self-transcendence in finite intellect. On his own, Aquinas identified intelligible species with intellectual habit to relate species to *intelligere* as form to *esse*, a parallel that supposes a grasp of the real distinction between finite essence and existence.[22]

This "real distinction" between essence and existence, ultimately rooted in the real distinction between understanding and judgment, was the core of Lonergan's own "intellectual conversion" in Bernard Leeming's course on the Incarnate Word in Rome in the mid-1930s.

---

[20]Ibid., 88.

[21]Ibid., 83–84. Cf. *Insight*, 411f., where he speaks of this Augustinian position as an empiricism on the third level of consciousness, some kind of "seeing" of the truth. At the same time, Augustine was limited, as was Newman—on the level of their times—to a common sense apprehension of human interiority. Cf. *Second Collection*, 227.

[22]Ibid., 188–89.

By the mid-forties and his studies of Aquinas he was arriving at expressing that distinction ever more clearly. The culminating step would be his writing of *Insight.*

An intellectual conversion is needed to grasp all this. So pervasive is "the native tendency to extroversion" that it appears in a multiplicity of guises. Typically it is found in conceptualist philosophies that are so focussed on concepts that they miss the intellect from which they emerge. "For intellectual habit is not possession of the book but freedom from the book. It is the birth and life in us of the light and evidence by which we operate on our own."[23] On the contrary, "Conceptualists conceive human intellect only in terms of what it does; but their neglect of what intellect is, prior to what it does, has a variety of causes. Most commonly they do not advert to the act of understanding. They take concepts for granted; they are busy working out arguments to produce certitudes; they prolong their spontaneous tendencies to extroversion into philosophy, where they concentrate on metaphysics and neglect gnoseology."[24]

The Aristotelian-Thomist program is not the simple matter of conceiving understanding as some kind of a "spiritual look" in the tradition of Duns Scotus and William of Ockham.

> We can have no knowledge of our intellects except by reflecting on our own acts of understanding. Evidently, the Aristotelian and Thomist program is not a matter of considering ocular vision and then conceiving an analogous spiritual vision that is attributed to a spiritual faculty named intellect. On the contrary, it is a process of introspection that discovers the act of insight into the phantasm and the definition as an expression of the insight, that almost catches intellect in its forward movement towards defining and its backward reference to sense for the concrete realization of the defined.[25]

Toward the end of *Verbum* Lonergan pays tribute to Aquinas' transposition of Aristotle, instead of taking up as his working philosophy the various forms of Platonism that were available. "Least of all could Aquinas have lost himself in the Platonist fog and at the same time steadily progressed from the *Sentences* toward the clear and calm, the economic and functional, the balanced and exact series of questions and articles of the *via doctrinae* in the *Summa,* in which the intellectualism of Aristotle, made over into the intellectualism of St. Thomas shines as unmistakenly as the sun on the noonday summer hills of Italy."[26]

[23]Ibid., 185.
[24]Ibid., 186.
[25]Ibid., 76–77; cf. 25–26 for a lengthy note on Scotus; also 187.
[26]Ibid., 219.

It is in conjunction with these *Verbum* articles that we find Lonergan's first use of the phrase "intellectual conversion." In an early draft of the articles, written around 1945, Lonergan discussed Cajetan's opposition to Scotus:

> But Cajetan was not born an anti-Scotist. He underwent an intellectual conversion. . . . But if Cajetan had to have a conversion to grasp the Aristotelian theory of knowledge by identity, may one not say that that theory is anything but obvious?[27]

In conjunction with these emphases in the *Verbum* articles, we can also point to some other brief statements in book reviews written in the late 1940s. For example, regarding a collection of commentaries on medieval issues, including the real distinction between essence and existence, Lonergan writes: "George Klubertanz, S.J., deals with the same question in St. Bonaventure, to find that *esse* and *essentia* do not differ, while *existere*, in its technical sense, meant for St. Bonaventure *esse hic et nunc*; it would seem that there is a patron saint for the naive epistemologists who are concerned exclusively with the real as 'something out there.' "[28]

In another review of Dom Illtyd Trethowan's *Certainty: Philosophical and Theological*, Lonergan criticizes the author's "dogmatic intuitionism." For Trethowan knowledge is intuitive apprehension of certainty, whether in the natural or supernatural order.

> Unfortunately the postulated intuitions do not seem to exist. In its first moment on each level, knowledge seems to be act, perfection, identity; such identity of itself is not a confrontation; confrontation does arise, but only in a second moment and by a distinct act, of perception as distinct from sensation, of conception as distinct from insight, of judgment as distinct from reflective understanding. On this showing confrontation is not primitive, but derived; and it is derived from what is not confrontation, not intuition, nor formal and explicit duality.[29]

Lonergan goes on to admit the difficulty of accepting the view he is proposing. It demands a momentous personal change. "Admittedly it is difficult to justify such derivation. Overtly to accept such difficulty is a basic and momentous philosophic option." Even the eminent historian of philosophy, Etienne Gilson, is not spared the critique of intuitionism. In a generally favorable review Lonergan adds the reser-

---

[27]Quoted in Frederick Crowe, "Tracking stray ideas in Lonergan: 'intellectual conversion,' " *Lonergan Studies Newsletter* 14 (March 1993) 9.

[28]Bernard J. Lonergan, review of *Medieval Studies* VIII (Toronto: Pontifical Institute of Medieval Studies, 1946) in *Theological Studies* 8 (December 1947) 706.

[29]*The Modern Schoolman* 27 (1949–1950) 155.

vation: ''Finally, the insistence upon a 'return to sense' and the affirmation of an intuitive experience of acts of existing (pp. 206 f.) are strangely reminiscent of something like Kierkegaard's esthetic sphere of existential subjectivity.''[30]

[30]Review of E. Gilson, *Being and Some Philosophers*, *Theological Studies* 11 (1950) 124.

Part Three
"Radical Intellectual Conversion"

"Intellectual conversion, I think, is very rare."

Foundations of Theology, 234

Chapter Ten

A Growing Focus on Scientific Method

In 1940 Lonergan finished his doctoral studies in Rome. "He had barely finished these when the May days of 1940 broke upon the world, and he had to tuck his thesis under his arm and head for a boat at Genoa, just escaping the boiling caldron that Europe was to become."[1] From 1940 to 1953 Lonergan taught theology at Jesuit seminaries in Canada: first, from 1940 to 1946 at L'Immaculée-Conception, the Jesuit seminary in Montreal, and then, in 1947 at Regis College, the Jesuit seminary in Toronto. In the extant notes from his theology courses during the 1940s it is evident that Lonergan's underlying concern is method: a focus on the nature of theological understanding. The seeds of what will emerge many years later as his *Method in Theology* can be seen in those early class notes.[2] Still, underlying his interest in theological understanding is his interest in understanding as such.

At this point Lonergan begins to focus more explicitly on the nature of modern scientific consciousness. After so many years in the study of the ancients, particularly Thomas Aquinas, Lonergan begins to take the methodologies of the sciences as the explicit focus of his reflection. Why? Well, for one reason, one could not just ignore the all-pervasive presence of the sciences in the modern world. Science was—and is—the paradigm for what it means "to know" in our world. Lonergan often quoted Herbert Butterfield, the historian of science, on the massive importance of the scientific revolution. "It outshines everything since the rise of Christianity and reduces the Renaissance and the Reformation to the rank of mere episodes, mere internal displacements, within the system of medieval Christendom."[3]

Indeed, the very success of the modern sciences was due to their declaring their independence from the ancient Aristotelian science that

[1]Frederick E. Crowe, "Bernard Lonergan's Intellectualism," *Spirit as Inquiry: Studies in Honor of Bernard Lonergan, Continuum* 2 (Autumn 1964) 16.

[2]Cf. Craig S. Boly, *The Road to Lonergan's* Method in Theology (Lanham, Md.: University Press of America, 1990).

[3]Herbert Butterfield, *The Origins of Modern Science, 1300–1800*, 2nd ed. (New York: 1966) 7; quoted from *Second Collection*, 56.

so penetrated into the warp and woof of Aquinas' thought, the very thought Lonergan had spent so many years studying.

> The world of Aquinas was very different from our own. His was a world of Babylonian and Ptolemaic ancestry, with the earth as its center, with its fixed species sustained by the benign influence of the heavenly spheres, with its short history of less than ten thousand years. How completely and intimately the thought of Aquinas was embedded in that world barely appears in summary accounts of his doctrine or in selected readings recommended to students. Modern science declared its independence from philosophy in general and from Aristotelian philosophy in particular.[4]

In the early 1970s Lonergan would write:

> For centuries the Christian's image of himself and of his world was drawn from the first chapters of Genesis, from Jewish apocalyptic and Ptolemaic astronomy, and from the theological doctrines of the creation and immortality of each human soul. That image has been assaulted by novel scientific traditions stemming from Copernicus, Newton, Darwin, Freud, Heisenberg. It has been the great merit of Teilhard de Chardin to have recognized the Christian's need of a coherent image of himself in his world and to have contributed not a little towards meeting that need.[5]

Lonergan's focussing on scientific consciousness in the early 1940s had the same end in mind. In addition, the rise of modern science was accompanied by post-Enlightenment philosophies that interpreted scientific consciousness in such a way as not to allow for the divine or for divine revelation. The basic issue was the nature of truth. As Lonergan noted some years later: "Thus I should maintain that the crop of philosophies produced since the Enlightenment are not open to revealed truths because they possess no adequate account of truth."[6]

In *Method in Theology*, after outlining the cultural changes brought about during the last four centuries by science, scholarship, and philosophy, Lonergan states: "These changes have, in general, been resisted by churchmen for two reasons. The first reason commonly has been that churchmen had no real apprehension of the nature of these changes. The second reason has been that these changes commonly have been accompanied by a lack of intellectual conversion and so were hostile to Christianity."[7] In other words, it is the presence or absence of intellectual conversion that is the core issue in the Church's under-

---

[4]*Third Collection*, 52.
[5]*Method in Theology*, 315.
[6]*Collection*, 186.
[7]*Method in Theology*, 317.

standing of what is going on in the world and the world's understanding of the meaning and realm of divine revelation.

In order to appreciate Lonergan's growing focus on the empirical sciences it is helpful to have at hand a schema he created years later in his *Method in Theology* on the three stages of human meaning: the stages of common sense, theory, and interiority. These stages can help us specify more clearly the cultural significance of Lonergan's own intellectual conversion and the further working out of that conversion in Lonergan's later writings. It has helped me to understand what was happening as I struggled with his *Insight* in the 1960s.

> The stages in question are ideal constructs, and the key to the constructing is the undifferentiation or differentiation of consciousness. In the main we have in mind the Western tradition and we distinguish three stages. In the first stage conscious and intentional operations follow the mode of common sense. In a second stage beside the mode of common sense there is also the mode of theory, where the theory is controlled by a logic. In a third stage the modes of common sense and theory remain, science asserts its autonomy from philosophy, and there occur philosophies that leave theory to science and take their stand on interiority.[8]

All of Lonergan's early study and his intellectual conversion in the mid-1930s had familiarized him with the breakthrough from the stage of common sense to the stage of theory. It was the breakthrough epitomized by Plato's dialogues that moved people beyond the realm of ordinary language and prepared the way for the systematic language of Aristotle. Because in these writers the "word," the activity of intellect, could effectively "challenge the evidence of the senses," the way was open for the world of theory: in the ancient world, the world of philosophy. To this world Stewart's book on Plato explicitly introduced the young Lonergan. Aristotle and Aquinas and the mathematical procedures of modern science represent the epitome of this second stage of meaning, the stage of theory. It is a world constituted by the relationships of elements, not to the sensing, emotional subject, but to all other elements in the context of a universal viewpoint. Thus, Aristotelian philosophy relates potency and act, matter and form, substance and accident, essence and existence, etc., in a total view of the constitutive principles of the universe. So the individual chemical

---

[8]Ibid., 85. "Such is the theoretical division. It is temporal in the sense that one has to be in the first stage to advance to the second and one has to be in the second to advance to the third. But it is not chronological: large segments of the population may have undifferentiated consciousness though a culture is in the second or third stage; and many learned people may remain in the second stage when a culture has reached the third."

elements of modern science are defined by their mathematical relations to each other in the total perspective that is the periodic table of chemistry.

Lonergan was well aware of the modern world's breakthrough to the second stage of human meaning, the stage of system and theory, through his own early studies in mathematics and logic and later through his immersion in the Aristotelian thought of Aquinas. As we noted, however, in Aristotle and Aquinas philosophy and natural science are almost inextricably bound up with each other. The discoveries of the modern sciences, on the other hand, to a large extent consisted in the emancipation from Aristotelian and medieval physics and consequently from Aristotelian philosophy. Modern scientists from Galileo on focussed on the empirical universe in an exclusive way. Science took over completely the theoretical treatment of the sensible world. It was a revolution in the world of theory.

With the rise of the modern sciences the situation of human philosophy was radically threatened. If modern science owes its success to its breaking free from Aristotelian physics and its exclusive taking over the explanation of the empirical world, what role is left for philosophy?

> Now the emergence of the autonomous sciences has repercussions on philosophy. Since the sciences between them undertake the explanation of all sensible data, one may conclude with the positivists that the function of philosophy is to announce that philosophy has nothing to say. Since philosophy has no theoretic function, one may conclude with the linguistic analysts that the function of philosophy is to work out a hermeneutics for the local variety of everyday language.[9]

For Lonergan, however, philosophy has not at all disappeared. It has its own realm and that is the realm of human interiority. The exploration of that realm was prepared for by many of the very philosophers who had influenced Lonergan as a young man, among whom were Augustine and Newman.

> Once consciousness has been differentiated and systematic thought and speech about mental acts have been developed, the capacities of ordinary language are vastly enlarged. Augustine's penetrating reflections on knowledge and consciousness, Descartes' *Regulae ad directionem ingenii*, Pascal's *Pensees*, Newman's *Grammar of Assent*, all remain within the world of commonsense apprehension and speech yet contribute enormously to our understanding of ourselves. Moreover, they reveal the

[9]Ibid., 94.

possibility of coming to know the conscious subject and his conscious operations without presupposing a prior metaphysical structure.[10]

In their own way, though separated by centuries, both Augustine and Newman prepared the way for a "third stage of meaning," that is, a stage consequent upon the successes of the modern sciences.[11] This third stage of human meaning is the stage in which the dynamisms of human interiority are analyzed in a *systematic* way.

> The Greeks needed an artistic, a rhetorical, an argumentative development of language before a Greek could set up a metaphysical account of mind. The Greek achievement was needed to expand the capabilities of commonsense knowledge and language before Augustine, Descartes, Pascal, Newman could make their commonsense contributions to self-knowledge. The history of mathematics, natural science, and philosophy, and, as well, one's own personal reflective engagement in all three are needed if both common sense and theory are to construct the scaffolding for an entry into the world of interiority.[12]

Certainly this is the reason why in the 1940s Lonergan began to turn his attention to an analysis of scientific consciousness. In his own way, on the level of his own scientific culture, he was doing what Augustine had done in the fourth century and Newman in the nineteenth.

In the following pages we will chronicle some of Lonergan's writings during the 1940s, and among them is found his own "personal reflective engagement" with mathematics, science, and philosophy. It was the working out of his own personal intellectual conversion at the level of his own times. In him the third stage of meaning was being born.

1. "The Form of Inference"

As we noted previously, Lonergan was interested in mathematics and the methodology of the sciences from his earliest years. The pedagogical methods of Fr. Charles O'Hara at Heythrop and his own work on logic had introduced him to the basic problematics of modern mathematics and science. That this interest remained with him is evident from an article he published in 1943 in *Thought*, "The Form of Inference." The title of the article is similar to his first *Blandyke Paper*,

---

[10]Ibid., 261.

[11]For the clear contrast between Augustine's psychological method and that of Aristotle, cf. the introduction to *Verbum*, vii–xv.

[12]*Method in Theology*, 261–62.

and its content is the development of his second paper, "The Syllogism."[13]

Lonergan takes as his starting point the fact that two of his mentors, H.W.B. Joseph in his *Introduction to Logic* and Cardinal Newman both are opposed to the idea of reducing knowledge to any particular form of syllogistic reasoning. On that basis, Lonergan asks if there is any general form of human thinking: "Is the human mind a Noah's ark of irreducible inferential forms? Is there no general form of all inference, no highest common factor, that reveals the nature of the mind no matter how diverse the materials on which it operates? Is everything subject to measure and order and law except the mind which through measurement and comparison seeks to order everything with laws?"[14]

His question is whether there is "some type of formally valid inference that possesses both the radical simplicity and indefinite flexibility necessary to embrace all other types of reasoning within itself." Through a detailed account of the various syllogistic and non-syllogistic types of reasoning, Lonergan finds the one underlying and common form of inference in the simple hypothetical argument of the type:

If *A*, then *B*
But *A*
Therefore *B*.

The body of the article consists in a very minute and detailed tracing of this form of inference throughout all the various types of syllogisms and logical thinking. In the conclusion to the article Lonergan relates his concern in this article to his overriding concern to articulate the basic structures of mind:

> We have not considered inductive conclusions. To correlate the movement from data through hypothesis to verified theory with the movement from implier through implication to implied, and both of these with the more ultimate process from sensa through intellection to judgment, is indeed a legitimate inquiry; but it is more general than the present and presupposes it. For the same reason we have not aimed at explaining inference but rather at finding the highest common factor of inferences no matter how they are explained. Indeed, it is precisely in our

[13]According to the editors of the *Collected Works* edition of *Collection*, this article probably originated in an article written between 1933 and 1937 for an English audience—originally rejected—and then touched up for the American readership of *Thought* in the early 1940s. The notes speak of seven pages of "logic fragments" in the Lonergan archives that probably date from the 1930s. Cf. *Collection*, 256–57.

[14]*Collection*, 4.

attitude towards the explanation of inference that we differ from the approach of the more traditional manuals of logic; the latter presupposes an explanation of conceptualization and of inference; we on the contrary have aimed at taking a first step in working out an empirical theory of human understanding and knowledge.[15]

2. "Finality, Love, Marriage"

Since Lonergan's interest was an "empirical" theory of knowledge, he turns his attention increasingly to the empirical sciences. Fortuitously, in the early 1940s he was joined in Montreal by Fr. Eric O'Connor, a mathematician who had just finished his studies in mathematics at Harvard, a person who proved to be an invaluable resource for Lonergan in the years to come.

> When I began teaching at L'Immaculee Conception [in 1940], Fr. Eric O'Connor returned from Harvard with his Ph.D. in mathematics and began teaching at Loyola College in Montreal. Later in a conversation it transpired that he was having difficulty in his efforts to teach; I asked him whether he was using the highly formalized methods then in vogue. He said that he was and I suggested that he concentrate on communicating to his students the relevant insights and that on this basis the students would be able to figure out the formalizations for themselves. My suggestion worked. The result was that I had an expert mathematician who also knew his physics (during the Second World War he helped out at McGill University and taught quantum theory there) whom I could consult when writing the earlier chapters of *Insight*.[16]

In 1943 Lonergan published an article in *Theological Studies* entitled "Finality, Love, Marriage" in which he presented an understanding of marriage in terms of an ascending order of sciences revealing different levels of the person (physical, chemical, biological, sensitive psychological, and intellectual) corresponding to ascending orders of human love: sexual attraction, friendship, human and divine love. There is a horizontal or essential priority of lower levels; but concomitantly, there is a vertical finality of lower levels toward higher realizations. Scientific perspectives are integrated into a personalist and religious thrust.

> In the recent fermentation of Catholic thought on the meaning and ends of marriage, the basic component of novelty would seem to be a development in biological science. Quite other factors, no doubt, account for the intense and widespread interest aroused; but the ground of the intellec-

[15]Ibid., 16.
[16]*Second Collection*, 267–68.

tual problem must be placed, I think, in a new scientific insight. To this Dr. H. Doms has given full prominence, and I cannot but agree that, if Aristotelian biology was aware of a distinction between fecundity and sex, it did not admit any systematic elaboration and application of that distinction. On the other hand, modern biology makes such elaboration and application inevitable. There results more than a suggestion that as fecundity is for offspring so sex has a personalist finality of its own.[17]

Into a systematic account of the relationship of the various scientifically discovered levels of reality Lonergan weaves an account of the vertical finality of lower levels to higher realizations. Modern thought discovers such finality operative in the statistical laws that allow "the fertility of concrete plurality" to open up to ever higher levels of realization. The whole is an almost "Teilhardian" view of the universe:

> Just as the real object tends to God as real motive and real term, just as the essence of the real object limits the mode of appetition and of process, so a concrete plurality of essences has an upthrust from lower to higher levels. But just as this fact is shrouded in the mists of Aristotelian science . . . so it is most conspicuous to one who looks at the universe with the eyes of modern science, who sees subatoms uniting into atoms, atoms into compounds, compounds into organisms, who finds the pattern of genes in reproductive cells shifting . . . to give organic evolution within limited ranges, who attributes the rise of cultures and civilizations to the interplay of human plurality, who observes that only when and where the higher rational culture emerged did God acknowledge the fullness of time permitting the Word to become flesh and the mystical body to begin its intussusception of human personalities and its leavening of human history.[18]

In an article written in the late 1940s, "The Natural Desire to See God," Lonergan contrasts the essentialist and conceptualist view of world order with the open intellectualist view he espouses. The essentialist view, rooted in a conceptualist view of mind as a "cerebral logic machine" grinding out conclusions, posits the ideas of finite natures as prior to world-orders. On the other hand, for an open intellectualism, "the world-order is an intelligible unity mirroring forth the glory of God. Because of this intelligible unity lower natures are subordinate to higher natures, not merely extrinsically, but also intrinsically, as appears in chemical composition and in biological evolution. Again, because of this intelligible unity finite natures are sacrificed for the

---

[17]*Collection,* 17.
[18]Ibid., 21–22.

greater perfection of the whole; thus there are extinct species and the toleration of many physical evils."[19]

The whole analysis in "Finality, Love, Marriage," aided by the analysis of the modern sciences, has a personalistic thrust:

> Now towards this high goal of charity it is no small beginning in the weak and imperfect heart of fallen man to be startled by a beauty that shifts the center of appetition out of self; and such a shift is effected on the level of sensitive spontaneity by *eros* leaping in [and] through delighted eyes and establishing itself as unrest in absence and an imperious demand for company. Next company may reveal deeper qualities of mind and character to shift again the center from the merely organistic tendencies of nature to the rational level of friendship with its enduring basis in the excellence of a good person. Finally, grace inserts into charity the love that nature gives and reason approves.[20]

3. "An Essay in Circulation Analysis"

We could not chronicle Lonergan's writings in the 1940s without mentioning his work on macroeconomics. That work did not come to fruition until the last years of his life. From his early years Lonergan had been interested in the analysis of economic activity. That interest resulted in 1944 in a manuscript on the circulation of money in a dynamic economy.

> My interest in economics goes back to the course on ethics when I was a student of philosophy at the Jesuit House of Studies at Heythrop in Oxfordshire. . . . I returned to Canada in 1930 to find the country in the pit of a depression. Theories and fads about what was wrong were current. In particular, there was a theory called Social Credit that argued that purchasing power was systematically deficient and that banks should issue and distribute money to make up for the deficiency. . . . The argument for Social Credit was clear and simple; the fallacy in the argument could be uncovered only through dynamic analysis. I tinkered with the problem of working out a dynamic analysis off and on; and finally about 1943 or '44 I had a 128 page manuscript.[21]

---

[19]Ibid., 85.

[20]Cf. ibid., 31–32: Cf. also 49: "The sexual extravagance of man, unparalleled in the animals, has its ultimate ground in St. Augustine's 'Thou hast made us for thyself, O Lord, and our hearts are restless till they rest in thee.' "

[21]"Macroeconomics and the Dialectic of Decline," unpublished notes prepared for a seminar at Boston College, 1978–1979, 1. Quoted from Michael Gibbons, "*Insight* and Emergence: an Introduction to Lonergan's *Circulation Analysis*," *Creativity and Method*, ed. Matthew Lamb (Milwaukee: 1981) 530.

That manuscript, *An Essay in Circulation Analysis,* with additions and revisions through the 1970s and early 1980s, will soon be published posthumously in the *Collected Works of Bernard Lonergan.* In 1944 he could find no one who could understand it and so he put it away for some years, that is, until after he had completed his *Insight* and *Method in Theology.* In 1977 he said: "I worked on one question for fourteen years, getting nowhere. I wrote one hundred and twenty pages, but didn't find anyone who could see any sense in it. Six or seven years later a colleague read it, found it extremely interesting and helpful, and agreed to collaborate—but he went off to Zambia to teach. The question is still genuine and authentic. Next term I shall be attacking it publicly."[22]

Lonergan's aim was a "systematic" analysis of economic phenomena. "Booms and slumps" are recurrent, and Lonergan's analysis seeks to show how they derive from an inadequate understanding of the nature of the productive process in an industrial economy. The dynamics of that productive process involve the relations between the three elements of production, exchange, and finance.[23] In the first section he distinguished between the production of consumer goods, clothes, for instance, and producer goods, sewing machines. Concomitantly, he distinguished between a consumer goods money circuit and a producer goods money circuit, crossover paths linking those circuits, and a redistributive area, the realm of banking and finance. The third section consisted in the analysis of the circulation of money in the different circuits. In this section there was a basis for a critique of the financial procedures which had caused the depression. As he once said to me, referring to many government economic policies: "People are stepping on the accelerator and braking at the same time!"

For our purposes, these analyses represent Lonergan's effort to allow his own personal intellectual conversion to flow into his analysis of the human world of economics. That intellectual conversion led him to seek to understand that world in systematic terms. The present writer is still trying to "reach up to" Lonergan's analysis of macro-economics.

4. "Thought and Reality"

In the fall and spring of 1945–1946 Lonergan taught a course in the Thomas More Institute for Adult Education in Montreal entitled

[22]Elaine Cahn and Cathleen Going, eds., *The Question as Commitment* (Montreal: Thomas More Institute Papers 77, 1979) 32; also 110.

[23]Cf. William Mathews, "Lonergan's Economics," *Method: Journal of Lonergan Studies* 3 (March 1985) 9–30.

"Thought and Reality." Years later he remarked on the receptiveness of his students to the course and on the encouragement it gave him to continue on the track he had begun. "In September there were about forty-five students coming; at Easter there were still forty-one. It seemed clear that I had a marketable product not only because of the notable perseverance of the class but also from the interest that lit up their faces and from such more palpable incidents as a girl marching in at the beginning of class, giving my desk a resounding whack with her hand, and saying, 'I've got it.' Those that have struggled with *Insight* will know what she meant."[24] An incident such as this, recalled many years later, was revealing to Lonergan the powerful effect of sharing with others the fruits of his own intellectual development. This "feed-back" was important to him.

Schematic student notes of this course are extant and they reflect much of what is present in the *Verbum* articles which he was working on at the time. The language and formulations are often Thomistic, but at the same time it is obvious that Lonergan is engaged in analyzing scientific understanding. Science represents the "value of the spirit of inquiry." Scientific understanding is "luminous." It is also pleasurable: it is "explosive when it changes your viewpoint." It has a synthetic power of grasping "all parts together in a simple view." Scientific understanding "puts in new rules and throws out old ones." This section ends with the following schematic jottings:

> Reflection on History of Scientific Development.
> Accuracy of Relevant Data (Which apply to the "why").
> Use of a Working Hypothesis—Constant Cross-dialectic running.
> Scientific work largely a matter of Collaboration.
> Exploring the Sub-Conscious—Helps to get the right phantasm.
> Science is Relative—Best theories are what is most probable at the present time (i.e., as the data are known) as it squares with the data.
> Does not follow that *Scientific Method* is relative or that understanding is relative.[25]

Those familiar with *Insight* will see in these jottings his developing understanding of the nature of empirical science. There is also the use of the term, "naive realism," with a dash next to it and the words, "first step in Philosophy." Next there appears to be a definition of naive realism: "You know real objects (sensibly) before you understand and before you think—as the animal knows."[26] Next he lists a whole

---

[24]*Second Collection,* 268.
[25]*Thought and Reality,* 8. (Notes taken by J. Martin O'Hara and transcribed by Thomas Daly.)
[26]Ibid., 10.

series of philosophies that flow from a naive realism: phenomenalism, Kantian criticism, Idealism, pragmatism, Platonism. With all of these he contrasts Aristotle: "Truth is the correspondence of judgment and reality. Reality is what corresponds to true judgment. It is what is."[27]

5. "A Note on Geometrical Possibility"

Lonergan's growing focus on scientific method is complemented by a continuing interest in geometrical questions. This is evident in an article published in *The Modern Schoolman* of 1949–1950, "A Note on Geometrical Possibility." The article is an analysis of Euclidean geometry from the viewpoint of metaphysical possibility. Lonergan mentions that Fr. Peter Hoenen had contended that, even in the light of non-Euclidean geometries and the modern developments of logic, only Euclidean three-dimensional extension is known as actually possible. Lonergan's aim in the article is to arrive at an understanding of Euclidean geometry from the viewpoint of intelligibility, since "intelligibility grounds possibility." Towards the end of the article he states: "We would meet with a distinction Fr. Hoenen's claim that we do not know whether or not N-dimensional spaces are possible: we do not know whether they are possible *simpliciter*, but it would seem that we do know that they are possible *secundum quid*."[28]

He concludes the article with the confession that he suspects that in the article there are a number of failures to hit things off with complete accuracy. It is in *Insight* that he will treat more fully the issues of relativity theory that are here touched upon from the viewpoint of geometrical possibility. Nevertheless, a number of issues that will reappear in *Insight* are first sounded in this article. For example, "Our basic assumption is that science primarily is understanding, that only secondarily in virtue of self-scrutiny and self-appraisal is scientific understanding expressed in definitions, postulates, deductions."[29] There follows the distinction between what he calls nominal and essential definitions. In *Insight* the latter will be called explanatory definitions.

> It follows that definitions are expressions of understanding and may be divided by differences in what is understood. But it is one thing to grasp the language proper to a science; it is quite another to grasp the nature of the object investigated in the science. Hence, definitions will be of at least two kinds, namely nominal and essential. Nominal definitions express one's understanding of a linguistic system, of how terms are

[27]Ibid., 11.
[28]*Collection*, 107.
[29]Ibid., 93–94.

to be employed, of what employed terms must mean. Essential definitions express one's understanding of a real system, of the necessary and possible and impossible relations of things, of why things are just the way they are. In both cases the understanding itself is real; but in nominal definitions the understood has only the reality of names; while in essential definition the understood has the reality of what names mean.

The function of nominal definitions in relation to essential definitions is illustrated by the human ability to create symbolic images of what transcends imagination. The issue is central to *Insight*.

> It may be well to indicate at once an incidental function of nominal definitions. It has been noticed that one cannot imagine a Euclidean point: one can imagine a minute speck, but if the speck really has no parts and no magnitude, then one's image disappears. Similarly, one cannot imagine a Euclidean line; one can imagine a very, very fine line, but if one imagines length from which all breadth is eliminated, one imagines nothing at all. Again, one cannot imagine the indefinitely produced straight lines of the definition of parallels: insofar as they are actually imagined, they are not indefinitely produced. On the other hand, one cannot do geometry without imagination and solely by using concepts. For the abstract straight line is unique; there are not two of them to run parallel to each other; and similarly whenever there is a question, and perpetually there is a question, of more than one geometrical entity of a kind, it is necessary for intellect to convert to phantasm. The solution to this anomaly is the symbolic image, that is, the image that stands for things it does not resemble. The geometer boldly imagines blobs and bars but understands them and thinks of them as Euclidean points and lines. The geometer does not bother producing lines indefinitely; he produces them a bit but understands them and thinks of them as indefinitely produced. He can do this because in between his images and his understanding there intervene his definitions, which settle for understanding and thought what the images stand for, no matter what they resemble.[30]

Next he turns to essential definitions. They presuppose nominal definitions of common matter at least symbolically represented in imagination. They proceed from acts of understanding in which is grasped the intelligible form of the common matter. The essence that is defined is the compound of form and common matter. The point that he had made in the *Verbum* articles is that the form is the *propter quid* that functions as the middle term between common matter and essence. "Why are these bones and this flesh a man? What is the middle term between the empirical data of bones and flesh and the conceived essence, man? It is the formal cause of a man, his soul." His next example is central

[30]Ibid., 95–96.

to the first chapter of *Insight:* "Or, to take an illustration from geometry, why is this symbolically imagined uniformly round plane curve a circle? What has to be grasped to effect the transition from empirically given uniform curvature to the essentially defined circle? It is the formal cause of the circle, what grounds both the circularity of the circle and, as well, all its demonstrable properties. But such a formal cause is the equality of all radii in the circle." He explains:

> If all the radii are equal, the plane curve must be round; if any are unequal, it cannot be round; and similarly for the other properties of the circle. The "must" and "cannot" reveal the activity of understanding; and what is understood is not how to use the name, circle, but circularity itself. Further, not only does understanding intervene, but it intervenes with respect to sensible data; the necessity results from the equality of all radii, but only sense knows a multiplicity of radii; the abstract radius is unique. Finally, from the understanding of sensible data, there results the definition: without understanding one can repeat the definition like a parrot; but one cannot discover the definition, grasp what it means, without understanding equality of radii as the ground of circularity.[31]

Finally, he aims at a definition of understanding itself, a definition of what of its nature grounds all definitions:

> Understanding itself is an irreducible experience like seeing colors or hearing sounds. It is what is rare in the stupid and frequent in the intelligent. It is the goal of inquiry, emerging upon the empirical, grounding the formation of concepts, definitions, hypothetical systems, pure implications. It is the grasp of unity (Aristotle's *intelligentia indivisibilium*) in empirical multiplicity, and it expresses itself in systematic meaning.[32]

---

[31]Ibid., 97.
[32]Ibid., 102.

Chapter Eleven
"Intelligence and Reality"

So far we have illustrated pieces of the puzzle: the gradual expression of Lonergan's own intellectual conversion. But there is a set of notes from 1951 in which he explicitly uses the phrase "intellectual conversion." These are the first clear accounts of what Lonergan will later call "the third stage of meaning," that is, the stage of human culture in which human interiority is systematically analyzed. The notes are an outline of a course of twelve hours taught at the Thomas More Institute between March and May 1951 and entitled "Intelligence and Reality."[1] This was during the time when he was well into working on *Insight* and the outline is reflective of what will emerge in *Insight*. The notes are typed by Lonergan in schematic form. We will highlight the elements that focus on what he here calls "radical intellectual conversion."

1. Experience, Understanding, and Judgment

Lonergan states his subject: not whether knowledge exits (a question he deems "a blind alley"), but rather, what is knowledge? He begins by highlighting many of the aspects of the act of understanding that he had highlighted in his previous writings. He distinguishes between the spontaneous insights in art, skills, crafts, technique, and the "analysed" [sic] insights of mathematics, science, and philosophy. Both are insights, but the latter involve analysis, allowing a person to facilitate the act of understanding in another "by talking to him." "Analysed" acts of understanding provide simpler and neater examples. This is a shorter expression of what he will say in *Insight* to justify his use of so many examples from mathematics and science.

---

[1]*Intelligence and Reality*, notes made by Bernard Lonergan for his course at Thomas More Institute, Montreal, 1951. Available at Lonergan Research Institute, Toronto. It is possible the course spanned the whole academic year of 1950–1951, but Lonergan's lectures came in the spring of 1951. There are also extant student notes from a third set of lectures focussing on insight that took place at Regis College, Toronto, in 1952–1953, but apparently very close to *Insight* itself as far as they go. Cf. Frederick E. Crowe, *Lonergan* (Collegeville, Minn.: The Liturgical Press, 1992) 70, 77–78.

In these notes he again employs his favorite geometrical example, the circle, in the analysis of understanding.

> Link between sensible data, imagined representations, and objects of thought. What is an object of thought? For the moment it is what you can think about but cannot see or imagine. Point: position without magnitude. Line: length without depth or breadth. . . . Geometers talk about them, cannot imagine them. How does one reach objects of thought? Imagine cart-wheel; ask why round (formal, not efficient instrumental material or final).

> Definition: parrot repetition *or* expression of understanding necessary and sufficient for uniform roundness grasped in imagined presentation.

He also illustrates the meaning of a "higher viewpoint" by understanding the movement from understanding arithmetic to understanding algebra. In *Insight* he illustrates this by showing how allowing the operations of arithmetic their full generality (to reveal the possibility of negative numbers, for example) provides "a virtual image" in which one can grasp the possibility of algebraic operations. Here he merely notes:

> Mathematical series of higher viewpoints
>
> image—insight—object of thought—symbol
> symbolic image—insight—higher object of thought

Toward the end of this first section on the act of understanding Lonergan describes intellectual mastery with regard to a particular set of "analysed" insights:

> Where others only see multiple incidental particular contingent
> Where others just read and pronounce the words
> Where others just gape at symbols
>> acquired mastery without hesitation
>> grasps unity in multiplicity, essential overruling incidental, universal illustrated in particular, necessary relating contingent

There is also a section on judgment which Lonergan defines by distinguishing questions for intelligence and questions for reflection. Among other things he notes:

> Present total increment a tiny fragment w respect to totality of true judgments. . .
> Habitual character of knowing: only one judgment at a time; either general and vague; or precise but particular. Woods or trees. We want to contemplate. We can only add.

The next section is on reflective understanding:

> Insight, meeting question for reflection, making judgment possible and rationally necessary.
>> grasps sufficiency of evidence; problem, What is sufficient?

At this point he introduces the notion of "the virtually unconditioned," that is, a conditioned whose conditions are understood *de facto* to be fulfilled. Among other examples he refers to concrete judgments of fact and there, in a parenthesis, he inserts "importance of Newman":

> All judgments have ultimately the same basis; virtually unconditioned. Kinds of evidence vary; possibility of expressing evidence varies. Act and criterion invariant.

> Opinions, if judgments, reduce to virtually unconditioned; eg best available scientific opinion, ie squares with known relevant data . . .

As a corollary he critiques the "escapism" of any ultimate appeal to logic, technique, method, rule, contrivance:

> Ultimate appeal has to be to inner acts, personal acts; your knowledge is your responsibility. Bear witness to truth. You cannot impose it.

Later he says:

> Real issue: existence theorem.
> Anyone may define terms and set up analytic propositions ad nauseam. Aquinas I, II, 65, 5, 4m: conclusions to principles; principles to terms; terms to wisdom.

> Wisdom—Habitual cluster of reflective insights with respect to ultimates. . . .

> Fundamental importance of Newman. Concrete judgment of fact, key to knowing existence, being in act.

2. Implicitly Defined

Early in these notes Lonergan treats of "explanatory abstraction," a more technical analysis of the act of understanding. Abstraction, he notes, is basically enriching. He appeals to the personal experience of grasping the *idea* of something, "the pre-conceptual, intelligible form emergent in sensible data." For example, in the example of the circle, enriching abstraction grasps that if the radii are equal, no bumps are possible; it must be a circle. Such necessity and impossibility are grasped in the image, not in general.

The "empirical residue," another term he will also use in *Insight*, is what is always left out in cases of explanatory abstraction: such as "instance, interference of different laws, continuum."

An "explanatory system" is a related set of explanatory abstractions. He distinguishes primitive and derived concepts. The derived are defined by the primitives:

> Primitive: terms and relations; relations fix terms;
>   terms fix relations; both from idea; both simultaneous

Here he touches on what is central to these notes and to *Insight*, implicit definition: the terms fix the relations and the relations fix the terms and both are rooted in insight. This technique, which in *Insight* he attributes to the geometer, David Hilbert, he here applies to understanding human knowing.[2]

For example, in a section of the notes entitled "Data, Images, Percepts," Lonergan defines these elements by their relationship to understanding:

> We cannot understand without understanding something.
> Ergo, there has to be a component in knowing that is presupposed and complemented by inquiry and insight.
> Ergo, definition of data, images, percepts by relation of presupposition and complementation to inquiry and insight.

After referring to the data sought in the empirical sciences, Lonergan refers to the data of consciousness: "acts of seeing, hearing, imagining, desiring, fearing, inquiring, understanding, conceiving, reflecting, judging, choosing." Direct understanding is to sensible data as introspective understanding is to the data of consciousness. There is no difference *qua* understanding:

> Begin from experience of understanding; relate to inquiry, presentations, concepts, in process of maths, class phase, statistical phase.

There are limiting experiences in this process:

> constructs also experienced; identity of experimenter, experimented on, experimentation.

Lonergan also mentions the "fallacy of amateurish introspection":

> Data images percepts are ineffable.
> Without distinction relation identification
> Hence indirect definition by relations
> Hence fallacy of amateurish introspection

---

[2]*Insight*, 37 (12–13). William Mathews claims that Lonergan might have been introduced to Hilbert's notion of implicit definition through Peter Hoenen's later articles in the *Gregorianum* in the late 1930s. Cf. ch. 6, n. 1.

What is this "fallacy of amateurish introspection?" Based on what Lonergan will write in *Insight*, I would contend that it would be any attempt at introspection based on a model of knowing as "taking a good look," so that introspection is conceived as "looking within ourselves." Genuine introspection is the heightening of our human consciousness that is involved in understanding the dynamic structure of our own knowing. Here he merely notes that the various levels of human consciousness are related by presupposition and complementation. Thus, in a section of the notes entitled "Structure of Knowing" he notes:

> Level of experience, of intelligence, of reflection. . .
> Levels related by presupposition and complementation. . .

The significance of implicit definition is its complete generality: it consists in explanatory definitions and omits nominal definitions. As he writes in *Insight*, "The exclusive use of explanatory or postulational elements concentrates attention upon the set of relationships in which the whole scientific significance is contained."[3]

3. Classical and Statistical Empirical Methods

Toward the end of an early section of the notes of 1951 on the act of understanding and its formulation in explanatory systems, Lonergan asks whether the relations involved in an explanatory system must be mathematical:

> Seems to be a secondary principle of relevance that requires relations to be mathematical with decreasing stringency as one advances from physics to chemistry, from chemistry to biology, from biology to human sciences.
>
> Chemistry defines hundreds of thousands of compounds by mere hundred elements. Defines elements by pattern of relations of periodic table. Periodic table not a mathematical series, though with many mathematical aspects and relations.

He then treats of "heuristic abstraction," which in *Insight* is clearly integral to what he calls the classical empirical method of science:

> Heuristic notion: a unknown b employed in making it known. eg x an equation involving x
> Basic heuristic notion "nature": a unknown, will be known when I understand; b employed in reaching understanding, for similars are similarly understood. . .

[3]Ibid.

Applied to *a* sensible similarity *b* similarities of conjunction, separation, sequence, sequences of proportions, etc., etc. Curve fitting.

He then goes on to define empirical method as "a method of ever closer approximation to complete account of the data that are given." Classical empirical method, which in *Insight* he associates with the names of Galileo, Newton, Clerk Maxwell, and Einstein, involves the selection of a possible explanatory system that fits the data in a given domain.[4] For example, a term such as "mass" is a non-mathematical higher term in the total explanatory system of modern physics. In the notes he writes:

> Masses are what stand in certain relations that are established experimentally. Lever, spring, balance, impact, free fall. Not "heavy" "light" "weight"; no direct experience; mass is a term defined by experimental relations between masses. Cp. "E" and "H" defined by Clerk-Maxwell's equations.

"Heavy," "light," and "weight" are common sense terms that denote things in relation to our sensitive being. They are not scientific or explanatory terms. In an article written soon after this, Lonergan makes the same point with regard to theological categories. "Just as the equations of thermodynamics make no one feel warmer or cooler and, much less, evoke the sentiments associated with the drowsy heat of the summer sun or with the refreshing coolness of evening breezes, so also speculative theology is not immediately relevant to the stimulation of religious feeling."[5]

In the same article, Lonergan uses the term "conjugate" to denote terms defined by their relations. Such conjugate terms are empirical when their defining relations admit experimental proof. Explanatory systems are relevant to empirical inquiry when their higher terms are empirical conjugate terms. In the concrete, explanatory "laws" are set forth with the proviso *caeteris paribus,* that is, "other things being equal." In fact, this is the recognition that things are not always equal and classical laws are realized according to schedules of statistical probabilities.

In the notes of 1951 Lonergan refutes the determinist viewpoint that would reduce the concrete world to a full set of abstractions:

> Misconception of concrete; it is not a full set of abstractions
> Misconception of explanation: initial situation unexplained, and so all subsequent concrete sit unexplained

---

[4]Ibid., 91 (68).
[5]*Collection*, 127.

Irrelevant to world in which we live: nothing in conclusions that not in premises; something in subsequent not in prior situations

Misconception of science. Prophet predicting miracles is not science. Science is comprehensive. Grasp of whole by clustering insights, mastery.

The reality of indeterminacy in chance aggregates opens the way to the statistical phase of empirical method. He illustrates indeterminacy through the analysis of a cast of dice:

not necessarily in data or in description of data   slow-motion picture of dice
possibility of assigning trajectory and momentum of every movement
but not possible to assign law governing relations between successive elements
just opposite of classical supposition

The intelligibility of the statistical phase of empirical method is probability:

Chance aggregate means aggregate as not understood
Probability aggregate means same as understood.

Probability means that the divergence of the concrete from the systematic must be non-systematic. An example: in a truly random outcome in the casting dice there is no *systematic* influence favoring any one of thirty-six possibilities. Any deviation from the probability 1/36 will be non-systematic; if there were a systematic deviation from that probability, one would search for a cause, such as the loading of the dice.

Later in the notes Lonergan speaks of the form of groupings of aggregates in the concrete universe as "emergent probability":

probability, because actual occurrence is governed by probability; emergent probability because events that actually occur affect the expectations of what is to occur.

The notes also have a section on "Things." In *Insight* Lonergan defines a "thing" as a unity, identity, whole differentiated by descriptive and explanatory conjugates. Here he speaks of the identity in temporally distinct data:

Differentiation by descriptive or conjugate terms; by probable expectations; individual, revert to data.
Unity and identity: presupposed by inquiry (change not annihilation, substitution, advent), by verification, application
3 invariants: identity, conjugate, frequency.

4. "Radical Intellectual Conversion"

In these notes the section entitled "Radical Intellectual Conversion" is immediately preceded by a section on "the pure desire to know." Such a pure desire to know, Lonergan states, is the wonder prior to our questions. It is not inhibited by a lack of interest in understanding. Nor is it interested only up to a point and for the sake of something practical. There is to this pure desire a "disinterestedness," that characterizes genuine science. It reflects the unlimited character of our ability to question and our desire for the absoluteness of truth. Error results from the interference of inhibiting and reinforcing desires with this pure desire to know.

Lonergan then makes a first approximation to explaining intellectual conversion by describing it as "turning from what seems to what is." Intellectual conversion is *incidental* if it is a turning "from a particular error to a particular truth."[6] In a somewhat extended sense Lonergan in his later years would often apply the term "intellectual conversion" to the great cultural break-throughs in the world of theory: for example, the Greek achievement in philosophy and the Christian Church's break-through to a systematic defense of the divinity of Christ at the Council of Nicea.[7] Lonergan often seemed to imply that the meaning of intellectual conversion varied according to the level of cultural development. That is, what at an earlier "stage of meaning" might qualify as an intellectual conversion, might at a later stage itself require a "radical intellectual conversion."[8]

In these notes *radical intellectual conversion* is an intellectual conversion that appropriates the dynamics of incidental intellectual conversion. Intellectual conversion is *radical* if it makes explicit and deliberate the pure desire to know and it acknowledges the existence and influence of inhibiting and reinforcing desires. Radical intellectual conversion effects the transition from the spontaneous to the explicit and the deliberate. It is, in fact, what Lonergan's whole work aims at ac-

---

[6]In some scattered notes found in the Lonergan archives and probably dating from around the time of "Intelligence and Reality" Lonergan writes of "spontaneous and systematic intellectual conversions. Spontaneous intellectual conversions are particular instances in which a person rejects what seems to be or what he wants to be and accepts what truly is. . . . . Systematic intellectual conversion is another matter. For it is a change, turning, not from a particular error to a particular though strange truth but from one general orientation to another general orientation. . . . It is turning from the world of sense to the universe of being." Quoted by Frederick Crowe in *Lonergan Studes Newsletter* 14 (March 1993) 10.

[7]Cf. "The Origins of Christian Realism," *Second Collection*, 239–61.

[8]Cf. *Method in Theology* on the "stages of meaning," 85–99.

complishing: not just the correction of one or other error, but the explicitation of the dynamic principle for combatting any error. Thus, fidelity to the pure desire to know effectively combats other inhibiting or reinforcing desires. It is not an adherence to some particular truth, but rather to the very principle whence truth is reached. Ultimately, it issues in a radical intellectual conversion.

By emphasizing the need for a radical intellectual conversion rooted in the pure desire to know, there is no danger of one's method being a mask for some particular favorite doctrine. The procedure is also invulnerable. As he writes in the 1951 notes, "to object is to appeal to obscurantism, to stupidity, to silliness."

Lonergan goes on to contrast radical intellectual conversion with Descartes' universal methodic doubt. The latter method is unreasonable for it involves an equal suspicion for the true and the false. If carried out, such doubt would result in mental infancy: "acquired habits of mind do not await our bidding to vanish." It also involves an excessive commitment: doubt everything means prove everything and for people in every walk of life such a "claim to omni-competence results in a charge of incompetence." *De facto*, Descartes did not himself return to mental infancy and become a pre-Socratic.

Finally, Lonergan in the same notes describes the function of radical intellectual conversion. First, it is a bludgeon against obscurantism, stupidity, silliness. Psychologically, it pulls one out of the flow of percepts, the memories and anticipations added to data that come from the orientation of efficiently and economically dealing with one's environment. It pulls one out of what Lonergan will later call "one's own little world." It pulls one out of the attitude that the world of sense is the criterion of reality; it pulls one away from deprecatory remarks about the "bloodless ballet of categories"; it pulls one away from spontaneous utilitarianism and pragmatism. Positively, the function of radical intellectual conversion is to head us for "whatever is intelligently conceived and reasonably affirmed." It is related to Aquinas' "natural desire to see God."

It seems obvious that in these notes "radical intellectual conversion" plays a role parallel to what will be the center of *Insight:* the explicit self-affirmation of the knower: "By 'self-affirmation of the knower' is meant that the self as affirmed is characterized by such occurrences as sensing, perceiving, imagining, inquiring, understanding, formulating, reflecting, grasping the unconditioned, and affirming."[9] In *Insight* all of these acts that constitute the content of

9*Insight,* 343 (319).

the self-affirmation of the knower flow from the pure desire to know. To the extent that the pure desire to know is operative, it issues in these acts and this content of self-affirmation. In effect, it is what the 1951 notes call "radical intellectual conversion": making explicit and deliberate the pure desire to know as the way of turning away from other inhibiting and reinforcing desires toward "whatever is intelligently conceived and reasonably affirmed." Such a radical intellectual conversion can provide a universally acceptable starting point for philosophy inasmuch as each philosophy is set forth as true.

In these notes radical intellectual conversion is also connected with the section on "the starting place of philosophy." There he says that philosophy begins with the invitation to radical intellectual conversion. It takes any person where they are and invites them to advance toward whatever is intelligently grasped and reasonably affirmed. Philosophy cannot be based on the arbitrary decisions of each person; it must be scientific and, as such, based on a fundamental set of concepts and relations. Such a basic set of concepts and relations must be such that:

a) Relations fix concepts and concepts fix relations.
b) Relations are not free constructions as in mathematics but have experiential basis as in empirical sciences.
c) Relations are universally accessible, for science is universally accessible.
d) Relations have a certain inevitability; they cannot be evaded . . .
e) Relations and concepts must be fruitful; supply a key to the integration of the whole sweep of human knowledge.
f) Relations and concepts must not be subject to radical revision; it must be possible to add refinements, developments; it must not be possible to change the whole shape of the picture.

Lonergan's thesis in these notes is that such a set of relations and concepts is supplied by an analysis of our knowing and by descriptive and "terminal," that is, explanatory, categories.

What is significant in these notes is the insistence on the fact that the self-knowledge generated by radical intellectual conversion is an explanatory knowledge. The method of "implicit definition" is invoked. Here this technique is applied to cognitional structure as such.

> We began from description of insight but moved on to analysis; i.e., relating insight to images and inquiry and definitions and explanatory systems. End result was a set of terms defined by the relations of a scheme; level of experience (sense data, perceptual images, free images; data of consciousness); level of intelligence (inquiry, direct understanding, formulation); level of reflection (questions for reflection, grasp of uncondi-

tioned, judgment). Each element explained by relations to others in terms of presupposition and complementation.[10]

These "relations" between the elements are experiential and universally accessible, that is, everyone has the conscious experience of these dynamisms of experiencing, understanding, and judging. The point is to arrive at an accurate knowledge of these dynamisms of human knowing. These relations also possess a certain inevitability, not on the level of the contents of our concepts and judgments, but rather on the prior level of the dynamism involved in coming up with any concepts or judgments at all. In the notes he invokes Aristotle's technique of dealing with the skeptic:

> Go to the root of the Aristotelian technique. What is to be done with the disputant that denies principle of contradiction? Get him to talk. I.e. intelligent and reasonable talking will make a man realize that he is committed to principle of contradiction. More deeply, it will make him realize that he cannot avoid experience, effort to understand, formulation of what he understands, reflection and judgment on formulation.

Just by being the person that one is, one is committed to experience, to intelligence, to reasonableness:

> Hermit can cut down on experience, but he cannot eliminate it. . . .
> One cannot intelligently repudiate intelligence; and one is committed by being what one is to reject unintelligent repudiation.
> One cannot reasonably repudiate reasonableness; and one is committed by being what one is to reject unreasonable rejection.

From such a procedure one can arrive at a metaphysics that moves beyond descriptive categories that describe what we do not yet understand to "terminal" or explanatory categories that implicitly define the objective differentiations within the universe of being. For example, the inevitability of the distinction between act, form, and potency arises from the inevitability of our cognitional process:

> Between Act and Form. Act corresponds to the "Yes" of judgment; it is what can be known only by the "Yes." Form corresponds to the intelligibility grasped and formulated by understanding.

> Between Form and Potency. Form corresponds to the intelligibility grasped by understanding. Potency accounts for the empirical residue, to what is abstracted from in all direct understanding. Instance, incidental, non-systematic divergence, continuum.

[10]Cf. ibid., 298–300 (273–74).

Inevitability restricted to proportionate beings. Angels without potency, just act and form. God, pure act.

The fruitfulness of this approach is that such relations are embedded in the correct understanding of any object on which we have data:

Embraces all positive science and mathematics.
Provides basis for human science.
Admits development to natural and dogmatic theology.

Such a procedure is beyond radical revision—for which we would need a new type of knowing. It combines the empirical with the *a priori*.

5. Objective Knowledge of Being

The notes of 1951 explicitate the notion of "being" as the objective of the pure and unrestricted desire to know. Such a pure desire penetrates all the contents of our knowledge; it places each content in the context of all the others; and it is open to ever further acquisitions. The pure notion of being is the pure desire to know inasmuch as it heads towards the absolutely universal and the absolutely concrete:

Plato, "If you ask because you do not know the answer, how will you recognize the answer when you get it?"
Process has begun; will proceed in determinate fashion to reach result under determinate conditions.

The composite notion of being is the pure desire to know in conjunction with the elements that leads toward answers:

Being is universe; a being is what pertains to universe. But what is universe? Depends on your formulations and judgments; and these are part of the composite notion of being.

Radical intellectual conversion opens one to the analogous notion of the composite notion of being. As Lonergan's early intellectual conversion was rooted in an understanding of the real distinction of essence and existence, so here he affirms the distinction within being of essence and existence:

Composite notion of being is analogous.
Notion is analogous 1) if component elements 2) if relation between components and 3) if this relation defines notion.
Notion of being has components "Is it?" and "It is."
There is a relation between them: essential to existential

Objectivity is rooted in the pure desire to know issuing in radical intellectual conversion:

Radical intellectual conversion commits us to realism; for conversion is to intelligently grasped and reasonably affirmed, therefore to what is known in true judgment.

In a realist philosophy, as distinct from a relativism, an empiricism or an obscurantism, an object is what is known in true judgment; hence "object" and "being" are equivalent terms. Lonergan rejects "the problem of the bridge," of getting from "in here" to "out there" as a false conception of the objectivity of human knowing:

> Realist objectivity is transcendent.
> Object is being, everything, all of everything.
> Nothing is left over from which to cross; no possibility of immanence.
> Object is being; but differentiation of being from within; hence "I" and "thing" are known through differentiating "being."
> Knowledge of real subject, real object, and real distinction is a set of judgments.
> "I am" "It is" "I am not it" "I make these judgments."

As he had affirmed in *Verbum*, such transcendence is rooted in the fact that our intellect is a created participation in uncreated light.

> *lumen intellectus nostri est participatio quaedam creata lucis increatae;* Thomist transposition of Augustinian vision of eternal reasons in incommutable light.

6. Conversion from Confrontationism

Opposed to such realism are many and varied forms of "confrontationism": roughly, that knowing is or should be "taking a look." Under this Lonergan again lists virtually all the schools of philosophy outside of critical realism. The "look" at the basis of confrontationism may be sensitive perception as in the various forms of empiricism, or some intellectual intuition that Kant sought for in vain and that naive realists dogmatically assert. It presupposes that human knowing is complete prior to judgment; judgment is merely affixing a rubber stamp on knowing as already complete. For confrontationism, knowledge is not primarily by identity between subject and object, a perfection in the subject, but dualistic: the object over against the subject.

For confrontationism the analysis of knowing is an impossible undertaking: to analyze knowing is to eliminate it. To take it apart is to make it impossible to put the pieces together again. This was, of course, Etienne Gilson's concern about any analysis of the conscious subject in Catholic philosophy, any "transcendental turn" to the subject.

The source of confrontationism is the fact that the human person is born an animal, and achieves animal integration spontaneously. For this reason the human animal is prone to make intelligence and reason merely another organ at the service of animal nature. Our orientation tends toward successful living in the world of sense.

On the other hand, there is for the human person the possibility of another orientation: that is, toward the universe of being by means of the pure desire to know and radical intellectual conversion. This is the significance of the "Platonist flight from sense, the Pythagorean five years of silence," and Lonergan adds in his notes, "relativity and quantum mechanics." The weakness of confrontationism is that it leads to fictitious intuitions, falsifications of knowledge, disappearance of knowing in immanence, idealism. As Lonergan writes,

> It can be asserted. It cannot be concluded. No reasons can be given for it except assertion that otherwise knowing would be impossible. No reasons can be given, because for confrontationist confrontationism has to be primitive and beyond analysis or explanation.

Significantly, as the young Lonergan had asserted in the Keeler review, so in these notes he asserts that confrontationism cannot deal with the fact of error:

> What is intuited a has to be there to be intuited (one cannot intuit what is not there) b cannot be corrected by second intuition (why should second look be any better than first, or if better, then why not third still better, fourth still better &c.)

Most of all, confrontationism leads to the arbitrariness found in so many philosophical schools:

> What are we confronted with?

> Most obviously sense presentations. If only that, then materialism.
> Essences, then Plato, Avicenna, Scotus, etc.
> Objects of thought, then idealism, immanence, with reaction to irrationalism.

7. Conversion from Mechanistic Science

A particular instance of confrontationism is found in the mechanical model of modern science which has had a profound effect on modern philosophy. In the 1951 notes Lonergan writes,

> Understand modern philosophy from influence on it of modern science; from recent advance of science return to phil. perennis.

Elsewhere Lonergan would say that scientific thought has provided the "undertow" to modern philosophy. To a great extent such an undertow has consisted in a mechanistic view of the universe. Here Lonergan brings out that such a mechanical model of the universe is rooted in the scientist's tendency to attempt to representatively imagine the objects of his inquiry:

> I see phenomena in cathode tube, cloud chamber, spectroscope, pointer reading; infer electron; very definite tendency to add to identity a set of imaginable qualities.
> Unverifiable, unless electron can be seen.

The scientist must be content with imagination as heuristic, as symbolizing the objects of his questions:

> Imagination as representative: no good. Scientist is scientist because hypothesis verified, not because of imagination; imagination for poets artists orators.

Like the presupposition of Kantian thought, modern science has been plagued by a confrontational model of knowledge, a model contradicted by recent scientific advances:

> Kant: denial that mechanical model, representative image, could be confrontationist knowing of thing in itself.

> Inability to reach significance of "being" because of failure to see that judgment results from grasp of unconditioned.

> Scientific thought has undergone a radical change.

> Relativity and Quantum mechanics eliminate representative images. Only remaining possibility is "being."

8. Philosophy and Radical Intellectual Conversion

Lonergan concludes his notes on "Intelligence and Reality" with a section entitled "What is the good of Philosophy?" He begins by saying:

> The unrestricted desire to know introduces the infinite into human life. Makes possible knowledge of the universe, conceptions and plans for the good of the universe, the unleashing of vast human energies in the executions of such plans, attainment of such ideals.

On the other hand, without the actual self-knowledge brought about by successful philosophy one's existence is precarious:

> Subject is thrown back on experience of self a) as self- regarding center b) as capable of ecstatic devotion to cause or person. Oscillates violently between extremes: a) contempt of liberal bourgeoisie b) materialist ideal with religious devotion c) new bourgeoisie of officials kept in line by delation and purges.

Only the pure desire to know—such as Augustine became aware of in reading Cicero's *Hortensius*—can help the person transcend stupid selfishness on the one hand, and blind and ecstatic devotion on the other. The pure desire to know is an achievement in the personal subject; but it is the root of objectivity and impartiality:

> Its goal is serene and objective apprehension of universe, of self in universe, of role of self in universe. Its consequence is agape, love of intelligible order of whole; neither self-regarding nor ecstatic; but joy in both good it brings me and the price I must pay.

Lonergan relates such philosophy rooted in radical intellectual conversion to the need for moral and religious conversion:

> Still philosophy does not provide final answer. Man can conceive an ideal for individual and society, but he cannot execute it. Necessity of grace. Xtian dogma; and secular experience: Ovid, Video meliora proboque, deteriora autem sequor. Man can become confused, fail to reach even philosophy. Descartes and rationalists. Kant and idealists. Kierkegaard and existentialists.

Ultimately the answer is religious conversion. Lonergan quotes a text from Romans 5 that he will often quote in his reflections on theology:

> Divine childhood: live by divine revelation and by divine grace. New knowledge beyond mastery of human understanding; centered in Xt our Lord. New love "poured forth in your hearts by Holy Spirit who is given you."

Chapter Twelve

Insight and Intellectual Conversion

I have recounted the historical origins of Lonergan's thought in his early interest in logic and mathematics and in the writings of Newman, Plato, Augustine, Aristotle, and Aquinas. The many hints and clues from these sources as to the nature of the human mind came together in Lonergan's intellectual conversion of the mid-1930s. That conversion found expression in his writings on Aquinas in the late 1930s and the 1940s. That event found expression in a growing focus on modern scientific method and in his notes on radical intellectual conversion in 1951. There he focusses on a systematic account of human knowledge, what he later will define as characteristic of the third stage of meaning, the stage of interiority.

By 1953, when he was scheduled to depart from Canada to teach in Rome, Lonergan had finished the writing of *Insight*. "I worked on *Insight* from 1949 to 1953. During the first three years my intention was an exploration of methods generally in preparation for a study of the method of theology. But in 1952 it became clear that I was due to start teaching at the Gregorian University in Rome in 1953, so I changed my plan and decided to round off what I had done and publish it under the title *Insight, A Study of Human Understanding.*[1]

Strangely enough, Lonergan never uses the phrase "intellectual conversion" in *Insight*. Even though the term "radical intellectual conversion" had played such a prominent role in his notes on "Intelligence and Reality," the term is not found in his "great work," *Insight*. Why? Perhaps because of the religious overtones of the word "conversion"? After all, *Insight* is written not just for believers, but for "any sufficiently cultured consciousness."

Lonergan states in the introduction, the aim of the book is pedagogical: to bring a person to the "startling" and "strange" breakthrough involved in coming to understand the structures of their own knowing. His primary aim is neither logical nor metaphysical, but rather

[1]*Second Collection*, 268.

a development that can begin in any sufficiently cultured consciousness, that expands in virtue of the dynamic tendencies of that consciousness itself, and that heads through an understanding of all understanding to a basic understanding of all that can be understood.[2]

It is obvious that Lonergan is aiming at effecting in the reader of *Insight* a similar breakthrough to the one he had experienced when he grasped the real distinction between essence and existence in connection with Bernard Leeming's course in the 1930s. But what is a "sufficiently cultured consciousness" that he envisions as the audience of *Insight?* There is no doubt that for Lonergan in *Insight* a "sufficiently cultured consciousness" is one that is familiar with the modern sciences. A "sufficiently cultured consciousness" today is a consciousness quite different than that of the early Christians; it is a consciousness quite different than the Aristotelian consciousness. Its most outstanding characteristic is the emergence of the autonomous modern sciences that are independent of modern philosophy. That is the reason why so much of the early chapters of *Insight* consist in the analysis of scientific and mathematical consciousness.

The ultimate aim of *Insight* is exceedingly high and wide, eventually encompassing metaphysical questions: questions about the nature of the universe and the existence of God; questions about the spirituality, immortality, and freedom of the human person, etc. But clarity on those issues begins with the clarity on one's understanding of one's own understanding. The point is to identify the act of understanding in one's own experience and to come to distinguish it from all the other mental operations that precede and follow from it. The point is also to discern and to distinguish between the act of understanding and all the other "existential" elements that can enter in and interfere with that act of understanding. "The point here, as elsewhere, is appropriation; the point is to discover, to identify, to become familiar with the activities of one's own intelligence; the point is to become able to discriminate with ease and from personal conviction between one's purely intellectual convictions and the manifold of other, 'existential' concerns that invade and mix and blend with the operations of intellect to render it ambivalent and its pronouncements ambiguous."[3]

Our aim in this chapter on *Insight* is not to review the whole book, an impossible undertaking. *Insight* is a work that must be read and wrestled with on its own. I myself have read it through a number of

[2]*Insight*, 22 (xxviii).
[3]Ibid., 14 (xix).

times and each time it is a new book filled with new treasures. Our aim here is rather to point out the significance of *Insight* in the light of Lonergan's own early intellectual conversion. Drawing mostly from the introduction, we aim to point out the significance of *Insight* as Lonergan's invitation to others to undergo the same intellectual transformation that took place in him within the mid-1930s.

1. Resolving "A Psychological Problem"

In the introduction to *Insight* Lonergan states that there is a major "psychological problem" involved in the process of coming to understand our own understanding. The problem, as he describes it elsewhere, is that we develop as animals before we develop as human beings and consequently, from our earliest years, we confuse our properly human knowing with the knowing we share with other animals. The confusion between these two kinds of knowing is at the origin of the various schools of philosophy.

> In each of us there exist two different kinds of knowledge. They are juxtaposed in Cartesian dualism with its rational *Cogito, ergo sum* and with its unquestioning extroversion to substantial extension. They are separated and alienated in the subsequent rationalist and empiricist philosophies. They are brought together again to cancel each other in Kantian criticism. If these statements approximate the facts, then the question of human knowledge is not whether it exists but what precisely are its two diverse forms and what are the relations between them.[4]

Because these two types of knowing exist in us, there result two main types of philosophical realism, one half-animal and half-human that is the basis for materialism and the philosophies of immanentism, idealism, relativism; the other a fully human realism, that has been called, in the context of our times, a critical realism. Speaking of what elsewhere he will call intellectual conversion, Lonergan says:

> For the appropriation of one's own rational self-consciousness, which has been so stressed in this Introduction, is not an end in itself but rather a beginning. It is a necessary beginning, for unless one breaks the duality in one's knowing, one doubts that understanding correctly is knowing. Under the pressure of that doubt, either one will sink into the bog of a knowing that is without understanding, or else cling to understanding but sacrifice knowing on the altar of an immanentism, an idealism, a relativism. From the horns of that dilemma one escapes only through the discovery (*and one has not made it yet if one has no clear memory of its startling strangeness*) that there are two quite different realisms, that

[4]Ibid., 11–12 (xvii).

there is an incoherent realism, half animal and half human, that poses
as a half-way house between materialism and idealism and, on the other
hand, that there is an intelligent and reasonable realism between which
and materialism the half-way house is idealism.[5]

Recall here Lonergan's early fear that he was becoming an idealist
when he broke through from his early nominalism. I experienced that
same fear as I wrestled with *Insight*.

Consequently, according to Lonergan, a major psychological
problem exists in our knowledge of ourselves, and because of that psychological problem, *Insight* is written from a pedagogical point of view:
to bring about the slow deliberate identification of the psychological
problem and its decisive resolution in the fully adequate affirmation
of ourselves as knowers. "The hard fact is that the personal psychological problem cannot be solved by the ordinary procedure of affirming
the propositions that are true and denying the propositions that are
false, for the true meaning of true propositions always tends to be mis-
apprehended by a consciousness that has not yet discovered what an
Augustine took years and modern science centuries to discover."[6] What
is needed is an overcoming of the psychological problem through an
adequate understanding of human understanding. *Insight* aims at
bringing about a development in the human person as he or she works
through the book. Lonergan constantly asks the reader to attend to
his or her own experience as they understand or fail to understand,
to substitute one's own examples for the examples used in the book,
to attend most of all to oneself in one's own conscious activities.

On a first level, the book contains sentences on mathematics, on science,
on common sense, on metaphysics. On a second level, the meaning of
all these sentences, their intention and significance, are to be grasped
only by going beyond the scraps of mathematics or science or common
sense or metaphysics to the dynamic, cognitional structure that is exemplified in knowing them. On a third level, the dynamic, cognitional
structure to be reached is not the transcendental ego of Fichtean specu-
lation, nor the abstract pattern of relations verifiable in Tom and Dick
and Harry, but the personally appropriated structure of one's own experiencing, one's own intelligent inquiry and insights, one's own critical
reflection and judging and deciding. The crucial issue is an experimental
issue, and the experiment will be performed not publicly but privately.
It will consist in one's own rational consciousness clearly and distinctly
taking possession of itself as rational self-consciousness. Up to that
decisive achievement, all leads. From it, all follows. No one else, no

[5]Ibid., 22 (xxviii). My emphases.
[6]Ibid., 17 (xxii–xxiii).

matter what his knowledge or his eloquence, no matter what his logical rigour or his persuasiveness, can do it for you.[7]

2. The "Already out There Now Real"

As we have noted, in the 1940s, after so many years in the study of the ancients, particularly Thomas Aquinas, Lonergan took the methodologies of the sciences as the explicit focus of his reflection. Why? Well, for one reason, one could not just ignore the all-pervasive presence of the sciences in the modern world. Science was—and is— the paradigm for what it means "to know" in our world. Indeed, the very success of the modern sciences was due to their declaring their independence from the ancient Aristotelian science that penetrated into the warp and woof of Aquinas' thought.[8] Modern science declared its independence from philosophy in general and from Aristotelian philosophy in particular. The basic thrust of modern science is empirical: to stake out the realm of sensible data as its own and to exclude from its purview any questions that do not have sensible consequences.

The problem for Christians, of course, has been that the successes of modern science seemed to support a materialist philosophy of the universe. On the other hand, in Lonergan's view the very development of modern physical sciences was leading beyond this view of science. Consequently, among the most prominent aspects of *Insight* are the numerous examples from modern mathematics and modern science. Just the sight of the differential equations can strike terror into someone who picks up the 785-page book for the first time! Nevertheless, in his introduction Lonergan gives three reasons for his prominent use of mathematical and scientific examples.

The first reason, as we mentioned previously, is clarity and exactitude: if one seeks a clear and distinct apprehension of the activities that mark the different levels of consciousness,

> . . . then one must prefer the fields of intellectual endeavor in which the greatest care is devoted to exactitude and, in fact, the greatest exactitude is attained. For this reason, then, I have felt obliged to begin my account of insight and its expansion with mathematical and scientific illustrations and, while I would grant that essentially the same activities can be illustrated from the ordinary use of intelligence that is named common sense, I also submit that it would be impossible for common sense to grasp and say what precisely common sense happens to illustrate.[9]

[7]Ibid., 12–13 (xviii).
[8]Cf. *Third Collection*, 52.
[9]*Insight*, 14 (xx).

The second reason for invoking scientific examples is the *criterion of the real* implicit in scientific operations. In a passage similar to the one above, Lonergan links Augustine's intellectual breakthrough in the spring of 386 with the project of modern science.

> For the present enterprise is concerned to unravel an ambiguity and to eliminate an ambivalence. St. Augustine of Hippo narrates that it took him years to make the discovery that the name, real, might have a different connotation from the name, body. Or, to bring the point nearer home, one might say that it has taken modern science four centuries to make the discovery that the objects of its inquiry need not be imaginable entities moving through imaginable processes in an imaginable space-time. The fact that a Plato attempted to communicate through his dialogues, the fact that an Augustine eventually learnt from the writers whom, rather generally, he refers to as Platonists, has lost its antique flavor and its apparent irrelevance to the modern mind. Even before Einstein and Heisenberg it was clear enough that the world described by scientists was strangely different from the world depicted by artists and inhabited by men of common sense. But it was left to twentieth-century physicists to envisage the possibility that the objects of their science were to be reached only by severing the umbilical cord that tied them to the maternal imagination of man.[10]

In the early chapters of *Insight*, Lonergan's analysis of scientific consciousness is at the same time a refutation of mechanistic determinism. The key issue is the personal and systematic appropriation of the distinction between imagination and insight. The key issue is the distinction between a naive understanding of knowing as "taking a good look" and a differentiated understanding of human knowing as constituted by activities of experiencing, understanding, and judging.

> The problem set by the two types of knowing is, then, not a problem of elimination but a problem of critical distinction. For the difficulty lies, not in either type of knowing by itself, but in the confusion that arises when one shifts unconsciously from one type to the other. Animals have no epistemological problems. Neither do scientists as long as they stick to their task of observing, forming hypotheses, and verifying. The perennial source of nonsense is that, after the scientist has verified his hypothesis, he is likely to go a little further and tell the layman what, approximately, scientific reality looks like![11]

The confusion of insight and visual imagination has been at the root of the disastrous interpretations of modern science during the last

[10]Ibid., 15 (xx–xxi).
[11]Ibid., 278 (253).

several centuries. But the development of modern classical and statistical science during the last several centuries has absolutely demanded this distinction. Thus, Lonergan points out the world of difference between a systematic unification of physical laws and an imaginative synthesis. "As systematic unification does not include imaginative synthesis, so it does not even guarantee its possibility. It is true enough that images are necessary for the emergence of insights, but images may be not representative but symbolic, not pictures of the visible universe but mathematical notations on pieces of paper."[12] The point is that we cannot reach a representative image of what scientific reality looks like. Scientific explanation of its very essence transcends imaginative representation: it relates things to each other in their systematic correlations and not to our visual imagination.

In *Insight* Lonergan analyzes the various canons or implicit rules in the practice of scientists that keep science on the track of explanatory understanding. One such canon, the canon of parsimony, forbids the empirical scientist from affirming what, as an empirical scientist, he does not know.[13] This has a relevance to the human tendency, present in the scientist as in anyone else, to try to visually imagine the objects of his science. For

> the canon of parsimony excludes any problem concerning the picture of objects too small to be sensed. For the image as image can be verified only by the occurrence of the corresponding sensation. Thus, the visual image of a small ball can be verified only by seeing a small ball, and the visual image of a wave can be verified only by seeing a wave. When the sensations neither occur nor can occur, all that can be verified are certain equations and the terms implicitly defined by such equations.[14]

The progress of empirical science is from description, that is, the relationships of things to us and to our senses, to explanation, the relationships of things among themselves. This possibility of moving from description to explanation implies the possibility of grasping "things," that is, "unities-identities-wholes" in which both descriptive and explanatory attributes or conjugates can be verified. It is understanding's ability to grasp "things" that makes it possible to go from description to explanation and from scientific explanation back to the concrete implementation of scientific insights.

But what is a thing? For starters, it is not a "body." A body is the correlative of our extroverted biological consciousness. It is, as

[12]Ibid., 116 (93).
[13]Ibid., 102 f. (78ff.).
[14]Ibid., 123 (99).

Lonergan says elsewhere, "the sure and firm-set earth on which I tread."[15] It is the sensible environment that is already constituted as the objective of biological desires and fears. It is "out there," full of sensuous dangers and opportunities. It is as "real" as a saucer of milk is real for a kitten while a painting of a saucer of milk, still less, the chemical analysis of milk, is, for the kitten, "unreal." "By a 'body' is meant primarily a focal point of extroverted biological anticipation and attention. It is an 'already out there now real,' where these terms have their meanings fixed solely by elements within sensitive experience and so without any use of intelligent and reasonable questions and answers."[16]

And yet human understanding can grasp dimensions of reality far beyond the possibilities of a kitten. A chemical analysis of milk can grasp real dimensions of milk that can have profound and far-reaching implications for the whole human family. The practice of the sciences illustrates that human understanding can penetrate to the "inwardness" of things—an imaginative term used in *Verbum* to indicate understanding's ability to go beyond imagination.

There are, then, two kinds of human knowing. One is a mixture of human knowing with the knowing we share with the higher animals; the other a distinctively human knowing. It adds understanding and, as we shall see, judgment, to human sensation and imagination.

> The problem set by the two types of knowing is, then, not a problem of elimination but a problem of critical distinction. For the difficulty lies, not in either type of knowing by itself, but in the confusion that arises when one shifts unconsciously from one type to the other. Animals have no epistemological problems. Neither do scientists as long as they stick to their task of observing, forming hypotheses, and verifying. The perennial source of nonsense is that, after the scientist has verified his hypothesis, he is likely to go a little further and tell the layman what, approximately, scientific reality looks like! Already we have attacked the unverifiable image; but now we can see the origin of the strange urge to foist upon mankind unverifiable images. For both the scientist and the layman, besides being intelligent and reasonable, also are animals. To them as animals, a verified hypothesis is just a jumble of words or symbols. What they want is an elementary knowing of the "really real," if not through sense, at least by imagination.[17]

This is the "psychological problem" spoken of in the introduction to *Insight.* Such is the origin of the "cover story" that has accompanied

---

[15]*Verbum*, 20.
[16]*Insight*, 279 (254).
[17]Ibid., 278 (253).

the successes of the natural sciences during the last few centuries. Mechanistic reductionism has interpreted the sciences as giving us pictures of the "already out there now real" atoms and sub-atomic elements that are the ultimate constituents of the universe. And the "cover story" continues as Carl Sagan repeats it for popular television audiences and Stephen Hawking writes a book on a popular "history of time" that, for the benefit of his audiences, contains no mathematical formulae! But the meaning of Einstein's relativity theory and Heisenberg's uncertainty principle is that an explanatory account of our universe transcends any imaginative synthesis we can invent. And the reason for this is that understanding transcends imagination. As Lonergan expressed the issue in 1955:

> Further, while this immanence of intelligibility in the sensible has been a potent factor in the traditional attachment of scientists to a mechanist view of reality, the outstanding fact of the contemporary scientific situation is that this deep-rooted tendency is now being overcome by the inner development of science itself. From the days of Galileo the real object of the scientist was thought to be some imaginable stuff or particle or radiation that moved imaginably in some imaginable space and time. But relativity has eliminated the imaginability of scientifically conceived space and time; and quantum mechanics has eliminated the imaginability of basic processes. Whether he likes it or not, the scientist has transcended imagination.[18]

3. Consciousness not an "Inner Look"

A third reason for the prominent use of scientific examples is that scientific method itself is just a specialized application of the object of Lonergan's interest, that is, the dynamic structure immanent and recurrently operative in human cognitional activity. The first half of *Insight*, then, is an analysis of myriad examples of both scientific and common sense knowing in terms of the three levels of cognitional activity: experiencing, understanding, and judging. Each level is defined implicitly: that is, by its dynamic relationships to the other levels. Thus, human understanding presupposes experience and completes it and is itself presupposed by experience and completed by judgment.

Bringing together all the various influences on his own thought, both ancient and modern, Lonergan sees all their positive elements exemplified in the elements of scientific method:

> Accordingly, it will be from the structural and dynamic features of scientific method that we shall approach and attempt to cast into the unity

---

[18]*Collection*, 138.

of a single perspective such apparently diverse elements as: 1) Plato's point in asking how the inquirer recognizes truth when he reaches what, as an inquirer, he did not know, 2) the intellectualist (though not the conceptualist) meaning of the abstraction of form from material conditions, 3) the psychological manifestation of Aquinas' natural desire to know God by his essence, 4) what Descartes was struggling to convey in his incomplete *Regulae ad directionem ingenii*, 5) what Kant conceived as *a priori* synthesis, and 6) what is named the finality of intellect in J. Maréchal's vast labor on *Le Point de départ de la métaphysique*.[19]

It is an amazing program: to use scientific method as a means of illustrating what ancient and modern philosophers had sought to express about the nature of our human spirits. It is a tremendously ambitious program: from an analysis of mathematical and scientific understanding to the wider context of common sense understanding with its personal and social implications; after treating things and human judgment to move on to affirm the invariant structure implicit in all knowing; to treat the notions of being and objectivity and the metaphysics and ethics that flow from the structure of human knowing; to conclude with an analysis of general transcendent knowledge, the existence of God implicit in our human knowing; and finally, to consider special transcendent knowledge, the structure of a divine solution to the problem of human living.

Hence, after working through chapters on the dynamic structure of experiencing, understanding, and judging present in scientific and common sense examples, Lonergan asks how it is possible for us to know ourselves as such. What is meant by "introspection"? Do we look into ourselves and intuit our inner being? To this, with more than a touch of irony, Lonergan replies: "Hence, while some of our readers may possess the rather remarkable power of looking into themselves and intuiting things quite clearly and distinctly, we shall not base our case upon their success. For, after all, there may well exist other readers that, like the writer, find looking into themselves rather unrewarding."[20] As he says elsewhere: "Thus if knowing is just looking, then knowing knowing will be looking at looking."[21]

On the contrary, human consciousness is not some kind of "inner look." It is, rather, our presence to ourselves on various levels that makes it possible to ask questions about our human knowing and deciding. It is the reality of consciousness that makes it possible for the reader to know whether what has been written is true. "To affirm

[19]*Insight*, 16 (xxii).
[20]Ibid., 344 (320).
[21]*Collection*, 208.

consciousness is to affirm that cognitional process is not merely a procession of contents but also a succession of acts. It is to affirm that the acts differ radically from such unconscious acts as the metabolism of one's cells, the maintenance of one's organs, the multitudinous biological processes that one learns about through the study of contemporary medical science."[22]

It is this experiential "self-presence" on various levels that constitutes the underlying unity of our cognitional activities.

> Indeed, consciousness is much more obviously of this unity in diverse acts than of the diverse acts, for it is within this unity that the acts are found and distinguished, and it is to the unity that we appeal when we talk about a single field of consciousness and draw a distinction between conscious acts occurring within the field and unconscious acts occurring outside it.[23]

> . . . What do I mean by "I?" The answer is difficult to formulate, but strangely, in some obscure fashion, I know very well what it means without formulation, and by that obscure yet familiar awareness, I find fault with various formulations of what is meant by "I." In other words, "I" has a rudimentary meaning from consciousness and it envisages neither the multiplicity nor the diversity of contents and conscious acts but rather the unity that goes along with them.[24]

4. The Self-Affirmation of the Knower

The first ten chapters of *Insight* present the structure of human knowing in both its scientific and common sense forms as containing the three cognitional levels of experiencing, understanding, and judging. But up to this point, on an explicit level, it has all been just an hypothesis: the hypothesis that every instance of truly human knowing consists of these three levels. Chapter eleven asks if the hypothesis is true: "Chapter eleven asks whether any true judgments occur and it attempts to meet the issue by asking whether I am a knower. The 'I' is the unity-identity-whole given in consciousness; a 'knower' is one who performs the operations investigated in the previous ten chapters; the reader is asked to find out for himself and in himself whether it is a virtually unconditioned that he is a knower. The alternative to an affirmative answer, as presented in *Method in Theology*, is the admission that one is a nonresponsible, nonreasonable, nonintelligent somnambulist."[25]

[22]*Insight*, 344 (320–21).
[23]Ibid., 349 (325).
[24]Ibid., 352 (328).
[25]*Second Collection*, 273.

What Lonergan is seeking to explain is the genuine meaning of introspection and self-knowledge. This process is significantly more complicated than "looking inside ourselves." As he wrote sometime later in an effort to present the core of *Insight:*

> Thus if knowing is just looking, then knowing knowing will be looking at looking. But if knowing is a conjunction of experience, understanding, and judging, then knowing knowing has to be a conjunction of 1) experiencing experience, understanding and judging, 2) understanding one's experience of experience, understanding, and judging, and 3) judging one's understanding of experience, understanding, and judging to be correct. On the latter view there follows at once a distinction between consciousness and self-knowledge. Self-knowledge is the reduplicated structure: it is experience, understanding and judging with respect to experience, understanding and judging. Consciousness, on the other hand, is not knowing knowing but merely experience of knowing.[26]

The process of self-knowledge, or the self-affirmation of the knower, consists in coming to know ourselves by paying attention to and coming to correctly understand those moments of "heightened consciousness" known as understanding and judging. On this account all our cognitional acts can be conscious yet none or only some may be known. Thus, most people know what seeing is, but are mystified when asked what understanding is. They do not know themselves as understanding, still less as judging. Such self-knowledge—the aim of all Lonergan's philosophy—is not easily come by.

> Different cognitional activities are not equally accessible. Experience is of the given. Experience of seeing is to be had only when one actually is seeing. Experience of insight is to be had only when one actually is having an insight. But one has only to open one's eyes and one will see; one has only to open and close one's eyes a number of times to alternate the experience of seeing and not seeing. Insights, on the other hand, cannot be turned on and off in that fashion. To have an insight, one has to be in the process of learning or, at least, one has to reenact in oneself previous processes of learning. While that is not peculiarly difficult, it does require 1) the authenticity that is ready to get down to the elements of a subject 2) close attention to one's own understanding and, equally, one's failing to understand, and 3) the repeated use of personal experiments in which, at first, one is genuinely puzzled and then catches on.[27]

[26]*Collection,* 208.
[27]Ibid., 208–09.

There is a clear distinction, then, between the self-knowledge that comes from genuine introspection and the conscious presence of the subject to himself or herself that is prior to such introspection: "I have been attempting to describe the subject's presence to himself. But the reader, if he tries to find himself as subject, to reach back and, as it were, uncover his subjectivity, cannot succeed. Any such effort is introspecting, attending to the subject; and what is found is, not the subject as subject, but only the subject as object; it is the subject as subject that does the finding."[28]

Lonergan calls this basis of philosophical method "self-appropriation." For our conscious activities are not "out there." We are involved in them whether we want to be or not, and the more we resist this conclusion, the more we employ those same activities to resist it. For these activities of experiencing, understanding, judging, and deciding with their concomitant activities *are* ourselves as empirically, intellectually, and rationally conscious. By them we constitute ourselves in the world.

Proper philosophical method, then, is basically pedagogical: calling attention to the activities that people are constantly engaged in without normally adverting to them. The fact that we are consciously constituted by these levels does not mean that we know them, or still less, live in the light of that knowledge. The central philosophical thrust, then, should be to show that these invariant anticipations and activities of human consciousness are in fact always operative in human living (art, science, common sense living, etc.) in such a way that even their denial involves their employment.

This appeal to the inevitabilities of reasonable self-knowledge is in line with Aristotle's method of analyzing the skeptic's statement that we cannot really know anything. If that were true, he asserts, the skeptic's only recourse would be the mute silence of the vegetable, not statements purporting to be intelligent and reasonable. Similarly, according to Lonergan, a cognitional schema of experience, understanding, and judgment cannot coherently be revised, for the very notion of such a revision implies these three levels of conscious activity.

> A revision appeals to data. It contends that previous theory does not satisfactorily account for all the data. It claims to have reached complementary insights that lead to more accurate statements. It shows that these new statements are either unconditioned or more closely approximate to the unconditioned than previous statements. Now, if in fact revision is as described, then it presupposes that cognitional process falls

[28]Ibid., 210.

on the three levels of presentation, intelligence, and reflection; it presupposes that insights are cumulative and head toward a limit described by the adjective, satisfactory; it presupposes a reflective grasp of the unconditioned or of what approximates to the unconditioned. Clearly, revision cannot revise its own presuppositions. A reviser cannot appeal to data to deny data, to his new insights to deny insights, to his new formulation to deny formulation, to his reflective grasp to deny reflective grasp.[29]

. . . Not only are the ''I'' and its cognitional operations to be affirmed, but also the pattern in which they occur is acknowledged as invariant, not of course in the sense that further methodical developments are impossible, nor in the sense that fuller and more adequate knowledge of the pattern is unattainable, but in the sense that any attempt to revise the patterns as now known would involve the very operations that the pattern prescribes.[30]

We have described Lonergan's model of the normative dimensions of human consciousness; we have tried to communicate the meaning he gives to the term ''self-appropriation.'' But, as we stated in the beginning, we will not have succeeded in communicating our meaning if the reader believes this be an easy task or one that can be accomplished in a short period of time. As Lonergan later says in *Method in Theology:*

Our purpose is to bring to light the pattern within which these operations occur and, it happens, we cannot succeed without an exceptional amount of exertion and activity on the part of the reader. He will have to familiarize himself with our terminology. He will have to evoke the relevant operations in his own consciousness. He will have to discover in his own experience the dynamic relationships leading from one operation to the next. Otherwise he will find not merely this chapter but the whole book about as illuminating as a blind man finds a lecture on color.[31]

In a footnote to the above quote Lonergan distinguishes between a presentation of the model of the levels of human consciousness and the slow process of self-appropriation: ''Please observe that I am offering only a summary, that the summary can do no more than present a general idea, that the process of self-appropriation occurs only slowly, and usually, only through the struggle with some such book as *Insight.*''[32] The value of Lonergan's *Insight* is precisely that it

---

[29]*Insight,* 359–60 (335–36).
[30]*Second Collection,* 273.
[31]*Method in Theology,* 7.
[32]Ibid.

was written with this pedagogical aim in mind: beginning with over three hundred pages of examples from mathematics, the sciences, and common sense living that illustrate the inevitable operations of human consciousness.

Because *Insight* aims at a personal development, it aims at what of its very nature is a slow process. "Essentially, it is a development of the subject and in the subject and, like any development, it can be solid and fruitful only by being painstaking and slow."[33] Several times in his writings Lonergan mentioned the many years John Henry Newman took to find his intellectual way to becoming a Roman Catholic. His own intellectual conversion took many years. It is indeed a painstaking and slow process. *Insight* was written to facilitate that process.

5. Metaphysics and Intellectual Conversion

Lonergan once noted that intellectual conversion, or the lack thereof, is objectified in terms of "positions" and "counter-positions." A basic *position* in metaphysics will be arrived at "1) if the real is the concrete universe of being and not a subdivision of the 'already out there now'; 2) if the subject becomes known when it affirms itself intelligently and reasonably and so is not known yet in any prior 'existential' state; and 3) if objectivity is conceived as a consequence of intelligent inquiry and critical reflection, and not as a property of vital anticipation, extroversion and satisfaction." On the other hand, it will be a basic *counter-position* if it contradicts one or more of the basic positions: "Let us say that Cartesian dualism contains both a basic position and a basic counter-position. The basic position is the *cogito, ergo sum*. . . . On the other hand, the basic counterposition is the affirmation of the *res extensa*; it is real as a subdivision of the 'already out there now'; its objectivity is a matter of extroversion. . . ."[34]

The counter-positions invite reversal, not merely because of an explicit contradiction with anyone else's stated thought, but in virtue of the implicit contradiction with the processes of one's own thought. "Thus, Hobbes overcame Cartesian dualism by granting reality to the *res cogitans* only if it were another instance of the *res extensa*, another instance of matter in motion. Hume overcame Hobbes by reducing all instances of the 'already out there now real' to manifolds of impressions linked by mere habits and beliefs. The intelligence and reasonableness of Hume's criticizing were obviously quite different from the knowledge he so successfully criticized. Might one not identify

[33]*Insight*, 17 (xxiii).
[34]Ibid., 413–14 (388–89).

knowledge with the criticizing activity rather than the criticized materials.''[35]

There is no getting around the place from which we start and that is the implicit intelligence and reasonableness of any assertions we make. ''The directives of the method must be issued by the self-affirming subject to himself.''[36] The key to any explicit metaphysics, then, is an adequate self-knowledge by which the latent metaphysics present in human operations becomes explicit.The key is an intelligible and true account of our intelligence and reasonableness.

> Metaphysics, then, is not something in a book but something in a mind. Moreover, it is produced not by a book but only by the mind in which it is. Books can serve to supply the stimulus for a set of precise visual experiences, to issue through experiences an invitation to acts of insight, to lead through the insights to a grasp of the virtually unconditioned. But books cannot constitute the visual experiences, nor necessitate the insights, nor impose the attainment of the high moment of critical reflection that through the unconditioned reaches judgment.[37]

In chapter sixteen of *Insight* Lonergan asks the question, ''Just what are the metaphysical elements? What are, for example, potency, form and act?'' He answers simply: ''They express the structure in which one knows what proportionate being is; they outline the mould in which an understanding of proportionate being necessarily will flow; they arise from understanding and they regard proportionate being, not as understood, but only as to be understood.''[38] There follows a very important corollary: ''If one wants to know just what forms are, the proper procedure is to give up metaphysics and turn to the sciences; for forms become known inasmuch as the sciences approximate towards their ideal of complete explanation; and there is no method, apart from scientific method by which one can reach such explanation.''[39]

My own scholastic philosophical training had implied that philosophers had some sort of ''intuition of forms'' or even ''intuition of being'' that others did not have. The metaphysician is exposed to the ever recurrent danger ''of discoursing on quiddities without suspecting that quiddity means what is to be known through scientific understanding.''[40]

[35]Ibid., 414 (389).
[36]Ibid., 423 (398).
[37]Ibid., 421 (396).
[38]Ibid., 521 (497).
[39]Ibid., (498).
[40]Ibid., 533 (509).

On the other hand, there is an extremely important role the philosopher or metaphysician can play in the unification of the sciences. "If the metaphysician must leave to the physicist the understanding of physics and to the chemist the understanding of chemistry, he has the task of working out for the physicist and chemist, for the biologist and the psychologist, the dynamic structure that initiates and controls their respective inquiries and, no less, the general characteristics of the goal towards which they head."[41] The danger for the scientist in a particular area, of course, is to pronounce on areas beyond his or her competence or on the structure of the universe as a whole. Only someone who has spent time on a metaphysics rooted in an adequate self-affirmation of the knower can do the latter.

The high and lofty aim of *Insight*, then, is summarized in the introduction in the following way:

> The last phrase has the ring of a slogan and, happily, it sums up the positive content of this work. *Thoroughly understand what it is to understand, and not only will you understand the broad lines of all there is to be understood but also you will possess a fixed base, an invariant pattern, opening upon all further developments of understanding.*[42]

It is in this sense, then, that all Lonergan experienced himself and all he wrote in *Insight* on the natural sciences and philosophy opened out to his study of the methods of historical scholarship and human science in *Method in Theology* and in his reflections at the end of his life on human economics:

> Kant's Copernican revolution marks a dividing line. Hegel turned from substance to subject. Historians and philologists worked out their autonomous methods for human studies. Will and decision, actions and results, came up for emphasis in Kierkegaard, Schopenhauer, Nietzsche, Blondel, the pragmatists. Brentano inspired Husserl, and intentionality analysis routed faculty psychology. A second stage of meaning is vanishing, and a third is about to take its place.[43]

6. "A Specifically Philosophic Conversion"

In an article published in 1958, "*Insight*: Preface to a Discussion," Lonergan replies to several questions raised by the publication of *Insight*. In the course of the article he distinguishes between two meanings of "the real world." On the one hand, it can mean the universe of being to be known by the totality of true judgments. On the

[41]Ibid., 522 (498f.).
[42]Ibid., 22 (xxviii).
[43]*Method in Theology*, 96.

other hand, it can mean "one's own little world": "In this sense each of us lives in a real world of his own. Its contents are determined by his *Sorge*, by his interests and concerns, by the orientation of his living, by the unconscious horizon that blocks from his view the rest of reality."[44] This horizon of "one's own little world" plays a powerful role in shaping one's consciousness.

> To each of us his own private real world is very real indeed. Spontaneously it lays claim to being the one real world, the standard, the criterion, the absolute, by which everything is judged, measured, evaluated. That claim, I should insist, is not to be admitted. There is one standard, one criterion, one absolute, and that is true judgment. Insofar as one's private real world does not meet that standard, it is some dubious product of animal faith and human error. On the other hand, insofar as one's private world is submitted constantly and sedulously to the corrections made by true judgment, necessarily it is brought into conformity with the universe of being.[45]

In an important footnote to the above, Lonergan speaks about the fundamental factor in the differentiation of philosophies in *Insight* as a specifically philosophic conversion: "I am inclined to believe, however, that this constant and sedulous correction does not occur without a specifically philosophic conversion from the *homo sensibilibus immersus* to the *homo maxime est mens hominis* (Thomas Aquinas, *Summa Theologiae*, 1–2, q. 29, a. 4c.). This existential aspect of our knowing is the fundamental factor in the differentiation of the philosophies in *Insight*."[46]

I have no doubt that the specifically philosophic conversion Lonergan refers to here is the radical intellectual conversion he first wrote of in 1951 and the intellectual conversion so prominent in his writing after the publication of *Insight*. Thus, although he never refers to it by name in *Insight* itself, still, years later in 1972, he will sum up the focus of his work in this way: "*Insight* insists a great deal on the authenticity of the subject, on his need to reverse his counter-positions and develop his positions, on the importance, in brief, of intellectual conversion."[47]

[44]Lonergan, "*Insight:* Preface to a Discussion," *Collection*, 148.

[45]Ibid.

[46]Ibid.

[47]*Philosophy of God and Theology*, 12. Similarly, Lonergan's Christology notes of 1956 refers to "conversio quaedam intima et radicalis, conscia atque deliberata" which is clearly intellectual conversion, and is related to the conversion which necessarily is the work of divine grace. Cf. editorial note in *Collection*, 287.

Conclusion

1. Intellectual, Moral, and Religious Conversion

Insight was finally published in 1957. In the meantime, in 1953, Lonergan began teaching in Rome and remained there until 1965.[1] "For the first ten years I was there I lectured in alternate years on the Incarnate Word and on the Trinity to both second and third year theologians. They were about six hundred and fifty strong and between them, not individually but distributively, they seemed to read everything. It was quite a challenge."[2]

A major part of this challenge came from a growing encounter with contemporary European thought, chiefly existential and phenomenolgical philosophies, and modern studies of history and hermeneutics. As in *Insight* Lonergan was up to the challenge of the modern sciences, so now he was up to facing the challenge of modern historical scholarship. Rooted in all the influences we have documented in this book, he had experienced in himself what modern European thought called "the turn to the subject" or "the anthropological turn."

> I had learnt honesty from my teachers of philosophy at Heythrop College. I had had an introduction to modern science from Joseph's *Introduction to Logic* and from the mathematics tutor at Heythrop, Fr. Charles O'Hara. I had become something of an existentialist from my study of Newman's *A Grammar of Assent*. I had become a Thomist through the influence of Maréchal mediated to me by Stefanos Stefanu and through Bernard Leeming's lectures on the *unicum esse in Christo*. In a practical way I had become familiar with historical work both in my doctoral dissertation on *gratia operans* and in my later study of *verbum* in Aquinas. *Insight* was the fruit of all this. It enabled me to achieve in myself what since has been called *Die anthropologische Wende*.[3]

All of these were a major source of challenge to Catholic theology and constituted the definitive beginning of a transition from a classical

---

[1]*Second Collection*, 268.

[2]Ibid., 276.

[3]Ibid. Lonergan refers to the study of Karl Rahner by Peter Eicher, *Die anthropologische Wende, Karl Rahners philosophischer Weg vom Wesen das Menschen zur personalen Existenz* (Freiburg/Schweiz: 1970).

to an historically conscious theology.[4] This change in the structure and procedures of Catholic theology had been long awaited. This new age in Catholic theology "dates not from 1965 when the second Vatican council closed, but rather from 1845 when Newman completed his *Essay on the Development of Christian Doctrine.*"[5]

This new context set everything Lonergan had done so far in a deeper and wider context. It fleshed out the human reality that a methodical theology would study. Such an historically conscious and critically grounded theology would facilitate the understanding of how divine revelation seeks influence in all areas of human life: "However trifling the uses to which words may be put, still they are the vehicles of meaning, and meaning is the stuff of man's making of man. So it is that divine revelation is God's entry and his taking part in man's making of man. It is God's claim to have a say in the aims and purposes, the direction and development of human lives, human societies, human cultures, human history."[6]

Eventually Lonergan's focus on human values, existential decision making and historical scholarship would result in a new breakthrough in his thought and the writing of *Method in Theology* in the late 1960s and its publication in 1972. In that work his treatment of religious and moral conversion in history, far from "dwarfing" his earlier work on intellectual conversion, only brings that work to "a far fuller realization."[7]

Method in Theology is about conversion: the apprehension of conversion through historical scholarship and the communication of the meaning and value of authentic conversion through a methodical theology. In this work he distinguishes clearly between intellectual, moral, and religious conversion. Intellectual conversion we have spoken of throughout this work. Moral conversion is the radical change in the criterion of one's decisions and choices from satisfactions to values. It involves the thrust of our human freedom toward authenticity. Finally, religious conversion is "being grasped by an other-worldly love." It is total and permanent self-surrender without conditions, qualifications, reservations. For Christians it is, as Paul put it in Romans 5:5,

---

[4]Cf. "Theology In Its New Context," *Second Collection*, 55–67. Elsewhere he pays tribute to Newman as marking the beginning of this new context in Catholic theology: unpublished paper, "A New Pastoral Theology," given at Yale University, February 11, 1974.

[5]Bernard Lonergan, "Change in Roman Catholic Theology," unpublished Larkin-Stuart lecture at Trinity College, University of Toronto, November 12, 1973, 22.

[6]*Second Collection*, 61–62.

[7]*Method in Theology*, 316.

God's love flooding our hearts through the Holy Spirit who has been given to us.

Lonergan explains the relations between intellectual, moral, and religious conversions in terms of Karl Rahner's notion of "sublation" in the sense that

> what sublates goes beyond what is sublated, introduces something new and distinct, puts everything on a new basis, yet so far from interfering with the sublated or destroying it, on the contrary needs it, includes it, preserves all its proper features and properties, and carries them forward to a fuller realization within a richer context.[8]

In other words, moral conversion goes beyond intellectual conversion by going beyond the value of truth to values generally. It sets the human subject on a new, existential level of consciousness. But this in no way should interfere with or weaken the subject's devotion to truth. "He still needs truth, for he must apprehend reality and real potentiality before he can deliberately respond to value. The truth he needs is still the truth attained in accord with the exigences of rational consciousness. But now the pursuit of it is all the more secure because he has been armed against bias, and it is all the more meaningful and significant because it occurs within, and plays an essential role in, the far richer context of the pursuit of all values."[9]

In a world in which alienation and ideology reign, intellectual conversion is extremely important for the social and cultural effectiveness of moral conversion. As Lonergan expressed it in the preface to *Insight*, "the very advance of knowledge brings a power over nature and over men too vast and terrifying to be entrusted to the good intentions of unconsciously biased minds. We have to learn to distinguish sharply between progress and decline, learn to encourage progress without putting a premium upon decline, learn to remove the tumor of the flight from understanding without destroying the organs of intelligence."[10]

Similarly, religious conversion goes beyond moral and intellectual conversion. In itself, it is an other-worldly falling in love that brings a joy that this world cannot give. At the same time it introduces a new orientation into intellectual and moral living. When a person realizes that they have been "grasped by an other-worldly love," then there is a new basis for knowing and valuing: "In no way are the fruits of intellectual and moral conversion negated or diminished. On the contrary, all human pursuit of the true and the good is included within

---

[8]Ibid.
[9]Ibid., 242.
[10]*Insight*, 8 (xiv).

and furthered by a cosmic context and purpose and, as well, there now accrues to man the power of love to enable him to accept the suffering involved in undoing the effects of decline."[11]

Lonergan preferred to explain intellectual conversion before explaining moral and religious conversion: "In an order of exposition I would prefer to explain first intellectual, then moral, then religious conversion."[12] The reason for this order of exposition, I surmise, is that intellectual conversion is the origin of the categories necessary to *explain* the dynamics of religious and moral conversion.

On the other hand, in fact, in the concrete, "there is no fixed rule of antecedence or consequence" among the different dimensions of conversion.[13] Still, ordinarily religious conversion precedes moral conversion, and moral conversion ordinarily precedes intellectual conversion: "In the order of occurrence I would expect religious commonly but not necessarily to precede moral and both religious and moral to precede intellectual."[14]

But "not necessarily"; because for someone like Augustine, and perhaps for some today, intellectual conversion can open the way to religious and moral conversion. Thus, to take two modern Catholic figures, both Thomas Merton and Avery Dulles included in the chronicle of their own religious conversions the important moments of some familiarity with scholastic philosophy.[15]

---

[11]Ibid.

[12]"Bernard Lonergan Responds," *Foundations of Theology,* ed. P. McShane (Dublin: Gill and Macmillan Ltd., 1971) 233.

[13] *Second Collection,* 66.

[14]McShane, *Foundations of Theology,* 233–34.

[15]Cf. Avery Dulles, *A Testimony to Grace* (New York: Sheed and Ward, 1946) where an insight into the notion of "being" was an important moment in his religious conversion. Cf. also the early chapters of Thomas Merton's *Seven Story Mountain* where the reading of the history of medieval philosophy was an important step in his religious conversion. Merton recalled picking up Etienne Gilson's *The Spirit of Medieval Philosophy* in the 1930s and reading there: "Beyond all sensible images, and all conceptual determinations, God affirms Himself as the absolute act of being in its pure actuality. Our concept of God, a mere feeble analogue of a reality which overflows it in every direction, can be made explicit only in the judgement: Being is Being, an absolute positing of that which, lying beyond every object, contains in itself the sufficient reason of objects. And that is why we can rightly say that the very excess of positivity which hides the divine being from our eyes is nevertheless the light which lights up all the rest: *ipsa caligo summa est mentis illuminatio."* *The Seven Story Mountain* (New York: New American Library, 1952) 171. Merton comments on this quote from Gilson: "I think the reason why these statements, and others like them, made such a profound impression on me, lay deep in my own soul. And it was this: I had never had an adequate notion of what Christians meant by God." Ibid., 172.

On the other hand, in a powerful exposition, Lonergan sets out "the causal viewpoint" that is at the basis of the "normal" sequence of conversions.

> Though religious conversion sublates moral, and moral conversion sublates intellectual, one is not to infer that intellectual conversion comes first and then moral and finally religious. On the contrary, from a causal viewpoint, one would say that first there is God's gift of his love. Next, the eye of this love reveals values in their splendor, while the strength of this love brings about their realization, and that is moral conversion. Finally, among the values discerned by the eye of love is the value of believing the truths taught by the religious tradition, and in such tradition and belief are the seeds of intellectual conversion.[16]

Was this Lonergan's own experience? Was this what brought him in Bernard Leeming's course on Christ to recognize the absolute necessity for the real distinction between essence and existence? Was it the underlying experience of God's love in Christ that eventually led him to his own intellectual conversion? Is this what led him in his theological writings to see intellectual conversion as implicit in the Christian Church's doctrine on the divinity of Christ?[17] Whatever the answer to these questions, it is certain that he regarded the acceptance of the Word of God as ultimately leading to intellectual conversion. "For the word, spoken and heard, proceeds from and penetrates to all four levels of intentional consciousness. Its content is not just a content of experience but a content of experience and understanding and judging and deciding. The analogy of sight yields the cognitional myth. But fidelity to the word engages the whole man."[18] Sometime later, in a discussion, Lonergan would put it this way:

> Well, there is a recent book on *Christ and Consciousness* and it says that Christians got their idea of reality from the resurrection of Christ. If Christ rose from the dead, there isn't just this world. It was the concrete understanding of what is meant by existence; it is what Saint Thomas meant by the third degree of abstraction which isn't an abstraction at all but a separation. The separation between the material and the immaterial and the real divides into the two. In other words, that is the way the Christians got hold of the Christian idea of spirituality.[19]

He then relates this to the search for "the unknown god" among the ancients, particularly in Plato and Aristotle: "Insofar as they reached

---

[16]*Method in Theology*, 243.

[17]Cf. "The Origins of Christian Realism," *Second Collection*, 239–61.

[18]*Method in Theology*, 243.

[19]Transcript by Nicholas Graham of discussion at Lonergan Workshop, Boston College, June 13, 1978.

the unknown god, they were already within the horizon of being, of being that is immaterial beyond all knowledge. And you have the long-winded approach in *Insight* because people today do not know about the unknown god. You have to open up their minds, let them find out what their own minds are before they can begin to be open to thinking of anything beyond this world." To an ensuing question on his own intellectual conversion, he added:

> Well that's when I accepted the distinction between essence and existence and I saw the necessity of it. But seeing the necessity of it was a matter of accepting Catholic dogma; and enabling people to accept that dogma was dealt with in a prior stage in *Insight*. We go through all this rigmarole of science, common sense and all the rest of it to help people find out what they have underneath their skulls—only it isn't underneath. Anything else?

2. Intellectual Conversion and the Human Situation

I have written this book with the conviction that intellectual conversion is central to understanding Bernard Lonergan's *Insight*. This event of intellectual conversion—the reality, not the term—was key in Lonergan's own life in the 1930s. It was the event he sought to facilitate in others in *Insight*. I have written this book with the further conviction that intellectual conversion is central to understanding all Lonergan's other writings: his writings in theology, his *Method in Theology*, other writings on method in science and scholarship, and his final writings on economics. Without personal intellectual conversion these writings cannot properly be understood.

Furthermore, I have written this work with the conviction that Lonergan's writings and the intellectual conversion he sought to facilitate in others have a profound cultural importance. In a very incisive chapter in *Insight*, Lonergan outlines the various "biases" that inhibit the pure desire to know and distort human consciousness. There is the "individual bias" or tendency to selfishness that rules out of court any questions whose answers might put a limit on one's own fears and desires. And there is "group bias" in which the passions and selfishness of the group rule out of court any suggestion that the group's well-being is excessive. But far deeper and more sinister is the "general bias" that rationalizes the "flight from understanding" and, under the cover of false philosophies and undignified myths of human life, considers "the really real" to be whatever fits in with the short-term practical needs and desires of human beings. The result is the gradual deterioration of the social situation and the inability of human beings to communicate on the basis of rational conviction. The majority of people, "instead of attempting rationalization themselves, are content to create an effective demand, a welcoming market, for more or less consistently developed counter-positions presented in myths and philosophies."[20]

In a powerful passage from *Method in Theology* Lonergan outlines this cumulative decline in the social situation: "What has been built up so slowly and so laboriously by the individual, the society, the culture, can collapse. Cognitional self-transcendence is neither an easy notion to grasp nor a readily accessible datum of consciousness to be verified."[21] In fact, Lonergan had spent many years searching for and finding this datum of consciousness in the classic writings of Newman, Plato, Augustine, and Aquinas.

Similarly, "values have a certain esoteric imperiousness, but can they keep outweighing carnal pleasure, wealth, power? Religion undoubtedly had its day, but is not that day over? Is it not illusory comfort for weaker souls, an opium distributed by the rich to quiet the poor, a mythical projection of man's own excellence into the sky?" The affirmative answer to such questions constitutes the breakdown of modern thought and culture, a breakdown that includes the disappearance of any genuine metaphysical vision.

> Initially not all but some religion is pronounced illusory, not all but some moral precept is rejected as ineffective and useless, not all truth but some type of metaphysics is dismissed as mere talk. The negations may be true, and then they represent an effort to offset decline. But also they may be false, and then they are the beginning of decline. In the latter case some part of cultural achievement is being destroyed. It will cease being a familiar component in cultural experience. It will recede into a forgotten past for historians, perhaps, to rediscover and reconstruct.[22]

Lonergan spent a major part of his life rediscovering himself and reconstructing for others a major "part of cultural achievement." That achievement he found in Plato, Aristotle, Augustine, Aquinas, Newman; and that achievement he reconstructed in *Insight* and *Method in Theology*. Without the continuing influence of that metaphysical vision, the conditions for genuine communication disappear.

> Moreover, this elimination of a genuine part of the culture means that a previous whole has been mutilated. . . . Increasing dissolution will then be matched by increasing division, incomprehension, suspicion, distrust, hostility, hatred, violence. The body social is torn apart in many

[20]*Insight*, 623 (600).
[21]*Method in Theology*, 243.
[22]Ibid., 243–44.

ways, and its cultural soul has been rendered incapable of reasonable convictions and responsible commitments. . . .

In these words Lonergan is describing the dissolution of meaningful conversation that, to a degree, he himself experienced in his own early study of philosophy. In such a world without basic shared philosophical convictions, believing others can lead to unbelief. "Then believing begins to work not for but against intellectual, moral and religious self-transcendence. What had been an uphill but universally respected course collapses into the peculiarity of an outdated minority."[23] In various ways through the years Lonergan identified the absence of intellectual conversion as one of the causes of the lack of human communication:

> Intellectual conversion does not hinder you at all dealing with simple people or ordinary people or anything like that; it helps you to understand them better, what their difficulties may be. It isn't anything narrowing; it is something broadening, simplifying, clarifying.[24] . . . You can misunderstand because the author is talking over your head. And when he is talking over your head in a very radical fashion, then conversion becomes very relevant.[25] . . . The real menace to unity of faith does not lie either in the many brands of common sense or the many differentiations of human consciousness. It lies in the absence of intellectual or moral or religious conversion.[26]

In Bernard Lonergan's thought and writings "some major part of cultural achievement" has been rediscovered and reconstructed. Lonergan's own reading in Newman, Plato, Augustine, Aristotle, and Aquinas led him to the project of recovering the metaphysical vision of the human person as constituted by the drive to be intelligent, reasonable, responsible, and loving; and correspondingly, the vision of the universe as constituted by an intelligent, reasonable, and loving God who calls human beings to be and to become themselves.

3. A Personal Experience

I began this book by describing the challenge to my own thought represented by Lonergan's *Insight*. That challenge was intensified by my doctoral dissertation in the late 1960s on the thought of Susanne K. Langer. Langer's concern in her writings on the human mind was

---

[23]Ibid., 244.
[24]Notes by Nicholas Graham from discussion session at workshop on method in theology, Regis College, Willowdale, Ontario, July 10, 1969.
[25]Ibid., July 14, 1969. Cf. *Second Collection*, 29–30.
[26]*Method in Theology*, 330.

to remain strictly "scientific." But her empiricist interpretation of science precluded giving any meaning to the words "soul" or "mind" that would be open to religious realities.[27] Both Langer's and Lonergan's work were "theories": both presented an explicitly articulated view of the universe supposedly in continuity with the modern sciences. But the crucial conflict was not that between conflicting viewpoints. The crucial conflict was that between any false theory of what constitutes human consciousness and the actual human performance of setting forth any theory whatsoever. The crucial conflict was between *content* and personal *performance*.

As I wrestled with Lonergan's thought, I slowly came to realize that not only was there a difference between Lonergan's view of human knowing and Langer's; there was also a difference between Lonergan's view of human knowing and my own spontaneous view of my own knowing. Indeed, that spontaneous view—in spite of years of scholastic philosophy—was, in its naive realism, closer to Langer's than to Lonergan's. As Lonergan put it, "some form of naive realism seems to appear utterly unquestionable to very many."[28] I realized that it seemed so for me.

Ultimately then, the issue was not between the views of Langer and Lonergan. Ultimately, the issue was the conflict between my own activities of understanding and judging and the naive views of knowing I had carried with me for years. At a certain point I realized that the answer could not be found just by more reading of Langer or Lonergan or anyone else. For "intellectual habit is not possession of the book but freedom from the book. It is the birth and life in us of the light and evidence by which we operate on our own."[29]

I knew what Langer meant—it was clear. It was clear to me that she assumed that scientific activity was reducible to imagination. It was clear that she was attempting to explain the more immediately accessible by an imagined view of what "science says."

I was wrestling with what Lonergan meant. That was less clear. But I sensed through the darkness that there was "something there." I was aware of the Lonergan "system," his explanatory account of the structure of human consciousness, the acts that presuppose and complement each other in a structured unity. I had memorized his "system" quite well! I once remember Lonergan in class recommending memorization as a *prelude* to understanding! Indeed, I was

---

[27]Cf. the quote from Langer mentioned in our introduction, n. 9.
[28]*Method in Theology*, 239.
[29]*Verbum*, 185. Cf. *Insight* 421 (396).

aware of the act of insight in myself, the act of catching on while reading a book, while reading *Insight* itself, the act of sizing up a human situation, of solving a problem. I could "feel" its importance as a source of the great works of culture and the achievements of civilization.

But I was not sure I had a real handle on it. What if Langer was right? What if every conscious act was reducible to imagination? I was not sure what insight was *like*. I was not sure I could situate it clearly in my own consciousness. I was not sure I "had" it. (Students of Lonergan's thought regularly go through this period of insecurity, of oscillating back and forth between imagined possibilities. Where does this insecurity come from?)

And that is when I remember having an "Archimedean experience." It was late one afternoon in Rome and I had been working at this stuff all day. In fact, I was, like Archimedes, relaxing in water—taking a shower! I remember saying something to myself like: "Where is this act of insight?" And then it occurred to me:

> *You're asking the wrong question!*
>
> Look at the question you're asking! You're asking a question that can't be answered! Asking "where" is an attempt to visualize what can't be visualized. You're attempting to imagine what of its nature goes beyond imagination—that is, insight!
>
> Indeed, you can be aware of the act of insight, understand it in its relationships with other cognitional acts, come to judge that understanding correct, but *you can't see it!* The very question you were asking was formulated in imaginative and visual terms and, as such, can't be answered.

It was an "inverse insight": an understanding that the question I was asking, that I spontaneously felt could be answered, could not be answered. I was in the shower, in a room, in a place that could be designated in spatial terms. But an explanatory understanding of my own understanding could not be so designated. I remembered Augustine's words from the *Confessions:*

> My mind was in search of such images as the forms of my eye was accustomed to see; and I did not realize that the mental act by which I formed these images was not itself a bodily image (*Confessions* 7, 1).

It was a moment of awareness that had been prepared for by many previous moments—indeed many questions and innumerable other "little insights." It would have to be reflected on, appropriated and applied in countless ways through succeeding years. Yet, it was a breakthrough. It was a moment that Lonergan aptly called an event of "startling strangeness." And "winter twilight cannot be mistaken for the summer noonday sun."[30]

Was this idealism? Like Lonergan, I found this question in myself. But it is idealism only if "reality" is thought of as the object of some sort of a look, an intuition, an *Anschauung*. Idealism still holds on (subconsciously, if you will) to "the already out there now real."

If, on the other hand, as Lonergan had learned so well from Newman and Aquinas and Maréchal and Leeming, reality is mediated by reasonable judgment, rooted in evidence of the virtually unconditioned, then we are in a realism. And such a realism can become a critical realism through the process of self-appropriation and intellectual conversion.[31]

Intellectual conversion is rooted in the intellectual breakthroughs most of us have had throughout our years of education.[32] But the full meaning of intellectual conversion is the full and conscious appropriation of our intellectual being, and indeed, our intellectual being in relation to the rest of our being—and to the universe. What I was implicitly looking for those days in Rome was the "already out there now real" insight—something I could imagine. What I realized that day in the shower is that this is different than understanding understanding—or for that matter, any cognitional act.

For even to fully and humanly understand imagination is not to imagine it; it is to understand it in its relations with the rest of our conscious acts and to judge that understanding correct. It was the growing sharp distinction between two types of knowing—one rooted in imagination, the other in intelligence—that was at the basis for my coming to know both the inadequacies of Langer's ultimate position in philosophy (in spite of her fine work on art), and the inadequacies of the scholastic philosophy I had been taught (in spite of its honoring of Aquinas).

The affirmation of an intellectual conversion in oneself can be taken as an arrogant assertion. I do not intend this. Intellectual conversion,

---

[30]*Insight*, 13 (xix).

[31]"To move from empiricism to idealism, one draws attention to the empiricist's failure to note all the structuring elements that are constitutive of human knowing yet not given to sense. However, while the idealist is correct in rejecting the empiricist's account of human knowledge, he is mistaken in accepting the empiricist notion of reality and so in concluding that the object of human knowledge is not the real but the ideal. Accordingly, to move beyond idealism to realism, one has to discover that man's intellectual and rational operations involve a transcendence of the operating subject. . . ." *Method in Theology*, 76.

[32]Analogous breakthroughs take place in every area of science and scholarship. Cf. Freeman Dyson's description of his students learning quantum physics:

as Lonergan spoke of it, is only a beginning. Its fruit must be extended to the whole of one's life.

> For the appropriation of one's own rational self-consciousness, which has been so stressed in this Introduction, is not an end in itself but rather a beginning. It is a necessary beginning, for unless one breaks the duality in one's knowing, one doubts that understanding correctly is knowing.[33]

And indeed, just as there are stages of moral and religious conversion, so one can speak analogously of stages in intellectual conversion, at least insofar as one allows intellectual conversion to influence all of one's intellectual life: "In any individual at any given time there may exist the abstract possibility, or the beginnings, or greater or lesser progress, or high development of intellectual or moral or religious conversion."[34]

In a phrase Lonergan was fond of using, the event of intellectual conversion should exert its influence "all along the line." Indeed, in his own life, his early intellectual conversion bore fruit not only in his understanding of modern science and scholarship, but even in the human science of macro-economics. Many of us are "still reaching up" to Lonergan's understanding in that area—and many other areas as well.

I end this book by noting that, although he began as my teacher, through the years Bernard Lonergan became my friend. He once wrote me a very treasured note congratulating me on a paper I had given

---

> The student begins by learning the tricks of the trade. He learns how to make calculations in quantum mechanics and get the right answers. . . . To learn the mathematics of the subject and to learn how to use it takes about six months. This is the first stage in learning quantum mechanics, and it is comparatively easy and painless.The second stage comes when the student begins to worry because he does not understand what he has been doing. He worries because he has no clear physical picture in his head. He gets confused in trying to arrive at a physical explanation for each of the mathematical tricks he has been taught. He works very hard and gets discouraged because he does not seem able to think clearly. This second stage often lasts six months or longer, and it is strenuous and unpleasant. Then, quite unexpectedly, the third stage begins. The student suddenly says to himself, "I understand quantum mechanics," or rather he says, "I understand now that there really isn't anything to be understood."

"Innovation in Physics," eds. Rapport and Wright, *Physics* (New York: Washington Square Press, 1965) 259–60.

[33]*Insight*, 22 (xxviii).

[34]*Method in Theology*, 326. Cf. also the first question of the discussion session at the Method in Theology seminar, Milltown Institute of Theology and Philosophy, Dublin, Ireland, August 10, 1971, where he takes up the question of "partial conversions."

on his *Method in Theology*. After my paper he made some remarks in response. In the note he expressed what I would also hope for from this book.

July 31, 1973

Dear Dick,

Many thanks for your note of July 1st.

Permit me to congratulate you again and most warmly on the very effective paper you read at the CTSA meeting. Like your book review in *America* it will contribute notably to the fortunes of *Method in Theology*.

I am glad some people found my jerky remarks at the end of the session acceptable. I would like to feel that they might serve to extricate me from the cocoon of abstractions in which, in the minds of some, I am supposed to dwell.

Wishing you all good things and keeping you in my prayers,

Bernie Lonergan

Bernard J. F. Lonergan
Selected Dates

1904	Born December 17 in Buckingham, Quebec, Canada
	Attended Christian Brothers School
1918–1922	Loyola College, Montreal
1922	July 29, entered Society of Jesus, Guelph, Ontario
1922–1926	Novitiate and classics, Guelph
1926–1929	Philosophy studies, Heythrop College, England
1930	B.A. Degree, University of London
1930–1933	Teacher, Loyola College, Montreal
1933–1937	Theological studies, Gregorian University, Rome
1936	July 25, ordination to Priesthood, Rome
1937–1938	Tertianship, Amiens, France
1938–1940	Doctoral studies, Gregorian University
1940–1946	Professor at L'Immaculée—Conception, Montreal
1944	Initial version of *An Essay on Circulation Analysis*
1945	"Thought and Reality" Thomas More Institute, Montreal
1946–1949	"The Concept of *Verbum* in the Writings of St. Thomas Aquinas"
1947–1953	Professor of theology, Regis College, Toronto
1949–1953	Writing of *Insight*
1953–1965	Professor of theology, Gregorian University
1957	*Insight: A Study of Human Understanding*
1957	*Divinarum Personarum Conceptio Analogica*
1959	"The Philosophy of Education," Cincinnati
1960	*De Verbo Incarnato*
1961	*De Deo Trino*
1965	Return from Rome for surgery
1965–1975	Research professor, Regis College
1967	*Collection*
1969	Member of International Theological Commission

1970	Companion of Order of Canada
1970	International Symposium on Lonergan's Thought, Florida
1971	Lonergan Research Center, Regis College
1971–1972	Stillman Professor, Harvard University
1972	*Method in Theology*
1972	John Courtney Murray Award, Catholic Theological Society of America
1974	*A Second Collection*
1975	Fellow of the British Academy
1975–1983	Visiting Distinguished Professor, Boston College
1983–1984	Retirement, Jesuit infirmary, Pickering, Ontario
1984	Died, November 26, Jesuit Infirmary, Pickering

Seventeen honorary doctorates were conferred on Father Lonergan

Bibliography of Works Cited

1. Works by Bernard Lonergan

We list here in chronological order the works of Lonergan cited in our text. A complete bibliography is available from the Lonergan Research Institute, 10 St. Mary Street, Suite 500, Toronto, Canada, M4Y 1P9.

A. Lonergan's Published Works

Grace and Freedom: Operative Grace in the Thought of St. Thomas Aquinas. Ed. J. P. Burns. London: Darton, Longman & Todd; New York: Herder and Herder, 1971. (Originally Lonergan's doctoral dissertation for the Gregorian University: Gratia Operans: *A Study of the Speculative Development in the Writings of St. Thomas of Aquin,* 1940.)

Verbum: Word and Idea in Aquinas. Ed. David B. Burrell. Notre Dame: University of Notre Dame Press, 1967. (Originally articles written for *Theological Studies,* 1946–1949.)

Insight: A Study of Human Understanding, Collected Works of Bernard Lonergan, vol. 3. Eds. Frederick E. Crowe and Robert M. Doran. Toronto: University of Toronto Press, 1992. (Fifth edition, revised and augmented of *Insight: A Study of Human Understanding,* first published by Longmans, Green & Co., London, Philosophical Library, 1957, with a second revised student's edition published in 1958.)

Understanding and Being: The Halifax Lectures on Insight, *Collected Works of Bernard Lonergan,* vol. 5. Eds. Elizabeth A. Morelli and Mark D. Morelli. Revised and augmented by Frederick E. Crowe with the collaboration of Elizabeth A. Morelli, Mark D. Morelli, Robert M. Doran, and Thomas V. Daly. Toronto: University of Toronto Press, 1992. (These lectures were originally given at St. Mary's University, Halifax, August 4–15, 1958).

De Verbo Incarnato. Rome: Pontificia Universitas Gregoriana, 1961.

Collection, Collected Works of Bernard Lonergan, vol. 4. Eds. Frederick E. Crowe and Robert M. Doran. Toronto: University of Toronto Press, 1988. (Second edition, revised and augmented, of *Collection: Papers by Bernard Lonergan,* ed. Frederick F. Crowe. New York: Herder and Herder, and London: Darton, Longman & Todd, 1967).

Doctrinal Pluralism. Milwaukee: Marquette University Press, 1971.

Method in Theology. London: Darton, Longman & Todd; New York: Herder and Herder, 1972. (Reprinted University of Toronto Press, 1990).

Philosophy of God and Theology. Philadelphia: The Westminster Press, 1973.

A Second Collection: Papers by Bernard J. F. Lonergan, S.J. Eds. W.F.J. Ryan and
    B. J. Tyrrell. London: Darton, Longman and Todd; Philadelphia: West-
    minster, 1974.
A Third Collection: Papers by Bernard J. F. Lonergan, S.J. Ed. F. E. Crowe. New
    York: Paulist Press; London: Geoffrey Chapman, 1985.

B. Published Articles by Lonergan Cited

"The *Gratia Operans* Dissertation: Preface and Introduction." *Method: Journal
    of Lonergan Studies* 3 (October 1985) 9–49. (This is the original preface and
    introduction to Lonergan's dissertation of 1940.)
Review of *Medieval Studies* 8 (Toronto: Pontifical Institute of Medieval Studies,
    1946). *Theological Studies* 8 (December 1947) 706–07.
Review of Dom Illtyd Trethowan's *Certainty: Philosophical and Theological. The
    Modern Schoolman* 27 (1949–1950) 153–55.
Review of Etienne Gilson's *Being and Some Philosophers. Theological Studies* 11
    (1950) 122–25; also in *The Ensign* (Montreal: May 28, 1949) 10.
"Respect for Human Dignity." *The Canadian Messenger of the Sacred Heart* 63
    (1953) 413–18.
"Method in Catholic Theology." *Method: Journal of Lonergan Studies* 10 (Spring
    1992) 10–11. (Lecture originally given to the Society for the Study of The-
    ology, Nottingham, England, April 15, 1959.)
"Bernard Lonergan Responds." *Foundations of Theology,* ed. Philip McShane.
    Dublin: Gill and Macmillan Ltd., 1971; and University of Notre Dame
    Press, 1972, 223–34.
"Reality, Myth, Symbol." *Myth, Symbol, and Reality,* ed. Alan M. Olson. Notre
    Dame, Ind.: University of Notre Dame Press, 1980, 31–37.
"Questionnaire on Philosophy." *Method: Journal of Lonergan Studies* 2 (October
    1984) 1–35.

The following articles mentioned in our text can be found in *Collection: Collected Works of Bernard Lonergan,* vol. 4:

    "The Form of Inference" (1943)
    "Finality, Love, Marriage" (1943)
    "On God and Secondary Causes" (1946)
    "The Natural Desire to See God" (1949)
    "A Note on Geometrical Possibility" (1949–1950)
    "Theology and Understanding" (1954)
    "*Insight:* Preface to a Discussion" (1958)
    "Metaphysics as Horizon" (1963)
    "Cognitional Structure" (1964)
    "Dimensions of Meaning" (1967)

C. Unpublished Works, Articles, Letters Cited

Letter to Henry Smeaton, June 20, 1927.
"The Form of Mathematical Inference." *Blandyke Papers,* no. 283 (January 1928)
    126–37.

"The Syllogism," Ibid., no. 285 (March 1928) 33–64.

"True Judgment and Science." A paper read before the Philosophy and Literature Society, Heythrop College, February 3, 1929.

Fragments of what may have been a lost essay on assent—evidently from the early 1930s. Fourteen pages.

Letter of January 22, 1935, to Rev. Henry Keane, S.J., Provincial of the Upper Canada Province of the Society of Jesus.

Essays on the philosophy of history written during the 1930s. Some of the titles of the essays are: "Analytic Concept of History"; "Sketch for a Metaphysic of Human Solidarity"; "Analytic Concept of History, in Blurred Outline"; "Essay in Fundamental Sociology"; "Philosophy of History"; "A Theory of History"; "Outline of an Analytic Concept of History"; "*Pantôn Anakephalaiôsis*, A Theology of Human Solidarity, A Metaphysic for the Interpretation of St. Paul, A Theology for the Social Order, Catholic Action, And the Kingship of Christ, in incipient outline."

An Essay in Circulation Analysis. Unpublished typescript, 129pp. 1944. Title added from later "editions."

Thought and Reality. Unpublished notes taken by J. Martin O'Hara of course at Thomas More Center, Montreal, 1945–1946. Later transcribed by Thomas Daly.

De ente supernaturale: Supplementum schematicum. Student notes 1946–1947. Regis College edition, ed. Frederick Crowe, Toronto, 1973.

De scientia atque voluntate Dei: Supplementum schematicum. Student notes 1949–1950. Regis College edition, ed. Frederick Crowe, Toronto, 1973.

Intelligence and Reality. Notes made by Bernard Lonergan for his course at Thomas More Institute, Montreal, 1951.

De intellectu et methodo. Notes taken by students and corrected by Lonergan of theology course, Gregorian University, 1959.

"The Natural Theology of *Insight.*" Unpublished paper given at the University of Chicago Divinity School, March 1967.

"The Scope of Renewal." The Larkin-Stuart lectures at Trinity College in the University of Toronto, November 15, 1973.

"Macroeconomics and the Dialectic of History." Notes prepared for a seminar at Boston College, 1978–1979.

D. *Interviews with Bernard Lonergan*

Caring About Meaning: Patterns in the Life of Bernard Lonergan. Eds. Pierrot Lambert, Charlotte Tansey, Cathleen Going. Montreal: Thomas More Institute, 1982. (Interviews with Bernard Lonergan.)

"What I Have Learned About Knowing Since Writing *Insight.*" February 25, 1969. Printed in Eric O'Connor, *Curiosity at the Center of One's Life.* Montreal: Thomas More Institute, 1987, 371–84.

"With *Method in Theology* Ready to Print." March 30, 1971. In Eric O'Connor, *Curiosity at the Center of One's Life.* Montreal: Thomas More Institute, 1987, 385–401.

"Grace After Faculty Psychology." December 30, 1971. In Eric O'Connor, *Curiosity at the Center of One's Life*. Montreal: Thomas More Institute, 1987, 402-13.

"Bernard Lonergan in Conversation." March 28, 1980. In Eric O'Connor, *Curiosity at the Center of One's Life*. Montreal: Thomas More Institute, 1987, 414-38.

"Questions with Regard to Method: History and Economics." March 31, 1980. In *Dialogues in Celebration*. Ed. Cathleen M. Going. Montreal: Thomas More Institute, 1980, 286-314.

Discussions with Eric Voegelin, Fred Lawrence, etc. 1977. Printed in *The Question as Commitment: A Symposium*. Ed. Elaine Cahn and Cathleen Going. Montreal: Thomas More Institute Papers/77, 1979.

Discussions at Lonergan Workshops, Boston College, June 13, 14, 1978; June 19, 1979; June 21, 1979. Transcripts by Nicholas Graham available at Lonergan Research Institute, Toronto.

2. Other Works Cited

Aristotle. *Metaphysics*, 7, 8; *De Anima*, 3. *The Basic Works of Aristotle*, ed. Richard McKeon. New York: Random House, 1944.

Augustine. *De vera religione* 39, 73. *Augustine's Earlier Writings: The Library of Christian Classics* 6, trans. John H. S. Burleigh. Philadelphia: Westminster Press, 1953.

_____. *The Fathers of the Church: Writings of Saint Augustine* 1. Ed. Ludwig Schopp. New York: Cima Publishing Co., 1948.

_____. *Confessions*. Ed. F. W. Sheed. New York: Sheed and Ward, 1942.

_____. *Confessions*. Ed. Henry Chadwick. Oxford: Oxford University Press, 1992.

Aveling, F. "Universals and the 'Illative Sense.' " *Dublin Review* 137 (October 1905) 236-71.

Biolo, Salvino. *La Coscienza nel "De Trinitate" di S. Agostino*. Rome: Libreria Editrice dell'Universitá Gregoriana, 1969.

Boly, Craig S. *The Road to Lonergan's Method in Theology*. Lanham, Md.: The Catholic University Press of America, 1990.

Boyer, C. *L'Idée de Vérité dans la philosophie de Saint Augustin*. Paris: 1941 (original ed., 1920).

Bremond, Henri. *The Mystery of Newman*. Trans. H. C. Corrance. London: Williams and Norgate, 1907.

Brown, Peter. *Augustine of Hippo*. Berkeley: University of California Press, 1969.

Burrell, David B. "Does Process Theology Rest on a Mistake." *Theological Studies* 43 (March 1982) 125-35.

Butterfield, Herbert. *The Origins of Modern Science, 1300-1800*. New York: The Free Press, 1957; 2nd ed. 1965.

Byrne, Patrick H. "The Thomist Sources of Lonergan's Dynamic World-View." *The Thomist* (46) 108-45.

Cameron, James M. *The Night Battle*. London: Catholic Book Club, 1962.

Crowe, Frederick E. "Lonergan and Thomas Aquinas: An Overview." Unpublished paper given at the Lonergan Workshop, Boston College, June 1990.

_____. *Appropriating the Lonergan Idea.* Ed. Michael Vertin. Washington: The Catholic University of America Press, 1989.

_____. *Lonergan.* Outstanding Christian Thinkers Series. Collegeville, Minn.: The Liturgical Press, 1992.

_____. "Obituary of Father Bernard J. F. Lonergan, S.J.," *Newsletter* of the Upper Canada Jesuit Province 60 (May–June 1985) 15–18.

_____. "Tracking stray ideas in Lonergan: 'intellectual conversion,' " *Lonergan Studies Newsletter* 14 (March 1993) 9–10.

Denziger & Schönmetzer. *Enchiridion symbolorum, definitionum et declarationum de rubus fidei et morum,* 35th ed. New York, 1974.

Dessain, Charles Stephen. "Newman's Philosophy and Theology." *Victorian Prose.* New York: Modern Language Association of America, 1973, 166–69.

Dulles, Avery. *A Testimony to Grace.* New York: Sheed and Ward, 1946.

Dyson, Freeman. "Innovation in Physics." *Physics.* Eds. Rapport and Wright. New York: Washington Square Press, 1965, 259–60.

Eicher, Peter. *Die anthropologische Wende, Karl Rahners philosophischer Weg vom Wesen das Menschen zur personalen Existenz.* Freiburg/Schweiz: 1970.

Fitzpatrick, J. "Lonergan and Hume I: Epistemology (1)." *New Blackfriars* 63 (1982) 122–30.

_____. "Lonergan and Hume II: Epistemology (2)." *New Blackfriars* 63 (1982) 219–28.

_____. "Lonergan and the Later Wittgenstein." *Method: Journal of Lonergan Studies* 10 (Spring 1992).

Flanagan, Joseph. "Psychic and Intellectual Conversion." (Unpublished paper given at Lonergan Workshop, Boston College, 1981.)

Gibbons, Michael. "*Insight* and Emergence: an Introduction to Lonergan's *Circulation Analysis.*" *Creativity and Method.* Ed. Matthew Lamb. Milwaukee: Marquette University Press, 1981, 529–42.

Gilson, Etienne. *Realisme thomiste et critique de connaissance.* Paris: Vrin, 1939. (English translation, *Thomist Realism and the Critique of Knowledge.* San Francisco: Ignatius Press, 1986.)

_____. *Being and Some Philosophers.* Toronto: Pontifical Institute of Medieval Studies, 1949.

Harper, Thomas. "Dr. Newman's Essay in the aid of a Grammar of Assent." *The Month* 12 (1870) 599–611, 677–92; 13 (1871) 31–58, 159–83.

Hefling, Charles C. "On Apprehension, Notional and Real." (Unpublished paper presented at the Lonergan Workshop, Boston College, March 18–19, 1988.)

Hoenen, Petrus. "De origine primorum principiorum scientiae." *Gregorianum* 14 (1933) 153–84.

_____. "De philosophia scholastica cognitionis geometricae." *Gregorianum* 19 (1938) 498–514.

_____. "De problemate necessitatis geometricae." *Gregorianum* 20 (1939) 19–54.

_____. *Reality and Judgment According to St. Thomas.* Trans. Henry F. Tiblier. Chicago: Henry Regnery Company, 1952.

John, Helen James. *The Thomist Spectrum.* New York: Fordham University Press, 1966.

Joseph, H.W.B. *An Introduction to Logic.* Oxford: The Clarendon Press, 1906; 2nd ed. 1916.

Joyce, George Hayward. *Principles of Logic.* London, 1920.

Keeler, Leo W. *The Problem of Error From Plato to Kant. A Historical and Critical Study.* Analecta Gregoriana 6. Rome: 1934.

Lamb, Matthew L., ed. *Creativity and Method: Essays in Honor of Bernard Lonergan, S.J.* Milwaukee: Marquette University Press, 1981.

Langer, Susanne K. *Philosophy in a New Key.* New York: New American Library, 1948.

_____. *Feeling and Form.* New York: Charles Scribner's, 1953.

_____. *Mind: An Essay on Human Feeling*, vol. 1. Baltimore: Johns Hopkins Press, 1967. (Vol. 2 and vol. 3 published in 1972 and 1982 respectively. Abridged edition of three volumes 1988.)

Lawrence, Fred. "The Fragility of Consciousness: Lonergan and the Postmodern Concern for the Other." (Unpublished paper given at the Lonergan Workshop, Boston College, June 1992.)

_____, ed. *Lonergan Workshop.* Atlanta, Ga.; 8 vols.

Leeming, Bernard. *Adnotationes de Verbo Incarnato.* Rome: 1936.

Liddy, Richard M. Review of Susanne K. Langer, *Mind: An Essay on Human Feeling*, vol. 1. *International Philosophical Quarterly* 10 (1970) 481–84.

_____. *Art and Feeling: An Analysis and Critique of the Philosophy of Art of Susanne K. Langer.* Ann Arbor: University Microfilms, 1970.

Maréchal, Joseph. *Le point de départ de la métaphysique.* 5 vols. Bruxelles: L'Edition Universelle, 1944–1949.

Mathews, William. "Lonergan's Apprenticeship." *Lonergan Workshop 9*, ed. Fred Lawrence. Boston College, 1993.

_____. "Lonergan's Economics." *Method: Journal of Lonergan Studies* 3 (March 1985) 9–30.

_____. "On Lonergan and John Stuart Mill." (Unpublished.)

McCool, Gerald A. "Neo-Thomism and the Tradition of St. Thomas." *Thought* 62 (June 1987) 131–46.

_____. *Catholic Theology in the Nineteenth Century.* New York: Seabury, 1977.

Merton, Thomas. *The Seven Storey Mountain.* New York: New American Library, 1952.

Meynell, Hugo A. *An Introduction to the Philosophy of Bernard Lonergan.* Toronto, University of Toronto Press, 1991.

Newman, John Henry. *Apologia pro vita sua.* London: Longmans, Green, & Co., 1913.

_____. " 'Biglietto' Speech." Rome: Libreria Spithöver, 1879.

_____. *Essays Critical and Historical*, vol. 1. London: Longmans, Green, & Co., 1895.

_____. *A Grammar of Assent*. London: Longmans, Green, & Co., 1913.

_____. *Letters and Diaries: The Vatican Council*, vol. 25. Oxford: Oxford University Press, 1978.

_____. *Philosophical Notebook of John Henry Newman*, vols. 1 and 2. Ed. Edward Sillem. Louvain: Nauwelaerts Pub. House, 1969–1970.

_____. *The Theological Papers of John Henry Newman on Faith and Certainty*. Eds. de Achaval and Holmes. Oxford: Clarendon Press, 1976.

Portalié, Eugene. *A Guide to the Thought of Saint Augustine*. Chicago: Henry Regnery Company, 1960. (This is the English translation of Portalié's article on Augustine published in the *Dictionnaire de Théologie Catholique*.)

Przywara, Erich. "St. Augustine and the Modern World." *A Monument to St. Augustine*. New York: Meridian Books, 1957; 1st ed. 1930.

Rice, Valentine. "The Lonergans of Buckingham." *Compass* (Journal of the Upper Canada Province of the Society of Jesus) March 1985, 4–5.

Schute, Michael. *The Origin of Lonergan's Notion of the Dialectic of History: A Study of His Early Writings on History*. Lanham, Md.: The University Press of America, 1993.

Stewart, J. A. *Plato's Doctrine of Ideas*. Oxford, 1909.

TeSelle, Eugene. *Augustine the Theologian*. New York: Herder and Herder, 1970.

Thomas Aquinas. *Summa Theologiae*.

_____. *De Veritate*.

Tracy, David. *The Achievement of Bernard Lonergan*. New York, 1970.

Urraburu. *Psychologiae, Pars Secunda*. Vallisoletti, 1896.

Voegelin, Eric. "The Gospel and Culture." *Jesus and Man's Hope*, vol. 2. Eds. Donald G. Miller and Dikran Y. Hadidian. Pittsburgh: Pittsburgh Theological Seminary, 1971, 59–101.

Watkin, E. I. *The Catholic Centre*. New York: Sheed and Ward, 1939.

Williams, George Huntston. *The Mind of John Paul II*. New York: Seabury Press, 1981.

Zucher, Joseph. *Aristotles' Werk und Geist*. Paderborn: 1952.

Index